A SHORT HISTORY OF HADDINGTON

A SHORT HISTORY

OF

HADDINGTON

BY

W. FORBES GRAY
F.R.S.E., F.S.A.Scot.

ASSISTED BY

JAMES H. JAMIESON
F.S.A.Scot.

SPA BOOKS

ISBN 0-907590-10-1

Publishing History:
This work was originally published in 1944 by the East Lothian
Antiquarian and Field Naturalist's Society. This new edition is
a facsimile reprint complete and unabridged.

Published by SPA Books Limited
PO Box 47
STEVENAGE
Herts

Printed by Antony Rowe Ltd, Chippenham

PREFACE

EXACTLY a century has elapsed since James Miller published his *Lamp of Lothian*, the only work that attempts seriously to review the Royal Burgh of Haddington in its historical aspect. Considering the period at which it was written, likewise the fact that the writer was a printer and not an historian, Miller accomplished his task with some credit. His path was beset with difficulties, some of them formidable. Miller had neither the time nor the facilities for writing the history of a town rich in memorials of the past, a town dating back to the time of David I. Moreover, he approached the subject from a wrong angle. Instead of placing Haddington in the forefront, he buries it beneath long-winded disquisitions on the general history of Scotland. Indeed *The Lamp of Lothian* may not incorrectly be described as a survey of our national story in which Haddington is introduced incidentally.

In the following pages an effort is made to reverse the process—to place Haddington in the centre of the picture, and to bring in just as much national history as is essential for rendering intelligible the part played by the town in events which affected Scotland as a whole. Written before the days of research as we know it, Miller's book not only suffers from false perspective, imperfect knowledge, and ill-arrangement, but omits aspects vital to an adequate presentation of the subject. Had a more extensive investigation of the sources been possible to him it would have revealed much fresh and illuminating material, which has been largely utilised in this work.

That there is urgent need for a history of Haddington on modern lines cannot therefore be doubted. Haddington is one of the earliest of the Scottish royal burghs. And its regal significance is evidenced by the fact that William the Lyon resided there, and that it is the town where his son Alexander II first saw the light. During Catholic times Haddington was of special importance not only ecclesiastically but from a strategic point of view, this royal burgh being in the line of march of the "auld enemy" —a fact worthy of emphasis, since Haddington was the scene of perhaps the most memorable siege in Scottish history, a detailed account of which is given here for the first time. This has been made practicable through the kindness of Captain W. N. Menzies, Edinburgh, who placed at my disposal a fully documented narrative of the siege of 1548–49, which he wrote after a careful examination of contemporary sources. The result is that I have been able to record, almost day by day, a realistic picture of the happenings of a siege which lasted eighteen months, during which Haddington was in the hands of the English, who were constantly subjected to attack by the Scots and their French allies. And in the midst of the turmoil the Scots Parliament convened in the Abbey, to the east of the town, and negotiated a treaty with the French whereby Mary Queen of Scots was to marry the Dauphin "to the perpetuall honour, plesour, and proffeit of baith the realms"—so at least it was fondly hoped.

Briefly, then, the work aims at presenting a concise, accurate, and consecutive story of Haddington from earliest times to the War of 1914–18. Original sources, such as the burgh records and the minutes of the trade incorporations (where these are available), have been drawn upon, while the whole range of Scottish historical literature has been ransacked for material throwing light on the town. This has led to one or two discoveries of outstanding interest. For example, how many students of Scottish history are aware that James VI narrowly escaped drowning in the River

PREFACE

Tyne at Haddington, an event which, had it ended fatally, would have changed the whole current of British history?

The work is in two parts. The first seven chapters set forth the reactions of Haddington to national affairs, while the remaining six treat of topographical features, as well as of municipal, industrial, and social life. In a work of limited scope it has not been deemed necessary to cite authorities in every instance, but all important statements are vouched for. Supplementary material of an interesting character is supplied in footnotes. The pictorial element includes rare and curious drawings depicting the burgh in bygone times, and there is a copious index.

As in the case of a previous publication of the East Lothian Society, I must place on record the valuable and unstinted service of Mr James H. Jamieson, F.S.A.Scot., who has co-operated with me from the beginning, though the narrative is wholly mine. Besides giving me the benefit of his unrivalled knowledge of the history of his native town, he has done a large amount of the research, read the manuscript several times, and assisted with the correction of the proof-sheets.

Acknowledgments are also due to Mr Robert Waterston, who shared with me the task of arranging for the printing of the work. I also am indebted to Dr W. R. Martine for allowing me to reproduce the illustrations of the "scene" in the parish church, the Drummer and Piper, and the Weavers' Flag; likewise to Mr Charles Stark, Haddington, for the use of his photograph of the picturesque old house in Nungate. The striking view of the buildings in Mitchell's Close is from the painting by Mr John G. Spence Smith, R.S.A., to whom, and to the proprietors of *The Scotsman* (in which it appeared), I tender thanks. Further, I place on record the courtesy of Messrs W. Green & Son, Ltd., in lending me blocks of Slezer's View of "Haddington in the Seventeenth Century" and Wood's "Plan of Haddington, 1819," both illustrations being from their publication *East Lothian*, by Charles E. Green.

Throughout the preparation of this volume I have freely drawn on the ample resources of the Signet Library, and to Dr C. A. Malcolm, the Librarian, and his assistants, I am particularly grateful.

W. F. G.

April 1944.

BIBLIOGRAPHICAL NOTE

APART from James Miller's *Lamp of Lothian* (1844; new ed., 1900), the only printed authorities dealing with the history and topography of Haddington are: (1) A long article contributed by George Barclay of Middleton to the first volume of *Archæologia Scotica* (1792). Dr Barclay was minister of Haddington and its earliest historian. His narrative is valuable in some respects but is not always accurate. (2) John Martine's *Reminiscences of the Royal Burgh of Haddington* (1883)—a collection of gossipy articles which originally appeared in the local press. The author was closely connected with the town and records a great deal of considerable interest about prominent inhabitants and events of his day. (3) John Richardson's *Recollections of a Haddington Octogenarian, 1793–1815*. This work (1905) extends to 53 pages, and may be classed with Martine's, though descriptive of an earlier period. (4) James Robb's *History and Guide to Haddington* (1883). A new edition, re-written and with additional matter, including extracts from the burgh records (*c.* 1421–1545), was published in 1891. Robb was an enthusiastic antiquary. (5) J. G. Wallace-James's *Charters and Writs concerning Haddington, 1318–1543*. Printed in 1895 for private circulation. Dr Wallace-James (a medical practitioner) made a transcript of the Burgh Court Book of Haddington. The deeds dealt with are, with certain exceptions, preserved in the Charter room of Haddington.

CONTENTS

PART I

CHAPTER   PAGE

I. THE ABODE OF KINGS (DAVID I TO HERTFORD INVASION) . . . 1

II. THE SIEGE OF 1548–49 10

III. CATHOLICISM AND THE KIRK 22

IV. UNDER THE STUARTS 39

V. BEFORE THE FORTY-FIVE—AND AFTER (1714–60) 53

VI. UNDER THE LATER HANOVERIANS 62

VII. THE VICTORIAN ERA—AND LATER (1837–1918) 72

PART II

VIII. TOWN AND PARISH 81

IX. MUNICIPAL AFFAIRS 94

X. CRAFTS—TRADE—INDUSTRY 106

XI. SOCIAL LIFE 119

XII. SCHOOLS AND SCHOOLMASTERS 128

XIII. BUILDINGS OLD AND NEW 139

INDEX 147

ILLUSTRATIONS

HADDINGTON IN THE SEVENTEENTH CENTURY	*facing page*	6
"SCENE" IN PARISH CHURCH	,, ,,	24
WOOD'S PLAN OF THE TOWN, 1819	,, ,,	64–5
HADDINGTON HOUSE, SIDEGATE	,, ,,	92
TOWN DRUMMER AND PIPER	,, ,,	98
WEAVERS' BANNER	,, ,,	112
NORMAN PALACE HIGH STREET A CENTURY AGO	,, ,,	120
OLD BUILDINGS IN MITCHELL'S CLOSE	,, ,,	134
"BOTHWELL CASTLE," HARDGATE	,, ,,	140
ANCIENT BUILDING IN NUNGATE	,, ,,	144

A SHORT HISTORY OF HADDINGTON—PART I

CHAPTER I

The Abode of Kings

THE high importance of the town of Haddington in early Scottish history has never been sufficiently realised. For long it has figured in the popular imagination as a quiet, the cynic would say a somnolent, county town with nothing to disturb the even tenor of its way—a town with interests chiefly agricultural. That such a conception is not without a modicum of truth may be admitted, but it has been too readily assumed that such a character has obtained from time immemorial. Haddington is so far from being a place with no history, that it may be said with absolute truth that some of the most stirring events connected with the dim ages of the national story happened there. In pre-Reformation times Haddington throbbed with the life of the Scottish nation.

Because of the unusual fertility of its soil East Lothian was, even in the twilight of history, as Hume Brown says, "a green spot amid the general barrenness and desolation of the country." [1] Food at all events was to be had there, which signifies a great deal when the whole kingdom was rent by warring factions and all was tumult and chaos. Furthermore, Haddington was of great strategic importance. When in remote centuries the inroads of the English were frequent, this royal burgh, situated on the direct route between Berwick and Edinburgh, had to bear the brunt of the impact. Again and again Haddington was pillaged and committed to the flames, and when the "auld enemy" had departed the havoc was often so widespread and devastating as to necessitate the rebuilding of the slim wooden houses with their thatched roofs which then constituted Haddington. Stone buildings, it may be explained, were not in use to any extent till near the close of the sixteenth century.

A fitful wave of prosperity passed over the southern portion of Scotland in the twelfth and thirteenth centuries and towns sprang into being. Haddington may well have been one of them. Anyhow the nucleus of a town existed in the reign of David I, for that king in referring in his charters to "my burghs" included Haddington. Strong presumptive evidence that David I was the founder of the town is afforded by the fact that his figure is engraved on the earliest known seal of the burgh, the style and design of which leaves no doubt of its being the work of the thirteenth or early part of the fourteenth century. [2]

On this fine seal David is shown crowned and enthroned. His right hand rests on a shield bearing the arms of Scotland, while his left grasps a sceptre terminating in a *fleur-de-lis*. The inscription reads: "*David Dei Gratia Rex Scottorum.*" The seal, which is appended to an Extract of Process in the Burgh Court of Haddington, dated 12th October 1518, displays on the reverse a goat reared on its hind legs, browsing (it is supposed) on an apple-tree. The background is diapered and of a lozenge pattern. It is inscribed: "*Sigillum Commun Burgi de Hadington.*" Another seal attached to a document relating to a debt due to Patrick Broun of Colstoun, dated 18th November 1578, differs from that of 1518 inasmuch as two goats are shown. A minute examina-

[1] *Life of John Knox*, i, 11.
[2] Henry Laing, *Supplemental Catalogue of Ancient Scottish Seals*, 1866.

tion convinced Henry Laing that both impressions are from the same die, and that the additional goat was engraved between the dates mentioned, probably to give symmetry to the design.

From the twelfth to the sixteenth century Haddington was the scene of events which gave a new direction to the history of Scotland. It was the abode of several of our kings, and at least one was born there—Alexander II. The regal significance of the burgh receives additional enforcement from the circumstance of its being an early creation and the recipient of various charters. A goodly proportion of the revenue of the Crown was derived from rents paid by the burgesses. There were also the dues upon exports and imports.

Haddington was for a considerable time the meeting-place of the Court of the Four Burghs (Roxburgh, Berwick, Edinburgh, and Stirling).[1] This body was presided over by the royal Chamberlain, whose duty was to visit each royal burgh once every year and inquire into burghal administration, especially the common good and the customs. The royal Chamberlain also saw to it that the legal code, known as the Laws of the Four Burghs, was strictly observed. In 1345 it came to the knowledge of Edward III that it had long been the custom in Scotland for appeals against findings of the burgh courts to be heard at Haddington by the Chamberlain and sixteen good men and true from the Four Burghs. All dooms disputed in burgh courts were also determined at Haddington before this royal official and four of the "maist discret" burgesses drawn from the Four Burghs.[2] Towards the end of the fifteenth century the Chamberlain's influence declined, and the royal burghs became pretty much a law to themselves as regards their property. As for the Court of the Four Burghs, it does not seem to have survived the early part of the sixteenth century.[3]

Another circumstance which gave Haddington a favoured position among royal burghs was that it appears to have been one of the principal seats of Catholic Christianity in Scotland. As will be more fully explained in the third chapter, the atmosphere of the town in the early centuries was predominantly ecclesiastical. If it was not the palladium of the ancient religion, it was certainly one of its energising centres. The religious buildings of Haddington were of great extent and magnificence, the streets swarmed with monks, friars, and nuns, and high dignitaries of the Church resided there.

Politically, too, Haddington was not without a considerable measure of importance. At a Parliament in its Abbey the destiny of Mary Queen of Scots was irrevocably fixed by a treaty with the French—a treaty that led almost directly to the Reformation. Nor can it be forgotten that the town was the scene in 1548–49 of as prolonged a siege as is to be met with in the annals of Scotland.

For the foregoing reasons, which will be stressed in the course of this narrative, it is demonstrably clear that the part played by Haddington in the development of early Scotland was in not a few respects outstanding.

The origin of Haddington is lost in the mists of antiquity. The phrase is hackneyed and often misapplied, but in the present instance is literally true. When the town arose, or precisely when it was given the status of a royal burgh, are matters of equal uncertainty, for its early records perished in the wars with the English. But we do know that when David I came to the throne in 1124 a community of some sort already existed, though, as has been already indicated, it probably was that monarch who

[1] Hume Brown, *History of Scotland*, i, 92.   [2] Acts, Scotland, i, 742.
[3] Theodora Pagan, *Convention of Royal Burghs*, 1926.

endowed it with a constitution. It is generally presumed, as has been stated, that David I granted Haddington a charter elevating it to the position of a royal burgh, and, considering that the burgh was a royal residence, this is not unlikely. Yet it might plausibly be urged that the charter emanated from his grandson, William the Lyon, who, apart from the fact that he founded many of the chief towns of modern Scotland, resided in Haddington. But whatever our attitude as to the rise of Haddington, it is a fact that from David's reign until 1216, when the place was burnt by the English under King John, the county town of East Lothian was the abode of royalty.

David I had several noteworthy links with Haddington. In 1135 he signed a charter there granting the lands of Swinton to his knight Hernulf. Four years later he gave Haddington and its lands to Ada, daughter of the Earl of Warenne and Surrey, when she married his eldest son, Prince Henry. And about the same time we hear of David granting St Mary's Church and its chapels, also a toft within the burgh, to the monastery of St Andrews.

Malcolm IV, grandson of David I, is rather a shadowy figure, which is not to be wondered at, for he came to the throne at the age of eleven and was dead before he had attained his twenty-fifth year. During this brief span he took part in a military expedition to France, and when in Scotland was continually on the move in an effort to repress turbulent nobles. So Haddington could not have seen much of Malcolm IV. Indeed there is but one recorded act that binds him to the burgh: in 1159 he granted a toft there to the monks of Kelso.

William the Lyon's connection with Haddington is more easily established. Unlike that of Malcolm IV, his was a long reign crowded with events that had a practical bearing upon the development of Scotland. The king resided much in the town, and there, in 1198, was born the prince who ascended the throne as Alexander II. In 1171 William the Lyon at Haddington, in presence of his mother (the Countess Ada), his brother David, and other noblemen, is reported to have granted a charter conveying the lands of Whitfield, near Hexham, to Robert, the chaplain, to be holden by him and his heirs of the canons of Hexham in fee and inheritance.[1] Again, in 1180, William the Lyon sat in a judicial capacity in Haddington and heard evidence in a dispute in which the retainers of the monks of Melrose and those of Richard de Morville were the parties involved. There, too, in 1191, William the Lyon gave his natural daughter in marriage to Robert de Ross. This king vied with David I in dutifulness to the Church, and through his instrumentality the monks of Coldingham became possessors of a toft in Haddington.

If the youth of Alexander II was spent in his native town, as may be reasonably supposed, Haddington must have had its share in moulding a shrewd and stable character. Among the most reputable of early Scottish kings, Alexander II was dogged by misfortune. His treaty with the English barons who opposed the misgovernment of John naturally incurred the enmity of that king, and there were remorseless reprisals. In 1216 John invaded the Lothians, and Haddington, probably for the first time, was subjected to pillage, destruction by fire, and various barbaric acts, an experience which the town was repeatedly to undergo during the next three centuries. Moreover, there were constant expeditions against refractory subjects. It need cause no surprise that after Alexander's accession Haddington saw little of him.

During his reign his native town was the scene of one of those murders which, owing

---

[1] John Hodgson, *History of Northumberland*, 1840, Part II, iii, 98.

to the internecine conflicts between noble families, were then of common occurrence. In 1242 Patrick, sixth Earl of Athol, "of the highest blood and kindred of Scotland, and himself a gallant youth," was treacherously murdered. The "palace" where he slept, in the west end of the High Street (then designated Crocegait), was burned to conceal the manner of his death. The instigator, if he was not the perpetrator of the crime, was William de Bisset, who belonged to an Anglo-Norman family, the members of which were powerful lords in Scotland under William the Lyon.

The murder of Athol took-place after a tournament in Haddington. Suspicion fell on Bisset, who was a member of the royal household. The story goes that Bisset persuaded the Queen to spend four days at his castle of Aboyne on her journey south from Moray, and this at the very time when Athol was slaughtered. Both Alexander II and his Queen befriended Bisset, the latter expressing her readiness to make oath of his innocence. But the murdered earl had also powerful supporters, and it may well be that the evidence implicating Bisset could not be overthrown. Anyhow the Bissets were banished, and obliged to take a vow to join the Crusade and never to return from the Holy Land.[1] Athol's remains were buried in consecrated ground within the Franciscan friary, which stood at the east end of the town.

Because of its strategic importance Haddington suffered more than most Lowland towns from the incursions of the English. We have seen how, at the outset of the reign of Alexander II, King John wreaked vengeance on the burgh. Then the latter's son, Henry III, intent on compelling the Scottish king to do homage to him, swept like a raging torrent over the fertile plains of Lothian and burnt the wooden dwellings in Haddington that had been hastily constructed after King John's visitation.

The district even then was noted for its cereal and fruit growing. "As early as the twelfth century the fame of the orchards of Haddington had gone beyond the limits of Scotland." [2] Writing in the sixteenth century, a French traveller refers to the town being "situated in a fruitful and pleasant country," [3] while Fynes Moryson speaks of "the pleasant village of Haddington." [4] A country, the richness of whose soil was widely acclaimed, proved a tempting prize to the English, and again and again they tried to obtain possession. In 1293 Edward I demanded of John Baliol that Haddington and Berwick be ceded to him, and at an English parliament in the following year, at which Baliol was present, the Bishop of Durham presumptuously claimed both towns with their appendages as belonging to his diocese.

The claim to the overlordship of Scotland, as is well known, was persistently and often powerfully maintained by successive English kings, notably Edward I. Haddington was, as matter of course, drawn into the vortex, and, until the Scottish War of Independence was fully matured, experienced much of the fighting, for was not the burgh "Scotland's wall," the place which, if once captured, would render the task of the invaders comparatively easy? No English king was more alive to this than Edward I. Haddington was given special attention when he resolved to attempt the subjugation of Scotland. Edward's peremptory demands were indignantly refused, with the result that he invaded East Lothian at the head of a large army.

Interesting details of the expedition are recorded in an anonymous chronicle of the period bearing the quaint title *Voyage of Kynge Edwarde*. On the "Wednesdaie Ascencion even (1296), the Kynge went to Hadyngton" and took forcible possession

---

[1] Cosmo Innes, *Sketches of Early Scotch History*, p. 438, footnote.
[2] Hume Brown, *Scotland in Time of Queen Mary*, p. 20.
[3] Jean de Beaugué, *Histoire de la Guerre d'Écosse pendant les Campagnes 1548-9* (Maitland Club), p. 23.
[4] Hume Brown, *Early Travellers in Scotland*, p. 82.

of the town, neither the civic nor the ecclesiastical authorities being able to withstand his extortions. The chief magistrate (the office of Provost was not yet created), one Alexander le Barker, was poltroon enough to swear fealty to the usurper and to sign Ragman Roll. Eve, Prioress of Haddington, also retained her position by acknowledging Edward's claim. This English king was again in the town on 19th August of the same year.

After the War of Independence the military importance of Haddington remained and was to be a disturbing factor for two centuries more. The frequent and ruthless onslaughts to which the town was subjected deprived it of its regal character and temporarily at least made it vulnerable. A place that was constantly liable to attack from a truculent enemy was obviously unsuited for a royal residence. Consequently the Scottish kings were compelled to find habitations elsewhere, and with them went much of the lustre that had been identified with Haddington since the time of David I.

The connection of William Wallace with the burgh was slight. In 1297, when in pursuit of Patrick, Earl of Dunbar, the great Scottish patriot marched his army through East Lothian by the old road along the ridge of the Garleton Hills. Wallace was in Haddington on 11th October of the same year when, with Andrew de Moray, he prepared a document addressed to the mayors of Lübeck and Hamburg.

The relations of Robert the Bruce with the town were closer. Haddington's earliest existing charter came from this king, or, more accurately stated, it was confirmatory of a previous one. Dated 6th December 1318, King Robert's charter renews the rights of the burgesses. They were to be exempt from tolls and customs, and to have exclusive trading privileges within the sheriffdom, while protection was afforded to all persons going to or returning from the burgh. One clause is eloquent of the early rise of industry. "We forbid . . . any one within our Sheriffdom of Haddington to buy wool or skins, or to trade in merchandise, or to make broad cloth, dyed or shorn, except our burgesses of Haddington." The latter might seize offenders, while goods that were wrongly bought were to be disposed of in Haddington. King Robert also threw his protection over "those conveying timber or merchandise" for the town's needs. "Any one daring to poind goods or to annoy them unjustly on our highway in going to the said town of Haddington, or in returning, shall incur our heavy displeasure." Finally, the burgesses were to possess "all common rights and common pasturage in moors, in peat mosses . . . and in all other easements rightly pertaining" to the town.

Haddington was in those long bygone times handicapped by the fact that progress towards evolving a prosperous industrial township was checked periodically by the ravages of the English. When, in 1329, David II ascended the throne, Haddington was but slowly recovering from the violence and havoc caused by the "auld enemy." Still the existence of certain streets is indicative of the fact that the burgh was a place containing numerous groups of houses. Moreover, some sort of municipal government prevailed, and there must have been a little trade, the local customs a short time after yielding £873 Scots.

But this little demonstration of trading activity was rendered futile by another English invasion. Edward III being now at war with France, the latter in the hope of easing the situation sent troops and money to aid the Scots in recapturing Berwick. Actually this project was accomplished, but in violation of a treaty concluded between the Scots and the English whereby the king of the former (David II) had obtained his freedom.

Edward III learnt the news of the fall of Berwick with indignant surprise. Returning hurriedly to England, he marched northwards at the head of an army numbering, a contemporary writer says, eighty thousand; but this is probably an exaggeration. Berwick reverted to the English, and Edward, in his thirst for revenge, laid waste the whole country as far as Edinburgh. Haddington did not escape. Its Abbey, and the church of the Franciscans or Minorites, were set on fire, and savage warfare went on in the streets. In Bellenden's translation of the Latin History of Scotland by Hector Boece, we read: "Nocht lang efter, King Edward came to Haddington to the great damage of all pepill lyand thairabout." Bower, on the other hand, alludes to the destruction of the church of the Franciscans, the real "Lucerna Loudoniae"— "a costly and splendid building of wonderful beauty." Edward III's attack happened early in February 1355–56 and was long remembered as "Burnt Candlemas."

Hard on this calamity came another of a different sort. On the eve of the Nativity of the Virgin, 7th September 1358, the river Tyne, swollen by excessive rains, overflowed its banks, causing immense damage and considerable loss of life. The suburb of Nungate was levelled to the ground and many houses in Haddington were swept away. Bower, the mediæval chronicler, relates that when the inundation approached the Abbey, one of the nuns took up a small statue of the Virgin and threatened to throw it into the water if the blessed Mary did not protect the sacred building. Whereupon the waters of the Tyne miraculously subsided. A pleasing tale with which to beguile the credulous of a superstitious age, though hardly consolatory to those who had lost their all.

Like his father, David II sought the well-being of Haddington. On 8th February 1369–70 he granted a charter conveying reciprocal rights of trade to Haddington and Dunbar in wool, hides, and skins throughout the sheriffdom and earldom of March. In 1378 Haddington, it is interesting to add, stood fifth among Scottish towns as regards the yield of its customs on wool.[1] Yet in uncertain and tumultuous times the transition from prosperity to the reverse occurred with startling suddenness. Ten years later, because of the town's "decayed state and poverty," a yearly payment of £15 sterling was remitted for four years, in terms of a charter by Robert II granting the burghers certain rights, together with the harbour of Aberlady. Again, on 3rd December 1389, Robert II granted to "our burgh" of Haddington small customs and, among other concessions, liberty to cultivate the King's Meadow and the right of working coal and quarrying stone.

During the reign of Robert II Haddington twice found the English in its midst. The first occasion might be described as an act of "peaceful penetration," but the second, when Richard II swooped down on the inhabitants, was as serious an inroad as had ever been experienced. The circumstances attending the former are interesting. In 1380 a peace movement between the Scots and the English was on foot. Negotiations on the English side were entrusted to John of Gaunt, Duke of Lancaster. In June 1381 Lancaster arrived at an amicable settlement, somewhat precipitately, England being then in dire need of all the forces it could muster to combat Wat Tyler's rebellion. In point of fact, the insurgents bore Lancaster no goodwill, and when tidings reached him that a return to England would be dangerous, he decided to remain in Scotland, where he was hospitably entertained and provided with a safe-conduct. So Lancaster kept out of troubled waters, passing the time pleasantly in Edinburgh and Haddington.

Hardly had the Scots and the English become reconciled when fresh trouble arose. On 26th January 1384–85 a truce was made between England and France, in which

---

[1] I. F. Grant, *Social and Economic Development of Scotland*, p. 308.

Haddington in the Seventeenth Century (Slezer's View).

[*To face p.* 6.

Scotland was invited to share by Charles VI of France, who dispatched an embassy to Robert II. But peace negotiations had been suddenly endangered by the Scots invading the territories of the Earls of Northumberland and Nottingham and carrying off immense booty. Robert II declared that the raid had taken place without his sanction, but so strange an excuse did not placate Richard II, who determined to be avenged before the Scots could claim the benefit of the truce. Accordingly the two aggrieved earls marched into Scotland with two thousand men-at-arms and six thousand bowmen. Edinburgh and Haddington, as well as a wide area round about, were subjected to fire and sword, and the Scots taught a stern lesson for their foolhardiness.

There was another hostile invasion in the reign of Robert III. Reviving the old claim of suzerainty over Scotland, Henry IV marched on Edinburgh in August 1400 to receive the Scottish king's homage. On the way thither he halted with his army at Haddington, where he remained three days. Royal quarters were found in the Abbey, and Henry was well entertained. So at least it would appear, if Bower is to be believed. This chronicler notes that the English king rewarded the sisterhood, and that he celebrated in Haddington the Assumption of the Virgin Mary.

Henry IV's invasion was distinguished from all others inasmuch as it was the last time that an English king led his army into Scotland in person. It was singular in another respect: it was comparatively harmless. Granted the not unimportant proviso that the Scottish king became his vassal, Henry IV was peaceably inclined. But dissension arose in the English army, and other troubles were looming ahead. Henry had therefore to be content with the vague promise that his demand would be considered, and he retired with what Hill Burton characterises as "the most bloodless and inoffensive army that ever entered Scotland." [1]

With such an indeterminate situation there was no guarantee that the two countries would not return before long to the arbitrament of war. Henry's claim of overlordship had been countered by simple evasion; the promise that the matter would be duly discussed was a hollow one. Scotland had no intention of surrendering to so fatuous a demand as overlordship, and well Henry knew it. Distrust and suspicion were manifest on both sides. The Scots, apprehensive lest fresh attacks should overwhelm them, believed a state of preparedness the wisest policy.

In accordance with this view, James II issued a decree that all fighting men east of Edinburgh were to assemble in Haddington, which John Hardyng, the chronicler, who was in Scotland "at bidding and commandement of the fifth King Henry," described as twelve miles from Edinburgh. The itinerary and map of Scotland which Hardyng appended to his metrical *Chronicle* shows considerable knowledge of the country, though he was rather out of his reckoning in his reference to Haddington, unless it be that English mileage differed from Scottish. But in spite of Hardyng's cloudiness about its position, the county town of East Lothian had lost none of its military importance, and when bands of armed men came trooping in from all quarters, it must have had the appearance of a huge camp.

Such a state of affairs ministered no doubt to the spectacular but proved a deterrent to the growth of trade. No town can flourish in face of perpetual insecurity. In 1451 James II made an effort to arrest the retrogressive tendency by granting the burgesses of Haddington exemption from payment of the customs on salt, likewise on certain skins. While the exemption was an acknowledgment of the burghers' "manifold good services done to us heretofore," it was also an indication of where the royal intervention would be most timely and helpful. The burgesses were also

---

[1] Burton, *History of Scotland*, 1905, ii, 377.

empowered to sell or buy, or take in exchange, "the merchandise of salt or the above-mentioned skins, and that with any persons as well foreigners or non-freemen."

In the earlier half of the fifteenth century Haddington was the fourth largest Scottish town; Edinburgh, Dundee, and Aberdeen were the only communities that took precedence. In addition to a relatively large population, the town was prominent in other respects. James III held a council there in 1482, and in the same year a large army was encamped outside ready to do battle for the rights of the Scottish Crown. Nor did this host remain long unemployed. In August the Duke of Gloucester (afterwards Richard III) invaded Haddington with three thousand archers. He had previously captured Berwick and had then marched on Edinburgh. But from the Scottish capital Richard soon retired to a safer position behind the river Tyne at Lethington (Lennoxlove).

Haddington does not bulk largely in the career of James IV. He was in the town on 31st July 1493 when, a youth of twenty, he signed certain documents. On his arrival the town bells were rung and "every ilk man put on his . . . cloak." A more particular occasion was in 1496. In that year James, having decided to support the claim of Perkin Warbeck, assembled an army and a train of artillery which set out in September with the intention of invading England. The Scottish king, accompanied by Warbeck, marched by way of Haddington, where the night of 14th September seems to have been spent. The *Lord High Treasurer's Accounts* disclose that among the cannon was the famous "Mons Meg," which must therefore have been drawn through the streets of Haddington. Another interesting fact derived from the same source is that payment was made "to a man at Haddington to gyde the gunners the best gait," or, in modern parlance, to guide the Scots army across the Lammermoors.

In 1503 Margaret Tudor, daughter of Henry VII, rested in Haddington on her way to Edinburgh to marry James IV. The princess was lodged in the Abbey, while her retinue was accommodated in the Franciscan friary. In Leland's *Collectanea*, Young, the herald, narrates the royal progress in quaint detail and quainter spelling.

The said Quene . . . drew her way toward Hadington; and in passyng before Dunbarre they schott ordonnance for the luffe of hyr. Shee was loadged that sam night in the Abbey of the Nonnes ny to Hadington, and hyr company at the said place . . . was ordanned provysyon at the Grey Freres as well as for the company as for the horsys.

In the early years of James V's reign, during the absence of Albany in France, Arran was appointed Governor of Scotland, to which subsequently was added the office of Warden of the Marches. Arran, who was now the most powerful man in Scotland, paid at least one official visit to Haddington, where he summoned the sheriffs to confer with him.

In 1529 James V escaped from the guardianship of Angus and set about reducing the noble castle of Tantallon. In June he held two councils in Haddington. The king again visited the town in the summer of 1531, and for having lodged him, Sir Patrick Mauchline [1] was granted an annual payment of £10 for life, the money to be abstracted from the burgh customs. When this king travelled to France, Haddington made the fifth largest contribution of any town towards the royal expenses, liberality which was tardily requited in 1542 by a grant of the office of sheriff within the burgh and its liberties to the provost and bailies.

In the immensely destructive inroads by Hertford's army in 1544—an invasion remarkable for its enveloping character, fire and sword being carried into almost every

---

[1] Rood priest and kirk master. Died 1544.

corner between Edinburgh and the Borders—Haddington, it need hardly be said, was in the thick of the carnage. Once again the community experienced an orgy of "frightfulness" which is but faintly reflected in the laconic entry in Patten's *Expedicion to Scotlande*. "We burned a fine town of the Earl Bothwell's called Haddington, with a great nunnery and a house of Friars." But if this be not conclusive evidence, we have Hertford's assurance to Henry VIII that both Haddington and Dunbar had been "well brent." [1]

Hertford's depredations notwithstanding, the town remained a prize for which no sacrifice on the part of Scotland's foe was too great, and in 1548–49 it was the scene of what a modern historian has described as the most memorable siege in all Scottish history. It lasted more than eighteen months during which the English garrison, it must be admitted, displayed a courage, endurance, and resourcefulness that has evoked general admiration.

Although there is no lack of material from which to construct a verbal picture of this famous siege, it has never received the attention it deserves. Moreover, the siege of 1548–49 is the most conspicuous event in the history of Haddington, and in a work like the present should receive space commensurate with its importance. It is therefore proposed in the next chapter to narrate as fully and accurately as possible, and from original sources, the story of the siege of Haddington.

[1] Hay Fleming, *Reformation in Scotland*, p. 331.

CHAPTER II

The Siege of 1548–49

AFTER the battle of Pinkie in September 1547 a large part of Lowland Scotland, with many of the castles, was in English hands. That the hold thus established should become permanent was the dominant aim of the conquerors. Henry VIII was recently dead, and as his successor, Edward VI, was only ten years old, the reins of government passed to Protector Somerset, whose savagery in the invasion of 1544 the Scots had good reason to remember. Nothing but complete subjugation would satisfy Somerset, and for this purpose a large army was assembled under Lord Grey de Wilton, whose military prowess at Pinkie had impressed Somerset.

As the English conquest extended as far north as Dundee, the permanent occupation of so extensive a territory was one of considerable difficulty. To garrison the whole area would have needed a much larger army than was available. All that could be done was to station formidable bodies of troops at strategic points. Two were fixed on: Broughty Ferry, as guarding the mouth of the Tay and the area round Dundee, and Haddington, the key to the fertile country of the Lothians and Edinburgh. Had Somerset been a free agent, he would have preferred Dunbar, but as that town was still occupied by Scots, Haddington was chosen instead. Without direct sea communication, it had yet one or two substantial advantages. In the words of Jean de Beaugué, who served with the French forces in Scotland, and wrote a graphic though not wholly reliable account of the siege, Haddington was situated at the heart of "a fruitful and pleasant country, near the capital city, not very far remote from the centre of Scotland."

The story begins in January 1547-48. In that month Lord Grey, with Sir Thomas Palmer as second in command, advanced from Berwick to Haddington, which, after much opposition, was captured. The *Diurnal of Occurrents* states that the English force numbered "tua thowsand men." All "the houssis of the Tyne" were taken possession of, but no damage was done, and everything was paid for. From the same source we learn that after capturing the town the English fortified it with "fowssis (fosses) and blokhous." Six weeks were spent in strengthening the defences, the work being supervised by Palmer. No traces of the fortifications remain above ground, but contemporary accounts suggest a quadrangular fort with bastions at the four corners, the whole being encircled with a ditch and broad rampart. Behind was a second ditch and rampart from which arquebusiers could fire in safety. This inner curtain, with turrets at the corners, enclosed the donjon. The defences were further strengthened by earthworks thrown up at some distance from the outer ditch on which guns of small calibre were mounted. In the matter of defence Haddington had also natural advantages, particularly its low-lying situation.

The main incidents of the siege are recounted in two contemporary accounts, one focussing the English point of view, the other the French. Both are sufficiently circumstantial to afford a vivid picture, though it would be unwise to place implicit trust in the veracity of either narrator. Indeed it is at times fairly obvious that each is drawing on his imagination, a thing not surprising in an uncritical age.

The English account, published in 1575, is from the pen of one Ulpian Fulwell. His "Discourse of the worthy service done at Haddington" forms an appendix to a scarce tract entitled *The Flower of Fame,* and is based on information conveyed to him by "certaine captaines" attached to the English garrison, who "seemed greatly to lament that so noble a piece of service as was done at Haddington should so lightly pass through the hands of cronographers." While one seems to detect the cloven hoof in Fulwell's remark that the French besiegers were fond of saying that there were "few good souldiers in England save those that took part in the siege of Haddington," Fulwell's story, second-hand though it be, probably is in the main trustworthy.

The French narrator, Jean de Beaugué, has this advantage over Fulwell, that he was an eye-witness of the events he describes. As has been already noted, Beaugué accompanied the French force, which was under the command of André de Montalambert Sieur d'Essé, and which was intended to aid the Scots in driving out the English from the territory in Scotland they had conquered. Beaugué's account was published in 1556 and translated in 1707 by Patrick Abercromby, author of *Martial Achievements of the Scots Nation.* It describes the methods of warfare adopted by the contending forces, but is vague topographically, and lacks the dramatic power and sense of actuality pervading Fulwell's narrative.

The English writer would have us believe that the French contingent comprised "lustre and gallant souldiers," but is seriously out of his reckoning in stating that the force was twenty thousand strong. Moreover, though the army sent by Henry II was predominantly French, it contained a fair proportion of Germans, Italians, and other nationalities. This force had with them, according to the *Diurnal of Occurrents,* "ane desone of cannonis with vther small pieces," [1] which certainly would be beggarly equipment for an army of twenty thousand men.

Early in May the fortifying of Haddington was complete. The English garrison, numbering two thousand foot and five hundred horse, was commanded by Sir James Wilford (or Wilsford), a man "apt for that chardge" and "of great diligence." [2] It was now in its quarters with two months' victuals and one month's fodder.[3] All was therefore in readiness for a siege which, it was generally feared, would be long and destructive. The garrison, however, appears to have been in good heart, Grey, who left Haddington on 12th June, informing Somerset that "there was never men less dismayed nor more desirous to see their enemies."

Meanwhile the Scots were chiefly concerned about the destiny of their young queen, but the arrival of the French levies made Arran, the Governor, aware that the English invasion also was of pressing importance. On 29th April he marched to Haddington with five thousand men and ten cannon, but retired without firing a shot. The English within the town had heard of the arrival of the French and were fully prepared to give them and the Scots a warm reception.

It is a curious fact that the garrison had the co-operation of the civilian population, who seem to have fraternised with their conquerors. Grey testifies that throughout the siege the townsfolk assisted the English in various ways. The burghers at that

---

[1] P. 46.

[2] A portrait of Wilford by an unknown painter is in the Scottish National Portrait Gallery. It is thus described in the *Catalogue* (1895): "Figure to below the waist . . . short, thick brown hair, brown moustache and beard . . .; black armour, with white collar and bands at wrist; his right hand holds a baton, and his left rests on a table . . ., on which lies his helmet." Perhaps the most interesting feature of the painting is that a view of the siege of "Haddington Tovn" appears to the right, with the inscription: "Taken and defended agaynst two beseages of the Scotes asisted by the Frenche bie the valeure of the Englishe men, this knighte being theyre captayne, Sir James Wilford." The portrait (from the Earl of Westmoreland's collection, and presented by a former Marquess of Tweeddale) is dated 1547, but as the siege did not take place till the following year, it may be presumed that the "view" must have been painted in after the portrait of Wilford was finished.

[3] *C.S.P.,* i, 105. The letters stand for *Calendar of Scottish Papers.*

time were mostly adherents of the ancient religion, though there appears to have been a sprinkling of converts to the Reformed faith, for Grey makes the request that preachers be sent to Haddington in the hope of spreading the new opinions.

No sooner had Grey returned to the English headquarters at Berwick than he received news that great numbers of the English horse at Haddington had deserted. These, however, were quickly replaced, and, accompanying the fresh relieving force, was additional equipment in the shape of weapons, tools, and ammunition.[1] By the third week of June preparations for the defence were far advanced. Practically all that remained to be done was the demolition of structures outside the fortifications which might impede defenders and besiegers alike.

On 30th June, Palmer, who had charge of the defences, wrote exultingly to Somerset: "The Haddyngtons hath doon ondres [wonders] in their fortifycacions, nothing left unperfected. So as on Thursday last they made holiday, and 2000 of them with their ensigns marched to the top of the hills in great triumph, hoping to have seen the enemy as they desired. . . . We shall now have hourly news I trust to rejoice your grace. Most men think kepying Haddynton ye wyne Skotland."[2]

Grey had orders to take down the parish church which, from its detached position south of the town, menaced the garrison. On 2nd July it was reported that the edifice was "in maner" demolished, which meant that the roof had been removed, the pillars cut and underpropped, and the building rendered insecure generally.[3] Still the damage was not such as to prevent the church playing an important part in the siege, for on the following day a body of besiegers were stationed behind the building, the hackbutters of which climbed the steeple and fired into the town. Yet Palmer was able to inform Somerset on 4th July that "our men have so beaten the church that no man dare show in it."[4]

Barely a week had passed since the arrival of the French before Haddington. On 29th June, Beaugué tells us that the advance guard appeared on the Garleton Hills, and that fifty lances were detached to entice the English beyond the fortifications. The ruse succeeded. Three hundred horse sallied forth but did not engage the attacking force who ventured no farther than the range of the English guns.

The besiegers now surveyed the defences, the garrison firing periodically, though with little effect. Next day French cavalry advanced to the north port (Hardgate), three hundred arquebusiers were posted at the Tyne, and d'Essé, in spite of the English cannon and the appearance of two hundred lances at the west port, carried out a leisurely reconnaisance. At the east end of the town English bowmen and arquebusiers, who had come from behind the barriers, had a tussle with the French stationed there. After a time the latter feigned a retreat until, on reaching the Garleton Hills, they were reinforced by troops that had lain in ambush. The English, thinking they were outnumbered, fled but were pursued and severely mauled, "the whole way" being strewn with slain and wounded. Wilford, the governor of Haddington, with two hundred lances and a small force of arquebusiers came to the rescue, but were compelled to retire.

For the moment the English had been repulsed. On 30th June the allies, consisting of eight thousand Scots and six thousand French, invested the town, and the siege was begun in earnest. The main force was concentrated at the west end of the town, the Scots headquarters being at Lethington (Lennoxlove), the French at Clerkington. A determined attempt was made to breach the fortifications, but, according to Fulwell, the fire from the ramparts was effective.

[1] C.S.P., i, 121. [2] Ibid., i, 133. [3] Ibid., i, 136 [4] Ibid., i, 138.

Because the gates of the town were not of any strength, our men were constrained to ram up the gates with earth, and to maintain the defence from the walls . . . and there were many assaults given, to the loss of both parties.   In the end, our enemies so beat the town with shot that they left not one whole house in which our men might put their heads; whereby they were constrained to lie under the walls. . . . Thus were the French able to come close . . . , there being no more distance between the two parties than the thickness of the wall. . . . One of the bulwarks was beaten down so flat that a man might ride in and out at the breach . . .

Fulwell gives an amusing instance of the primitive means adopted by the garrison to beat back the besiegers.

It grieved the English to see their neighbours so near their noses.   Whereupon a blunt countryman . . . invented a way to beat them from the walls with flails.   He tied a heavy plummet of lead to the end of a rope, fastening the other end to a good truncheon to hold in the hand, and with such flails they slew and maimed a great number of them.

Most of the cannon of the attackers were trained on the south-west corner of the town, and here at times the fighting raged furiously.   At the base of the Garleton Hills were three pieces of artillery, but seven brass guns on the north bulwark "beat them so hotly" that the besiegers withdrew.[1]   On 1st July the French dug trenches against the west and south defences and next day made another attempt to breach the walls.   Germans serving with the French shot "cutthrottis" from the church tower into the town, but the English made their position untenable.[2]   "Their hack-butters," writes Palmer and Holcroft, "go to the top and shoot into the town at random, but our men lie close and shoot to some purpose."   Indeed so deadly was the fire of the English that the French had difficulty in finding men willing to work at the "uncomfortable labour" of trench-making.

Convinced that the re-taking of Haddington would be no easy matter, the besiegers requisitioned additional cannon from the French fleet in the Firth of Forth.   These were landed at Aberlady and Dunbar, and, posted at Gimmersmills, in Nungate, fired into the town.   The French camp was situated "beside the mills of Haddington next Clerkington," their battery, which at first consisted of only two cannon, being "placed in a little cornfield."[3]

On 4th July a Scots army, four thousand strong and commanded by Argyle, arrived at the scene of action.   Hitherto co-operation between Scots and French had not been cordial, despite the fact that the French regarded their allies as "very good company." They were amazed, however, at their appearance—"almost naked" and with "painted waistcoats and a sort of Woollen Covering, variously coloured."[4]   Equipped with bows, broadswords, and targes, the Scots proved good fighters.   Even before they had encamped, several hundreds were detached from the main body and attacked the English guard at the west port.   But when the garrison's cannon thundered forth, terror seized them.   Beaugué declares that they "shut their ears and threw themselves on their bellies at each shot of the cannon."

The fire of the English had become a disturbing factor, so much so that the besiegers threw up counter-fortifications at the Abbey (or east) port, which by 4th July were within forty feet of those of the enemy.   The speed with which these military works

---

[1] *C.S.P.*, i, 133.   [2] *Ibid.*, i, 137.

[3] Miller in his *Lamp of Lothian* refers to traces of an old fortification, south-west of the town, which existed in his day.   Circular in form, it was known as the "New Wark."   In the burgh records, under date 19th July 1576, there is mention of the "gait (road) passand to ye new wark."   It has been suggested, and with some degree of probability, that the tower was constructed by the French for the purpose of mounting cannon. The New Wark, which stood in the playing field of the New School buildings, was pulled down in the first half of last century.

[4] Beaugué, 18.

were got ready was due to the impressment of five hundred slaves from French ships lying in Aberlady Bay. These victims of forced labour ran the gauntlet of the English musketry, and that the casualties were high is testified by an English spy who states that "they carry them off hourly in carts, dead and wounded." [1]

On the following morning six large guns pounded the defences at the south-west corner, the reverberations of which, Beaugué reports,[2] "awakened those in Haddington with a vengeance." But though the cannonade was intense, it did little damage, most of the shot being buried in the earth composing the outer curtain. Consequently the besiegers, desiring to be more effective, removed their artillery farther east. Here another two hundred rounds were fired at close range, but again with meagre results. Still the bastions at the west end were "condamnit," and the Tolbooth injured.[3] When the firing had ceased, an assault was begun, the French placing scaling-ladders against the ramparts on the west and south. But little was accomplished, the damage being speedily repaired and the defences pronounced stronger than ever.[4]

Up to this point the task of besieging Haddington had been largely, if not wholly, in the hands of the French. Although, as we have seen, a large Scots army had arrived under Argyle, the relations between the allies were not cordial. D'Essé had assigned a place to the Scots in the plan of attack, but the latter declined to co-operate. They are said to have expected the town to be retaken without their assistance, but if that were so, why was a formidable Scots army sent to Haddington? Perhaps the true explanation is that the Scots feared that the French would not implement their bargain, *i.e.* the expulsion of the English garrison, their main concern being the completion of the treaty for the marriage of the young Scottish queen to the Dauphin of France. As the retaking of Haddington was made the condition of their signing the treaty, the Scots apparently had resolved to hasten slowly in the matter of assisting the French. The latter therefore for a time carried on the siege under the critical eye of the Scots.

Happily the affair of the treaty, which had such an important bearing on the siege, was settled at last. On 7th July 1548 momentous happenings took place in the Abbey of Haddington. There the Scots Parliament had assembled, together with the Queen-Mother (Mary of Lorraine) and Arran, when D'Oysel, the French ambassador, made known the kind of requital his master (Henry II) expected in return for coming to the aid of the Scots. "The maist Christian king of France," moved by the ancient alliance and "the mortall weires, crudelities, depredatiounis, and intollerabill injuris done by our auld enemeis of Ingland," had "set his haill harte and minde for defence of this realm" of Scotland, and, for "the more perfect union and indissoluble amity of France and Scotland," desired that Mary Queen of Scots and the Dauphin be married "to the perpetuall honour, plesour, and proffeit of baith the realms."

The assent of the Estates to this treaty is said to have been given "in ane voice," but in truth there were influential dissentients, notably Arran. In hardly an agreeable atmosphere therefore was brought about one of the epoch-making treaties of Scottish history. But many were sceptical as to whether the French alliance was a well-chosen policy. Might they not be paying too high a price if it meant, as indeed it did mean, that Scotland was being used by France merely as a tool wherewith to aid in the subjugation of England? Moreover, a considerable body of Scots sincerely wished a religious awakening similar to that in progress south of the Border.

But the Treaty of Haddington was firmly supported by the Queen-Mother, and Arran could do nothing but approve, at least outwardly. The treaty was signed

---

[1] *C.S.P.*, i, 137. [2] Beaugué, 22.
[3] *Scot. Corres. of Mary of Lorraine*, 248–249. [4] *C.S.P.*, i, 139.

accordingly, but with the proviso that the French king should defend the liberties and laws of Scotland, which implied that the whole armed strength of France now in Scotland would be utilised for the expulsion of the English.[1] Nor was this condition to be interpreted in any formal sense, for on the day on which the Treaty of Haddington was signed Arran relinquished the Regency in favour of d'Essé, who was invested with the Scottish regalia which the Queen-Mother had brought with her from Edinburgh.[2]

The treaty notwithstanding, the French were tardy in resuming military operations in Haddington. For this they probably were not entirely to blame. No working agreement between them and the Scots seemed possible. Worse still, if Beaugué is to be believed, some of the Scots were secretly co-operating with the English in return for hard cash.[3] In such a predicament the French were not prepared to bear the brunt of the fighting without being substantially reinforced.

Meanwhile the English were furnishing supplies to the garrison in Haddington, and, on 7th July, Grey, with Sir Robert Bowes, Warden of the Middle March, and Sir Thomas Palmer, set out from Berwick with a supporting force of two thousand men. On reaching Linton Bridge four hundred mounted arquebusiers were sent in advance with supplies for the beleaguered garrison. Crossing Nungate Bridge, they reached the east port without mishap, and, on raising the welcome cry of "Socours,"[4] were admitted. Only now was the alarm sounded in the camp of the besiegers, who hotly pursued a body of arquebusiers returning to the main force at Linton Bridge with the horses of their comrades who had remained behind to strengthen the garrison.[5] Beaugué says[6] that the arquebusiers passed within two hundred yards of the Scots camp which, if true, was an unflattering comment on the vigilance of the Scots. The French were "much moved and called it treason."[7]

Strengthened numerically and replenished with food and munitions, the English put fresh vigour into their efforts to frustrate the plans of their enemies. The latter mined the south-west bastion and its collapse was expected, but the English, fearing the worst, isolated this bulwark. A mound of earth was substituted, and was kept low so that it could not be seen by the attacking force. From this mound as well as from the flanking walls the English poured a deadly fire. And when the besiegers "had tastyd of such an assault or twayne, ther were no doubt but they would be found coole enough."[8]

By this time intensive siege operations were in progress. Cannon were trained on the centre of the town. Some of these were mounted at the parish church, but so hot was the garrison's reply that this position had to be abandoned.[9] By 10th July the French had dug some twenty feet into the earthworks on the south and had constructed a trench alongside the ditch. "Mynners" at work outside the fortifications were defended by seven cannon,[10] but the English marksmanship was such that it was with difficulty that the French could induce men to do this work.[11] As it was, two cannon were dislodged on the west, while a mine on the south was rendered ineffective. We also hear of sixty arquebusiers and twenty pikemen from the garrison escorting harvesters engaged in cutting corn outside the north port.[12]

D'Essé planned a general assault for 14th July, but when the day came many Scots

[1] C.S.P., i, 139.   [2] Ibid., i, 139.
[3] Beaugué, 23–24; Leslie, History of Scotland (S.T.S. ed.), 310.
[4] C.S.P., i, 140.   [5] Hamilton Papers, ii, 598–599.   [6] Beaugué, p. 28.
[7] Calendar State Papers (Domestic), 1601–1603, and Addenda, 1547–1603, 390.
[8] Hamilton Papers, ii, 599.   [9] C.S.P., i, 146.
[10] Hamilton Papers, ii, 602–603.   [11] Ibid., ii, 603.   [12] Ibid., i, 146.

had deserted. Consequently the French were but half-hearted in their attack, with the result that about eighty were killed and many injured. D'Essé made overtures to Arran for assistance, but the latter was not enamoured of the prowess of the French, who "did nothing but destroy the country." The French leader, on his part, accused his allies of ingratitude.[1] After an interview, at which both Arran and d'Essé were present, a thousand Scots left Haddington.[2]

D'Essé now let it be known that no further effort to retake the town could be made till 17th July when Argyle was expected to arrive with a fresh body of troops. The garrison, however, believed that the French were about to depart,[3] colour being given to the rumour by the removal of the greater part of the ordnance to Edinburgh.[4] But the whole affair was a ruse, and when the English sallied forth they were attacked and driven back into the town.

Presently the French, aware that a fresh English army, under Grey and Palmer, was advancing on Haddington, made hurried preparations for an inevitable encounter, while the Queen-Mother went through the streets of Edinburgh inciting French and Scots soldiers to return to Haddington and drive out the English. Beaugué states that the Queen-Mother's appeal was not in vain. "In an hour's time there was not one soldier of either nation (excepting sick) to be seen in the city."

D'Essé seems to have done everything to check the advance of Grey and Palmer. The south bank of Tyne was lined with French and Scots, the trenches were guarded by eight hundred Germans, while an equally strong force was posted at Clerkington. Grey was not ignorant of what was in store for him. Wilford was anxious that the advance should be delayed till prospects of success were brighter, but either the advice of the captain of the garrison did not reach Grey in time, or he saw reason to reject it.[5] In any case, the clash of opposing forces was not long delayed. When a detachment of mounted arquebusiers reached the outskirts of the town they found further progress barred by French cavalry, numbering one hundred and fifty. The English, however, had the best of the skirmish and the French fled.[6] This success heartened Grey's main force, which marched to the far side of the Tyne.

And now occurred the incident known as "Tuesday's Chase," so named because the day happened to be a Tuesday. Some of the English mistook a body of French horse for a portion of Grey's forces and there was a sharp engagement close to the Franciscan friary. The garrison under Wilford, in an attempt to rescue their comrades, suffered heavy losses and Palmer was taken prisoner. The losses are variously enumerated. Beaugué puts them as high as eight hundred killed and two thousand prisoners. In Birrel's *Diary* the statement is that "money (many) was taken and slaine," which sounds a more moderate computation and probably in accordance with fact. While the French horse are credited with pursuing the English for eight miles,[7] the latter fought with great gallantry, and doubtless derived some consolation from the circumstance that while the relieving army was being chased, the garrison raided the French camp, carried away some cannon, and destroyed the scaling ladders.

Next day, 18th July, the Queen-Mother paid another visit to Haddington, principally to congratulate the French, but also to reconcile her fellow-countrymen with her refractory subjects. She also inspected the French camp, and even mounted the tower of the parish church to see how matters fared in the town. But she was seen

---

[1] C.S.P., i, 147.   [2] Ibid., i, 147.   [3] Ibid., i, 148; Hamilton Papers, ii, 614.
[4] Calendar State Papers (Domestic), 1601–1603, and Addenda, 1547–1565, 391; Scots. Corres. of Mary of Lorraine, 250–251.
[5] C.S.P., i, 148.   [6] Hamilton Papers, ii, 614–615.   [7] C.S.P., i, 148.

by the English gunners who were ungallant enough to fire a volley of "chayne and other haile shot as slew and hurt a great nombre about hyr."

"Tuesday's Chase," though disastrous for the English, still left the crucial problem unsolved—the expulsion of the English from Haddington. The defences had been greatly strengthened, and it seemed as if the only way to achieve success would be to blockade the town and bring about submission by starvation. On 22nd July Wilford wrote that the town was five times as impregnable as it was when the siege began,[1] which seemed convincing proof that the capture of Haddington by assault was surrounded with almost insuperable difficulties.

Intensive blockade at any rate was resolved upon. As a step in this direction it was suggested, says Beaugué, that the French should make their headquarters at the Abbey. The French did remove their camp, but whether they found a new lodgment at the Abbey is not so certain. Anyhow the new position was regarded as less dangerous from the English point of view, for the garrison frequently ventured beyond the fortifications, not, however, as a sign of strength but of weakness.[2]

The truth is supplies were running low, and if relief did not come quickly, the state of the English would be as desperate as their enemies could wish. In response to Wilford's despairing appeal, a new army of nearly two thousand men, and carrying food supplies, reached the beleaguered town on 23rd July, only, however, to be severely mauled by the besiegers, who, says the *Diurnal of Occurrents*,[3] killed a hundred and took twelve hundred prisoners. But other authorities indicate that the English losses were considerably less.[4]

This defeat drove home the truth that the encircling army was not to be beaten off by spasmodic and somewhat trifling displays of armed power. Hitherto the English had underrated the resilience of the attacking force, and it was now obvious that if the garrison was to be relieved, a large army would be required. But to attain this object was by no means easy. For one thing, the army of occupation was stationed nearly four hundred miles from London, which signified a great deal in an era of primitive transport; and for another, malversation was rampant. Holcroft mentions the staggering fact that in five months no less than £14,000 of public money had been disbursed for food, all of which had been diverted into the pockets of the officers. These formidable handicaps notwithstanding, a huge expeditionary force was organised, which was to have the assistance of the fleet. Besides transporting the troops, the ships were to carry food for the garrison. The port of Aberlady was to be the landing place. But in the midst of preparations this fair prospect was overcast by Somerset's announcement of a policy of strict economy. Shrewsbury was instructed to reduce the army intended for Haddington by several thousand men. A compromise, however, was brought about when it was known that Argyle with "all the power of Scotland" was marching on Haddington, determined to make a final attempt to oust the English.[5]

On 18th August the fleet set sail from Berwick, and not before time, with fifteen thousand men, mostly infantry, on board.[6] Little or no food supplies were reaching the town owing to the vigilance of the besiegers, though a party of "assured" Scots smuggled in small quantities. This episode raises the interesting question as to how the inhabitants comported themselves during the siege. Certain it is that the practice was sufficiently notorious to lead to the circulation of an order calling upon the East

---

[1] *C.S.P.*, i, 149.   [2] Beaugué, 47.   [3] Page 47.
[4] *Calendar State Papers (Domestic), and Addenda, 1547–1565,* 392.
[5] *C.S.P.*, i, 158.   [6] Hume Brown, *History of Scotland,* ii, 34.

Lothian lairds to see that no help was given to the English garrison on pain of being "hanged, drawn, and quartered" and "landes and goodes" forfeited.[1]

By 22nd August the expeditionary force was encamped near Aberlady and, meeting with no opposition, entered Haddington two days later. But their stay was short. Beaugué tells us that after leaving four hundred horse to make good the losses of the garrison, and presumably food as well, they returned to Berwick. That all this should have been accomplished without one blow being struck on either side may be explained in several ways. The French, disappointed at the paltriness of the aid sent by Arran in compliance with an urgent appeal from d'Essé, were not prepared to risk an engagement in which they would be largely outnumbered. Several French detachments had already retired to Leith to hasten the fortification of that seaport, while others were preparing to return to France. As for the Scots, both Shrewsbury and Grey informed Somerset that they were at vanishing-point. In these circumstances d'Essé, to his "inexpressible regret," was obliged to retire with his forces to Musselburgh, and to abandon the fortification of Aberlady and Dunbar.[2]

A period of inactivity supervened. September was a blank month so far as the siege was concerned, and early in October the French had taken up their winter quarters. But d'Essé could not reconcile himself to the *status quo* and decided to make another attempt to expel the English. Resolving on a night attack, he brought his forces from Musselburgh by a "convenient and secret avenue," and arrived before the town on 10th October. In his *History of the Reformation* Knox furnishes a vivid account of what appears to have been a thrilling episode. The Reformer was then toiling in the French galleys but heard the story from eye-witnesses. Knox describes how the French approached Haddington shortly after midnight when only the English sentinels were awake. D'Essé's men advanced "so secreatlye that thei war never espyed till that the formar war within the basse courte, and the haill company in the churchyard, nott two payre of bout's lenth's [3] distant from the toune." Then the English, roused by the cries of the watch, rushed to the attack with "bowes and billes," and a fierce conflict ensued near the east port. Beaugué's version is that the alarm was given by the attackers overpowering the guard and making "the walls resound with the name of France." Knox's version makes it clear that the French had marched by the south of the town, and, passing through the churchyard (on the north side of which there was then a road), finally took up a position between Lady Kitty's Garden and Nungate Bridge, *i.e.*, the Sands or, as Knox says, near the east port. To continue the Reformer's homely vernacular:—

One [soldier] amongis many cumes to the Easte porte, whare lay two great pieces of ordnance, and whare the ennemies [the French] war known to be, and cryed to his fellowes that war at the yett macking defence, "Ware befoir"; and so fyres a great peace (*sic*) and thareafter another, which God so conducted, that after thame war no farther persuyt maid; for the bullates redounded fra the wall of the Freir Kirk to the wall of Sanct Katherine's Chapell, which stood direct foiranent it, and fra the wall of the said Chapell to the said Kirk wall agane, so oft, that thare fell mo than ane hundreth of the French. . . . Thei schott oft, but the French reteired with diligence and returned to Edinburgh without harme done, except the destructioun of some drynkin bear, which lay in the saidis Chapell and Kirk.[4]

And from Knox we pass to a modern version of the happenings at Haddington on this memorable day. It is from the brilliant though not always accurate pen of Froude.

[1] *Hamilton Papers*, ii, 617.   [2] *C.S.P.*, i, 160.
[3] The signification of the phrase "bout's lenth" is difficult to determine. One of the meanings of "bout" given in the *Oxford English Dictionary* is "the going and returning of the plough," which may supply a clue.
[4] Knox's *History*, ed. Laing, ii, 403-411.

The sentinels (says this Victorian historian) had but time to give the alarm before they were killed; the watch was driven in, and some of the French entered with them, in the confusion. . . . These, seizing the gates and keeping them open, the assailants behind were thronging after them in force, when a cannon, loaded with grapeshot was fired by an unknown hand into the thick of the crowd, and destroyed a hundred men upon the spot. The check gave the English time to collect. While the attacking party were still reeling under the effect of the discharge, they poured down upon them through a postern. The gun was again charged and fired; the gates were closed, and all who remained inside were cut down or killed in jumping from the battlements. Furious at his failure, d'Essé again led up his troops to the assault . . . but the whole garrison were by this time under arms. Three times the French came up to be driven back with desperate loss.[1]

Viewing his situation as hopeless, d'Essé drew off his men and returned to Edinburgh, "sair lamenting," as Bishop Lesley puts it, "that out of his hands in a maner was reft sa gude ane occasionne of victorie." [2]   Arran, too, deplored the turn of events. He had rejoiced "not a litell" when news was brought him that Haddington had been taken and that the whole garrison had been put to the sword, save a few near the south wall. Not only so, but he had assembled a body of horse and rode to the help of the French. His chagrin therefore was great when, after starting from Edinburgh, a second message reached him that the French had been defeated. Nevertheless Arran continued the march in the vain hope that the posture of affairs would not be as bad as was represented. Before long, however, he had ocular demonstration that the first tidings were untrue, for suddenly he came upon the retreating French. Whereupon Arran turned about and with his horsemen rode back to Edinburgh.

The French had indeed suffered disaster, but a more frightful enemy was now at the gates of Haddington. The plague had broken out and soon appalling conditions prevailed in the beleaguered town. By November the garrison, whose exhausted state made them easy victims of the scourge, could count on less than a thousand men capable of carrying on the defence, and even they were "more like to be sick than the sick to mend," for they were housed in "cabins," without beds and without sufficient clothing. Food too was scanty, bad weather having ruined the crops.[3]

Such was the woeful tale that Wilford, governor of Haddington, imparted to Somerset. That it was not exaggerated is shown by another letter to the Protector, dated 14th November, in which the writer says that "the sick soldiers from Haddington, etc., are shut out of houses and die of want in the streets." [4]

Knox asserts that the English departed in the "spring tyme" of 1549, but he is clearly in error. They would have gladly evacuated the town at an earlier date than they did. Unfortunately, the ravages of the plague riveted them to the spot. Fulwell gives a distorted view when he affirms that "neither the want of clothes, nor the severity of the plague, which was hot among them (i.e. the English), nor the lack of ammunition, nor the sharp sauce of hunger, could make them yield up the town." In point of fact, there was every reason for the evacuation, for by this time the English hold on the conquered territory in Scotland had been loosened, the chief places held by them having been recovered.

At the beginning of 1549 the centre of military operations had shifted to Broughty Ferry. Less importance therefore was attached to the retention of Haddington. Be this as it may, the English had occasional skirmishes with the Scots who manned Dunbar Castle. In one of these Wilford and about fifty mounted arquebusiers were surrounded close to the fortress. Fierce fighting ensued, and Wilford, who was wounded, surrendered along with the bulk of his force. Wilford was sent a prisoner

---

[1] Froude, *History of England*, iv, 325–326.   [2] Leslie, *History of Scotland* (S.T.S.), ii, 317.
[3] *C.S.P.*, i, 166.   [4] *Calendar State Papers (Domestic), 1601–1603, and Addenda*, 394.

to Stirling Castle, and he was succeeded in the governorship of Haddington by Sir James Croft.[1] Soon after, important changes also took place in the French command. D'Essé gave place to Paul de Termes. Arran seems to have been mainly responsible for this replacement, since he complained that d'Essé wasted his forces in unprofitable ventures, that he was "more injurious to his friends than enemies," and that his men were so overbearing, "that by reason of the intestine discord all was like to be ruined." With de Termes came fresh troops to replace the Germans who had gone home. D'Essé's successor was firmly convinced that Haddington could only be reduced by a blockade. Accordingly, he fortified Aberlady[2] to prevent English supplies being landed there. A fort was also erected at Luffness, the remains of which may still be seen. By this means, and with the help of the Scots garrison at Dunbar Castle, the English position was soon precarious enough.

Early in August the defenders of Haddington found the pressure so great that it was actually proposed that the town should be evacuated, and that the conquered land to the south be divided among those who had served in the campaign.[3] In this way the English border would be strengthened. But apart from this, something had to be done, seeing that the sterner and more insidious enemy—"the pest and hungar was rycht evill amangis tham":[4] disease was thinning the ranks of the defenders, while "wind and rain [were] too much to write of."[5] In September the English command at Berwick was informed that the garrison would "no longer abide their misery," and as repeated and piteous appeals for help were made, reinforcements were again got ready. The fresh army numbered fully three thousand men, included horse and foot and "tag and rag of all sortes," and was commanded by the Earl of Rutland. Its object was to bring off the garrison in Haddington, likewise what munitions remained.

On the night of 13th September the English reinforcements encamped at Innerwick. The French and Scots, numerically stronger, were posted at East Linton. The opposing forces therefore were within measurable distance of each other. Next morning the French and Scots unaccountably withdrew to Tranent, a move that did not help the English so much as might have been expected. For one thing, the Tyne was in flood "as the like hath byn syldom sen," and for another, Linton Bridge had been broken down by the allies. These hindrances notwithstanding, Haddington was reached before the day closed. Once behind the fortifications, Rutland's army set fire to the town; Lethington also was committed to the flames. Arms and munitions were placed on wagons, and preparations for evacuation were completed. Authorities differ as to when the English quitted Haddington. The *Diurnal of Occurrents*[6] mentions 14th September, which is manifestly wrong, if the relieving force did not reach their destination till that date. It is difficult to suppose that they would leave within a few hours of their arrival. Joseph Bain in his Introduction to the *Calendar of Scottish Papers* says that the English remained "till at least 17th September," while Thomas Fisher, in a letter to Cecil, conveys the impression that it was the 18th. Again, the writer of the Introduction to the *East Lothian* volume of the Ancient Monuments Commission asserts, on the strength of letters reproduced in *Select Illustrations of Scottish History*, that the English were still in Haddington as late as the 27th. Buchanan assigns a later date still—1st October. Certain items in the *Accounts of the Lords Treasurer of Scotland*,[7] however, indicate that the Scots and French were in possession

[1] *Scot. Corres. of Mary of Lorraine*, p. 355 n.
[2] Leslie, *History of Scotland* (S.T.S.), ii, 329.
[3] *C.S.P.*, i, 177.
[4] *Diurnal of Occurrents*, 48.
[5] *C.S.P.*, i, 179.
[6] Page 48.
[7] ix, 341.

of the town by 20th September. Anyhow the evidence seems conclusive that the English finally departed from the "evill taken towne" of Haddington in the latter part of September 1549.

The fluctuating course of events, which lasted eighteen months, has been traced with a wealth of detail made possible by abundance of material. The siege of Haddington is the most famous in Scottish history, whether we have regard to its protracted duration, or the skill and thoroughness with which the town was defended, or the strange and wayward conjunction of Scots and French in an effort to bring about its fall.

CHAPTER III

Catholicism and the Kirk

IN the middle of the sixteenth century the Reformation movement in Scotland, despite the zealous preaching of George Wishart, was making slow progress. Catholic Christianity still held sway over the vast majority of the people. There were few signs of the growth of that Protestant teaching which, in less than twenty years, was to leaven two-thirds of the entire population. This adherence to the old religion did not rest on doctrinal grounds, for the Catholic Church in Scotland had long been bankrupt in faith and morals, and had justly earned the contempt of good men. The attachment to the pre-Reformation type of religion was a purely political affair. With all its defection from the truth and right living, the ancient Church yet stood for national independence. Not only was it a strong barrier against English domination, but it strove in its own indeterminate way to end the warring factions which, all too plainly, were sowing the seeds of Scottish disintegration. Usually the Catholic Church supported the monarch in his efforts to subdue the nobles, many of whom were intriguing with the English.

Paradoxical it may well seem, yet nowhere in Scotland with the important exception of St Andrews was Latin Christianity more strongly entrenched, nowhere perhaps was the mediæval ritual more imposingly practised, nowhere was there more reluctance to relinquish the old religion, than Haddington, which may virtually claim to be the birthplace of John Knox—the man who, as we are reminded, was to raise the Reformation from a "slough of financial and political chicanery into a burning and tremendous religious issue." [1] Hume Brown testifies that in few districts of Scotland was the mediæval Church more prosperous than in Haddington.[2] From the twelfth century to the upheaval in the sixteenth there were within its borders numerous religious establishments controlled by powerful ecclesiastics who drew their wealth from the fertile Lothians. A testament of 1432 refers to the document having been "confermyt with ye seyl of ye office of ye Dene of ye Cristianite of Hadyntoun." In the east end of the town the Grey Friars had a monastery which John Major protested against as displaying more grandeur than was consistent with the rule of the Order. Haddington had also several chapels, while just outside the town was a parish church richly endowed with altars and chaplainries, likewise a Cistercian abbey.

Nor was the spectacular side of Catholicism forgotten. At frequent intervals the streets of Haddington were the scene of crowded animation by reason of elaborate ceremonials, and displays of a less exalted kind, in which the Church joined forces with the secular element. Knox in his youth must have witnessed the local craftsmen holding their pageants on the occasion of the feasts of Corpus Christi, Candlemas, and St Nicholas. And besides elaborate religious processions, there were miracle plays—those entertainments of the "rough and tumble" order, in which the Abbot of Unreason, as organiser and director, gave rein to various forms of festivity and merrymaking. Undoubtedly the entertainment was crude and coarse, but it enlivened the dull, monotonous lives of the burghers. Needless to say, the popularity of the Abbot of Unreason and the shows identified with his office were anathema to George Wishart, who, in a sermon in the parish church, inveighed against such exhibitions as contrary

[1] C. H. Warr, *Presbyterian Tradition*, p. 254.　　[2] Hume Brown, *Life of Knox*, i, 13.

to true religion. "I have heard of thee, Hadingtoun, that in thee wold have bein at ane vane Clerk play two or three thowsand people; and now to hear the messinger of the Eternall God, of all thy toune nor parishe can not be nombred a hundreth personis. Sore and feirfull shall the plagues be that shall ensew this thy contempt." [1]

Gradually the office of Abbot of Unreason fell into disrepute in Haddington. Although it was a heinous offence to refuse to take part in a Church festival, three burghers who in 1536 had been nominated for the office had the courage to do so. For their contumacy they were each made to pay forty shillings to the kirk master. This episode led eventually to the raising of the question as to whether the Abbot of Unreason was not a survival of Church life which had outlived any usefulness it ever had. But the master of the civic revels was not to be dethroned just yet. The office continued some time longer, though, it is noteworthy that an inducement to accept the duties had to be offered in the shape of a payment of forty shillings Scots, together with a burgess-ship. On the other hand, those who declined were penalised to the extent of forty shillings each. One of the fines was awarded to the person who became Abbot of Unreason. But the end of the mummery came in 1552 when the magistrates discharged "all Abbots of Unreason in tyme cumin."

Rather garish were the Corpus Christi displays when the craftsmen under their respective banners marched through the town, the rear of the procession being brought up by the ecclesiastics carrying the Host. In 1532 the Masons and Wrights disputed with the Baxters as to precedence in the procession, and after a deputation had been sent to Edinburgh to discover the practice there, it was decided that the Masons and Wrights, together with the Smiths and Hammermen, should pass in the procession on Corpus Christi Day and in all others "ane of ye ta crafts and ane of ye uther together in oxteris (arm in arm) as breithers." The Masons and Wrights, Smiths and Hammermen were to march immediately in front of the Host (and therefore were given the place of honour), the Baxters preceding them.

The religious processions of festival days, likewise the unedifying entertainments which followed and which were keenly relished by the groundlings, were the visible embodiment of the strength of Catholic tradition in Haddington on the eve of the Reformation. Here was a stronghold of the Roman Church which Scottish kings patronised and even the Papacy deigned to notice. From the reign of David I to that of James V the religious establishments within the burgh or immediately outside were numerous, rich, and wielded far-reaching influence. Their splendour, it is true, was often dimmed and their opulence dissipated by English burnings and English spoliation; but a remarkable recovery was usually accomplished.

Of the numerous edifices which made Haddington of great ecclesiastical prominence during Knox's youth only two remain—the hoary chapel of St Martin, east of Nungate, which carries us back to the earliest period of the town's history, and the more impressive but less venerable parish church of St Mary, whose lone position in the broad and fertile belt stretching away to the Lammermoors, likewise the solemn grandeur of the ruined choir and tower, arrest the eye as does no other building. The Church of St Mary is not the "Lamp of Lothian," a designation which belongs to the friary of the Franciscans, but it ought to have been. Through five centuries it has borne aloft the torch of religion, has witnessed to the incommensurable things. A link with the far distant past, it still functions in the ever living present. St Mary's was the town's church under Catholic auspices, and for nearly four hundred years it has

---

[1] Laing's ed. of Knox's *Works*, i, 138.

ministered to the spiritual needs of the community as interpreted by the doctrines of the Reformation.

Haddington's parish church occupies what is believed to have been the site of an earlier place of worship, also dedicated to the Virgin. About 1139 David I granted this building, together with the lands of Clerkington, to the Augustinian or Black Canons of St Andrews. No description of this earlier church is known to exist and no part of the structure has been preserved. It is surmised to have been a small Norman building occupying the choir of the present structure, the nave and probably transepts of which were probably built over part of the mediæval churchyard. This view is strengthened by the fact that when St Mary's underwent considerable alteration in 1891 large quantities of human remains were found beneath the floor. It was also discovered that the external walls of the present church were actually resting on graves. There is therefore some reason for supposing that the church of David I occupied the eastern portion of the existing building and that what is now the nave was then a burial place.

St Mary's is " one of the largest [Scottish] churches built in the great building period of the late fourteenth to the late fifteenth century, of which its ordinance and detail are typical." [1] Its erection no doubt was occasioned by the destruction of the previous church by Edward III in 1356. Built as a parish church, St Mary's is frequently referred to as such in the books of the Burgh Court of Haddington; and in the *Buke of the Auld Register of Haddington* (1426), which contains a record of gifts to the church, occurs the phrase "Paroche Kirk." The fabric is built of a mixture of red and grey stone. The former, which is prominent in the eastern portion, is from quarries near Garvald. The church is cruciform, and is composed of choir, nave, wide side aisles, and transepts without aisles. At the crossing is a tower ninety feet high, which, it is believed, was at one time surmounted by an open stone coronal similar to that of St Giles', Edinburgh. In this tower hung the bells which were carried away by the English in 1549. The main doorway in the west front is divided by a central pier, the whole being set within a semi-circular arch. On the capital of the central pier is a beautifully carved shield bearing the emblems of the Passion—crown of thorns enclosing a heart, hands, feet, nails—arranged heraldically. Those inexperienced in Scottish architecture might at a venture assume the doorway to be Norman, whereas the retention of the round-headed arch was a characteristic of the fifteenth century. The tracery of the windows inclines to the flamboyant and, although there has been much renewal, it still resembles the original design. On the exterior are many curious carvings, the work of the builders. Grotesque human faces are set alongside various animals, including a pig, dog, fox, goose, and squirrel. On one of the buttresses is a representation of a man playing the bagpipes. Numerous mason marks are to be found throughout the church, and on one of the piers is carved a clam shell; while on the face of another is an incised cross of eight limbs within a circle.

At the Reformation the church, which had become dilapidated mainly as the result of the battering it received in the siege of 1548-49, was repaired "fra stepill to the west end," to quote the wording of the burgh records. The nave was now transformed into a Presbyterian place of worship. Subsequently the choir and transepts were walled off and allowed to become ruinous. At the same time the edifice was cleared of all mediæval altars, images, and other appurtenances of Catholic worship, while the various trade incorporations, who had formerly contributed to the upkeep of the altars, later on built themselves lofts or galleries. The magistrates also erected a

[1] *Historical Monuments (Scotland) Commn., East Lothian vol.*, p. 38.

Convener of Trades Asserting his Claim to sit in Magistrates' Seat in St Mary's.

[*To face p.* 24.

gallery. In this condition St Mary's remained till about 1811 when further alterations took place, the nave arcade being heightened, the aisle roofs reconstructed at a higher level, and the whole interior gutted. Capacious galleries replaced the private lofts of the trade incorporations, the pulpit was given a southward position, and a door, which was made in the north wall, served the galleries. In 1891–92 the interior was once more entirely gutted, the north door built up, the magistrates' seat placed in front of the west gallery, an organ introduced, and the whole interior made to conform to present-day conditions. Between 1892 and 1920 eight windows were filled with stained glass, while the pulpit, communion table, and baptismal font were the gift of the Misses Aitchison of Alderston. Repairs have been carried out from time to time on the derelict choir and transepts, so as to preserve them from utter destruction. In the first half of the nineteenth century the walls were propped up with wooden beams, which by 1864 had become a mass of unsightly and decaying timber. These were then replaced with iron rods. The latest renovation was carried out in 1926–30 under the direction of the Ancient Monuments Commission, when the ruin was strengthened so thoroughly as to ensure its safety for many years.

The history of St Mary's is so crowded with events, ecclesiastical and secular, that a whole volume would be needed to do it justice. Only a very brief outline can be sketched here. One of the earliest references is that of 1453 when Pope Nicholas V issued a bull decreeing that the perpetual vicarage of the church be reserved to James Gray. Nine years later the burghers of Haddington, as *dominos* of the parish church, granted a receipt to the prior and convent of St Andrews for £100, which the latter had bound themselves to pay for the repair of the choir and replenishing the furniture of the high altar.

In or about 1539 St Mary's was given a collegiate constitution at the instigation of the town council, who at their own expense set up a college of priest-choristers, the master (later named "president") of whom was responsible to the burgh. It was the duty of this functionary to preserve discipline, draft rules, and levy fines. He also supervised the clergy officiating at the altars and in the chantry chapels. Like most pre-Reformation churches, St Mary's contained numerous altars dedicated to various saints. These were supported either by private donors or by trade incorporations. The ornaments and furnishings were often costly. In 1426 John of Furde presented a silver chalice to St Peter's altar. Then we read of John Crummye and his wife enriching the altar of the Holy Rood with a like gift, together with a paten inscribed with the word "Jesus." The Sinclairs of Stevenson were patrons of the Holy Blood altar, while one of the chaplains at the altar of St John the Baptist was Sir William Cockburn. The Cordiners' craft naturally supported the altar of St Crispin, the Hammermen, St Eloi's. Another altar, dedicated to the Three Kings of Cologne, had Sir Thomas Kerrington for chaplain. One of the celebrants at the altar of Our Lady was Sir Thomas Mauchlyn, who was remunerated by the town. A close bond existed between the burgh and the parish church, as was shown in 1556 when certain clergy were summoned to the tolbooth for consultation with regard to the improvement of divine service.

The conspicuous part played by St Mary's in the siege of 1548–49 has been narrated in the preceding chapter. On the eve of the Reformation the walls of the church resounded with the eloquence of George Wishart who, not long before his martyrdom, preached there on two consecutive days. Knox, who was with him on both occasions, tells us that Wishart before the first service walked to and fro behind the high altar. No evidence has been found that Knox himself preached from the pulpit of St Mary's, but it is more than likely that he did. The Reformer was in receipt of certain tithes from the parish.

Besides the chantry chapels in the parish church, there were at least six others in various parts of the town and vicinity, the majority of which were linked with the mother church of St Mary's. These were dedicated to St Martin, St Ann, St Katherine, St John, St Ninian, and St Laurence. With the exception of the chapel of St Martin, all have long since disappeared, and information concerning their history and appearance is either non-existent or extremely scanty.

St Martins, to the east of Nungate, the outer walls of which still remain, is the oldest ecclesiastical edifice in Haddington. Dating from the beginning of the twelfth century, this chapel belonged to the Abbey till the Reformation, when it passed into the possession of the town and was used for Presbyterian worship, an arrangement that lasted into the seventeenth century. At a later period it became derelict, a condition in which it has been ever since. The chapel displays Norman work and was originally a small rectangular structure comprising nave and chancel. The latter no longer exists, but the nave and a portion of its vaulted roof are still to the fore. There were two doorways—one to the north and the other to the south. It is supposed that the chapel had some connection with Alexander de Martin, Sheriff of Haddington, who received various lands from the Princess Ada, daughter-in-law of David I; but reliable evidence is wanting. What is certain is that the nunnery held courts *apud Ecclesiam S. Martin* in Nungate. After the Reformation St Martin's was conjoined with the parish church, the minister of which had also the oversight of Athelstaneford. For a long period the building was entirely neglected, and last century a proposal was actually brought forward for erecting a parish school on its site. Fortunately wiser counsels prevailed. The ruin, renovated in 1913 by H.M. Office of Works, is surrounded by a burial ground in which, however, there have been no interments for many years.

Half a mile to the west of Haddington, and close to the village of St Laurence, stood until 1906 the remains of a religious establishment which is said to have contained not only a chapel but a leper hospital,[1] both dedicated to St Laurence, whose special care was the poor and sick. The hospital was endowed by James V and had for its preceptor one of the royal chaplains—Walter Ramsay. This institution was founded by Richard Guthrie, Abbot of the monastery of St Thomas the Martyr, Arbroath, and in 1533 was incorporated with the "monastery of the Order of St Katherine of Sciennes" in Edinburgh.[2] The revenues amounted to £9 sterling, but the Franciscans of Haddington, the spiritual directors of the hospital, augmented this sum with twenty shillings paid over by the magistrates from the royal fermes.[3] To the Hospital of St Laurence belonged eighty-two acres, which probably included the Spittelrig at Haddington. On 15th February 1562–63 the nuns of St Katherine in the Sciennes disposed of these lands to Sir John Bellenden of Auchinoule, whose relative, Sir Lewis Bellenden, conveyed the property on 23rd March 1587–88 to Sir Thomas Craig, the well-known feudalist, and Helen Heriot, his wife.

Our account of the parish church of St Mary has taken us prematurely into the

---

[1] At the demolition of this building in 1906, the beams of the roof were found to be held together with hand-made nails. Through the west gable wall, four feet thick, ran a wide chimney from a fireplace in the basement. From built-up windows and doors it was evident that the structure had been much altered. A row of stones projected from the south wall.

[2] *Liber St Katherine*, pp. 41–48.

[3] *Exchequer Rolls*, 23rd July 1530.

post-Reformation period, and we must now return to the days of Catholic Christianity about which there is still much to be said.

When, early in the thirteenth century, St Francis of Assisi founded the great religious order bearing his name, he ordained that the brotherhood should place poverty in the forefront. At first this rule was faithfully observed, but in course of time it was variously construed. Some friars strove to adhere strictly to the Franciscan view of life; but others relaxed the discipline. The former became known as Observantines, the latter as Conventuals. Each branch founded religious houses in which the respective interpretations of the rule were practised. In Haddington there was founded a Conventual friary. Probably its first appearance on the page of history was in 1242 when the Earl of Athole, who (as narrated) was murdered in the town, was buried within the Franciscan precincts. The Friary, consisting of "church, houses, edifices, gardens, dovecots," occupied the site of the Episcopal Church and adjoining ground. A charter of 1560 gives the boundaries as follows:—

On the north by Friar Gowl; on the east by the water of Tyne and a mill-pond immediately below Nungate Bridge; on the south by the road leading from the town to the parish church (now Church Street); and on the west by land, partly waste and partly built upon, belonging to the burgh and known in the sixteenth century as the Rudis of the Friar Wall.

Subsequently the Franciscans owned ground described as the "Commone Douket called the Frier Douket," likewise an acre in the "Capoun Flatt" and a croft at Poldrate. Then in 1478 Sir James Cockburn of Clerkington gifted to the friars the "Kingis Yaird," which lay south of Church Street. This ground, on which grain was grown, was held on condition that the friars said Masses annually for the soul of the donor.

The Friary was then the most imposing building in Haddington. Although the rule of St Francis favoured plain buildings, its ornateness is attested both by the chronicler Bower, a native of the town, and John Major, who received his schooling there. Bower speaks of its splendour and, in particular, of the beauty of the translucent light streaming through its windows. Hence the Friary was called the "Lamp of Lothian," an epithet that has been erroneously applied by historians, both ancient and modern, to St Mary's. It is Major, too, who takes umbrage at the "sumptuous magnificence" of the Franciscan friaries, and hazards the opinion that when Edward III burnt the Haddington house in 1356 it may have been a divine rebuke of the careless lives of the brotherhood.[1]

Not much was known of the Franciscan establishment at Haddington till the researches of Dr Moir Bryce [2] brought together a mass of material that enabled its history to be told with considerable fullness. The Friary depended much on royal grants. By Robert the Bruce's charter the town became a creditor of the Scottish Exchequer for twenty merks annually derived from the Castlewards of the Bailiary of Haddington. From this source the Friary drew a weekly allowance of three shillings. James IV was another benefactor. In 1490 he granted the brethren three bolls of wheat and certain sums from the privy purse, and when in 1507 this monarch stayed at the Friary he granted forty-two shillings for "the King's Belcher in the Freris." But it was from the private donor that the Franciscan house benefited most. In 1287 an anonymous person granted six merks yearly from the local lands known as "Ralph Eglyn's Acres" for "furnesing of wyne, walx, ale, and other necessar thingis within thare kirk." Then, previous to 1293, Sir William Lindsay of Luffness presented the friars with one merk annually on the morrow of the Feast of Pope St Gregory

---

[1] *History of Great Britain* (S.H.S.), p. 297.   [2] *Scottish Greyfriars*, i, 168–198.

provided they celebrated Requiem Mass on that day for the soul of Lady Margaret Lindsay, his mother. And the parents of Sir John Congilton having been buried in the church beside the altar of St Duthac, their son, in the year of Bannockburn, supplied bread and wine to this altar in return for a yearly Mass. Again, in 1337, Sir Alexander Seton granted twenty shillings annually for the ornaments and vestments of the church, which sum was increased to three pounds by William, first Lord Seton. Another donor was Sir David de Annand, who authorised the friars to remove from his barony of Tranent as much coal as they could use.

The interest of the family of Sir William Haliburton of Carlowry in the Franciscans of Haddington was shown in 1478 when Sir John Haliburton, vicar of Greenlaw, selected them to administer his charity for the poor of East Lothian. To the warden and the eight friars then resident he assigned a tenement in Poldrate and another in Northgate. A portion of the former was converted into an almshouse with three beds, while the remainder was burdened with certain annual rents for its support. The benefits of the charity were for "bodies borne or upbred of the Barony of Dirltoun." The right of presentation to two of the three beds was reserved to Haliburton during his lifetime and thereafter to the lairds of Dirleton. If there was neglect to present a pauper within twenty days from the date on which the bed became vacant, the burgh of Haddington was to "gif the said person or persones to the said beddis." The warden had the disposal of the third bed. The beneficiaries were bound to recite the Psalter of Our Lady three times daily, and, "ilk nycht at the bel of curfur [curfew]," they were to say "five Pater Nosters, five Aveys and a Crede." If they were "litterit," they were also to repeat the "De profundis." Another condition of the Haliburton charity was that the friars were to distribute forty pence worth of bread among the poor on Candlemas Day. King James III formally approved of the Haliburton almshouse in a Charter of Confirmation.

From this time onwards the Franciscans increasingly enjoyed the munificence of the burghers and others. For example, the altar of St Clement was endowed by Walter Bertram, who was Provost of Edinburgh more than once in the fifteenth century. Bertram's gift was bestowed in circumstances which illustrate the friendly relations subsisting between the Franciscans and the Seculars, the friars agreeing to the appointment of a secular chaplain to this altar at a salary of £9, 2s. 8d., with a further allowance of two pounds for ornaments and upkeep. Bertram also granted to the Friary an annual rent of ten shillings in order that High Mass might be celebrated on every vigil of St Francis, the Mass to be preceded by a placebo and dirge, after ringing of the bell through the town.

A decided shrinkage in endowments occurred after the siege of 1548–49. The town properties from which the friars hitherto had drawn rents were now for the most part uninhabitable and even ownerless. Consequently arrears accumulated, and in 1553 the warden initiated a series of poindings to recover payment of an annual sum representing about one-fourth of the income from endowments. It was clear, however, that a retrograde course was being pursued. On 10th October 1555 the brotherhood granted a Letter of Alienation of their house to the magistrates, and this disposition was confirmed in a Precept of Sasine granted by Warden Congilton because of "the singular favour, good deeds, help, and protection accorded to us by the aforesaid provost, bailies, councillors, and community against the invaders of our Order and our foresaid convent during the present calamity (i.e. the Reformation)." In the following year the King's Yaird was conveyed to the burgh, in 1571 the superiority of the church and conventual buildings, as well as the Franciscan lands, were vested in the Crown, and in 1572 the Friary was pulled down. The pavement was removed to the parish church, the east gable with its lofty window was presented to Sir Thomas Cockburn of Clerkington, while three roods of the Friary site were feued to John Gray.

Dr Moir Bryce, to whose labours this account of the Friary is much indebted, furnishes the names of eight wardens (probably there were more) and those of the brethren who constituted the Chapter from 1478 to 1559. He also gives summaries of the endowments and annual rents whose existence is known from the records of the burgh court, 1530–59.

From the Franciscan Friary we pass to the Cistercian Abbey of Haddington, founded between 1153 and 1178 by the Countess Ada (mother of Malcolm IV and William the Lyon), and dedicated to the Virgin Mary. The seal of the Abbey, appended to an agreement between the nuns and the prior of St Andrews in 1245, shows the Virgin crowned, with the infant Jesus on her knee. A later seal, dated Nunraw, 4th September 1569, figures the Virgin wearing a crown and seated beneath a canopy. Her right hand holds a sceptre, while the left supports the infant Jesus on her knee. In the lower half of the seal is a half-length figure of a monk praying. The inscription is: "S. Capituli Sante Marie de Hadintun." This seal is appended to Precept of Clare Constat by Isabel Hepburn, Prioress of the Abbey of Haddington, for infefting David Forrest, as heir to his father, John Forrest, Provost of Haddington, in Gimmersmills and certain lands in Nungate.

Not a stone of the Abbey remains above ground. It was situated on rising land on the north bank of Tyne, about a mile to the east of Haddington. The design and size of the building are matters of uncertainty. At the Reformation there were only eighteen nuns. While safe deductions cannot be made from this circumstance as to the relative importance of the Abbey, it seems tolerably clear that the establishment did not rank among the larger religious houses of Scotland. Probably it stood higher in point of wealth, for at its dissolution, or shortly before, its revenues amounted to £308, 17s. 6d. annually.

Looking to the period at which it was built, the Abbey would in all likelihood be of Norman design. While the structure has totally disappeared, the bridge maintaining communication between it and the territory to the south of Tyne still survives. A cherished historical monument of East Lothian, this bridge is not, however, contemporaneous with the origin of the Abbey. It is believed to have been erected in the earlier half of the sixteenth century, and consists of three pointed arches the under faces of which are ribbed with courses of polished masonry. On the Abbey the royal foundress bestowed the lands of Begbie, Clerkington, and other properties, also the church of Crail in Fife. Private persons also made gifts. In 1318 Patrick, son of Roger of Popil (Popple), presented a toft and eleven acres. Further, a charter, dated 21st May 1349, tells how, in consequence of the English invasions, the Abbey had been plundered and its muniments destroyed. These misfortunes led to supplications to the Bishop of St Andrews to confirm to the nuns churches, teinds, and tenements, a petition which was granted. In 1514 a further connection between the Abbey and the church of Crail was established. By a bull of Leo X, Sir William Myrton, perpetual vicar of the parish of Lathrisk (Kingskettle), and Janet Hepburn, "the abbess of St Clare's monastery at Haddington," were authorised to admit Alexander Dunbar to be vicar of Crail. Thereafter the Fife church was, at the instance of the abbess and Myrton, erected into a collegiate establishment.[1] And in further

[1] Rogers, *Register of Collegiate Church of Crail*, p. 4.

token of goodwill, the abbess presented the church with a silver cross, chalice, and vestments.

The duties of the prioress were unusually varied. Sometimes she was obliged to transact business seldom coming within the orbit of female administration. In July 1523 oxen for the army were demanded of her, and in October bread, ale, beef, and corn.[1] Occasionally she resisted what seemed to her extortionate demands, as when in April 1532 she declined to pay the wapinschaw tax. In 1535 the prioress and convent bestowed land in Nungate on Sir Hugh Bald. An undated deed, but belonging to the period 1550–60, is signed on behalf of the prioress and convent (fifteen names in all) by William Walterson [Waterston], notary public. This document is a tack in favour of Mr Alexander Forrest, parson of Logymontrose, a native of Haddington, granting their corn mill of Gymmersmylnes and certain acres in Nungate on a nineteen years' lease. In addition to the money rent, Forrest had to supply the sisterhood with ten capons yearly, also with two horses to convey victuals from Aberlady. The prioress and nuns on their part undertook to provide their tacksman with "wood leif of greit tymmer [timber]."

Even military duties fell to the prioress. An order having gone forth that all castles in the Lothians were to be adequately garrisoned, she was charged with the "caire and keiping of the place and fortalice of Nunraw" against their "auld ynimeis [enemies] of England and all utheris." Nunraw (or Nun's Row), the peel tower at the foot of the Lammermoors, was the grange of the Abbey of Haddington and a refuge in turbulent times. What this signified may be judged from the fact that if the prioress was unable to carry out instructions, she was to "cast doun and destroy the samyn, swa that na habitationer salbe had thereintill from [that] thym furth." The fate of Nunraw was finally decided on 23rd February 1547–48 when Lord Grey of Wilton informed Protector Somerset that the fortalice had capitulated.

It is amusing to learn that the Abbey prided itself on its educational facilities, considering that most of the nuns could not even write their names. Yet in this capacity the institution obtained aristocratic, even royal patronage. In 1463 the Princess Margaret, second daughter of James II, entered the Abbey solely for her education. Her governess was Dame Alison Maitland, presumably of the Lethington family. On 13th February 1474–75 James III assigned Dame Alison five merks yearly for life as a reward for the tuition she had given his sister. The pension was paid by the customar of Haddington, whose accounts show that the princess remained in the Abbey till July 1477. Hither, too, came the daughter of the Regent Arran, probably with the same purpose.[2] In the *Lord High Treasurer's Accounts*, under date 24th April 1544, occurs this entry: "To his Grace's douchter, Gene [Jean] Hammiltoun, at her departing to the Abbey of Haddington." Then follows a list of clothing with which she had been supplied.

On 20th October 1567, by which time the supremacy of the Roman Church in Scotland was doomed, the prioress, with consent of the Chapter, disposed of the greater part of the Abbey lands in favour of William Maitland of Lethington, secretary to Mary Queen of Scots. Randolph gives a different version. Writing to Cecil in 1563, he declared that Lethington had taken possession "of the whole Abbacie which the Quene had given him, so that he is now equal with any man that hath his whole lands in Lodian." But if Queen Mary invested Lethington in the manner described, she is also reported, two years later, to have assigned the abbatial endowments to Bothwell, the rival of Lethington. In another letter to Cecil, dated 4th April 1566, Randolph

---

[1] *Lord High Treasurer's Accounts*, v, 216.   [2] *C.S.P.*, ii, 275.

mentions, curiously enough, the appointment of an abbess "with all the vile ceremonies that in the most blindness was used." This was Dame Isabel Hepburn, the last official head of the Abbey. She appears to have held office for only a few months. After her departure the conventual buildings quickly became ruinous. Dame Isabel eventually conformed to the new religion and married Andrew Schetholme. She and her husband were alive in 1588.[1]

The Queen-Mother (Mary of Lorraine), as stated in the previous chapter, attended a momentous meeting of the Parliament in the Abbey, and it is not unlikely that her daughter, Mary Queen of Scots, visited the convent more than once. In a letter of Bedford to Cecil, written on 4th April 1566, allusion is made to Queen Mary "solemnly, with all the old wonted toys," investing a nun and placing her in the Abbey of Haddington.

Probably enough has been said in support of the statement with which this chapter opened, namely, that Haddington was a place of more than ordinary significance when the Catholic Church was all powerful in Scotland. It was in this citadel of the ancient religion that Knox grew up, and although the Reformer emancipated himself from the yoke of the older type of Christianity, it was only after much spiritual travail. Hume Brown, the scholarly biographer of Knox, points out that in all likelihood it was because Haddington was so impregnated with the Catholic atmosphere, had surrendered so fully to Roman doctrine and practice, and was so beset with powerful clergy and conventual houses that it was behind other Scottish towns in accepting Protestant teaching. But if the Reformation was slow in establishing itself in Haddington, its fruits were unmistakable, abundant, and lasting once it had taken root. In due season Protestant zeal shone as conspicuously as had Catholicism in earlier times.

The sharp contrast between the old regime and the new is witnessed to by Wishart and Knox. In spite of Wishart being "singularly learned in godly knowledge" and "clearly illuminated with the spirit of prophecy," Knox instances Haddington as an exception to the rule that the common people heard him (Wishart) gladly. And the personal experience of the early Reformer tends to confirm this view, for when, in January 1546-47, he came to Haddington on his last preaching tour, he found most of the inhabitants in no mood to receive the Reformed faith. No doubt the lukewarm reception was partly political, Wishart having had dealings with certain Scottish nobles who were known to be in the pay of Henry VIII, and committed to the downfall, if not the murder, of one who was the chief representative of Catholicism in Scotland as well as of national independence—Cardinal Beaton. But this partiality for the old religion involving, as things were then, political implications dear to the heart of the Scottish people generally, gave place by degrees to a standpoint more in accordance with the new Christian order.

The change, however, was not perceptible till Wishart had passed from the earthly scene. His so-called subversive doctrines were preached in the parish church to a mere handful of listeners, "where," writes Knox, "it was supposed the greatest confluence of people should be." At the forenoon service on 15th January 1546-47, "the auditouris" were "nothing in comparisone of that which used to be in that kyrk." And when Wishart preached again in the afternoon "many wondered" because "the auditure was so sclender." It is Knox, too, who paints a realistic picture of Wishart pacing to and fro behind the high altar, his "verray countenance" and "visage"

[1] *Liber Conventus S. Katherine Sinensis*, p. 70.

31

revealing "the greaf and alternatioune of his mynd." Then from the pulpit Wishart rebukes the townsfolk for their Laodicean spirit.

The precise date of Knox's conversion is unknown, though his close association with Wishart shows that in 1546–47 he was veering towards Reformation principles. But there were other friends in Haddington who, on his own testimony, influenced his later religious opinions. It was from Thomas Guylliame (Williams), a native of Athelstaneford, that the Reformer first received "any taste of the truth." Whether Knox had much personal contact with Williams, who was at first a well-known Dominican, we do not know, but he is loud in his praise. "The man," he declares, "was of solid judgment, reassonable letteris (as for that age), and of a prompt and good utterance: his doctrine was holsome, without great vehemency against superstitioun." Williams became chaplain to Arran, but the Regent's defection from the new teaching led to his inhibition as a preacher, and he departed for England.

Another local pioneer of Protestantism was David Forrest, whose family acquired from the nuns of the Abbey the flour mills known as Gimmersmills. In the *Lord High Treasurer's Accounts, 1562–72*, Forrest is designated "General of the Cunzie-house." Knox characterises him as "ane man that long hes professed the trueth and upoun whom many in that tyme depended." Wishart was the guest of Forrest, and Knox, on returning to Scotland in 1555, renewed acquaintance with this member of the Gimmersmills family. We read: "Last came John Knox in the end of the harvest . . . who first being loadged in the house of that notable man of God, James Syme [apparently in Edinburgh], begane to exhorte secreatly in that same house, wharunto repared the Laird of Dun, David Forrest, and some certain personages of the toune." Forrest, too, was in Knox's company in 1558 when the image of St Giles was smashed by the Edinburgh mob. And it was he who tried to allay the excited passions of the citizens, or, as Knox has it, "laboured to stay the brethrein."

In 1559 Knox, in a letter, enumerated eight towns where "the ministry is established," but Haddington is not one of them. "In the native district . . . of him who beyond every other individual was to be the instrument of her ruin, the ancient Church of Scotland had struck her very deepest roots, and offered the most obstinate front to the storm that broke upon her." [1] Hume Brown's statement notwithstanding, the year 1559 witnessed an important step towards undermining the fabric of Catholicism in Haddington. It was then, as we have seen, that the Franciscans handed over their property to the magistrates, though the latter, it is true, came under a notarial obligation to the brotherhood of restitution in the event of the friars being again permitted to live according to their Rule.

Two years later we come upon the first definite evidence that the old order was passing and that Protestantism was in the ascendancy. The repairing in 1561 of the parish church is hardly susceptible of other explanation than that the building was being made suitable for the new mode of worship. Further indications were the forfeiture of the chantry chapels to the Crown, the sequestration of the fruits of the vicarage, the appointment of a Reader of the Scriptures, and the burning of "mess clothes and bukes." More important still, John Aytoun, Provost of Haddington, and Bernard Thomson were dispatched to Edinburgh in March 1570 to obtain the services of a minister, who, by the way, was to be escorted to the burgh by John Douglas, one of the bailies. The remuneration of the Reader of the Scriptures, or "exhorter of the common prayers," as he was sometimes called, was derived from the revenues of the chaplaincies and annual rent. On weekdays he acted as schoolmaster. Probably

---

[1] *Life of Knox*, i, 15.

the first Reader was Walter Balcanquhall, who was given "fifty merks in the year" for reading "the common prayers in the kirk at vii hours before noon in summer and viii hours in winter, and that on Sunday, Wednesday, and Friday." The rest of the time was spent in discharging the functions of "clerk in the [kirk] session and doctor in the school." In 1574 bread and wine were obtained for the communion; in 1575 a pulpit and seats were introduced; and in 1581 the "auld scule" was prepared as a dwelling for the minister.

The first Protestant pastor was Patrick Cockburn. He had studied at the University of Paris and was called to the Chair of Oriental Languages there. Cockburn, who was appointed to Haddington in 1562, wrote various works in Latin, but his scholarship was eclipsed by his successor, James Carmichael, one of the most famous ministers the parish ever had. Carmichael was the friend of Andrew Melville, who, in a letter to his brother James, writes: "What is the 'profound Dreamer' (so I was accustomed to call him when we travelled together in 1584)—what is our Corydon of Haddington about? I know he cannot be idle. Has he not brought forth or projected anything yet, after so many decades of years?" Carmichael was minister of Haddington from 1570 to 1584, and again from 1587 till his death in the reign of Charles I. In 1571 his pastoral duties were extended by his being presented to St Martin's in Nungate, and still more in 1574 when the churches of Athelstaneford and Bolton were combined under Carmichael who had the assistance of two readers. Furthermore, from 1572 onwards Carmichael was schoolmaster of Haddington, an office, however, from which he was relieved in 1576 "in consideration of his great burden in the ministry."

Till 1584 Carmichael discharged his duties normally, but having refused to acknowledge the bishop as his ecclesiastical superior, he had to relinquish his charge. He fled to England, and for eighteen months was the most prominent among the Scottish Presbyterian exiles, the band including the two Melvilles and James Lawson, the successor of Knox in St Giles'. When the evil days were overpassed, Carmichael resumed his ministry in Haddington. In 1606 he was made perpetual moderator of the Presbytery. Carmichael helped to revise the Second Book of Discipline, compiled a Latin grammar which was dedicated to James VI, abridged the Acts of General Assembly, and, at the request of the Privy Council, revised Sir John Skene's *Regiam Majestatem*.

In the seventeenth century Haddington was as fervently Presbyterian as it had once been definitely Catholic. When James VI inaugurated his prelatic policy, which was carried much further by Charles I, it was vehemently opposed by the burgesses. What seems to be the earliest instance of clerical dissension occurred in 1607 when George Grier, minister of St Martin's Chapel, was summoned to appear before the High Commission for not preaching on holy days and refusing to dispense the sacrament to kneeling communicants. Carmichael, as became the friend of Andrew Melville, the founder of the Presbyterian polity, was a tower of strength in withstanding the insidious advances of Episcopacy. Against this uncompromising attitude, however, we must place the disconcerting fact that George Gladstanes, Archbishop of St Andrews, after attending a meeting of the Diocesan Synod of Lothian at Haddington in November 1610, was made a burgess. Not only so, but seven ecclesiastics who accompanied the Archbishop were, at his instigation, also admitted, likewise the Chamberlain of St Andrews, and Mark Gladstanes, presumably a relative. The incident may be susceptible of a satisfactory explanation, but on the face of it the matter raises perturbing thoughts as to the genuineness of Haddington's allegiance to Presbytery.

CATHOLICISM AND THE KIRK

But however we may account for such concessions to Episcopal domination, there is the indubitable fact that in 1633, the year of the coronation of Charles I at Holyrood, Robert Kerr, minister of Haddington, refused to conform to Prelacy. Nor is there any uncertainty as to where the burgesses stood as regards the National Covenant and the events that led up to it. They were imbued with strong Covenanting sympathies and played their part worthily in the war of religion which was the central feature of the time. In September 1637 Laud's Service Book was petitioned against by the Presbytery. Here are the terms of the resolution drawn up under the guidance of Robert Balcanquhall, the Moderator—a resolution which, it was hoped, would bring to naught a "great evil":—

That quhair we have all conceavit ane great fear to be prest, baith minister and people, to practize in our churches a lait book, intitulat a Book of Common Prayer for the Church of Scotland, and we foirseing . . . the great evill and hurt quhilk will inevitable ensew by the fearfull disturbance and rent that will follow . . . be reasone that the foirsaid book being stylit a book for a satlie forme of divyne worship, quhilk in no natione nor kirk . . . was ever receavit in a christian estait under a christian king but by a Nationall Assemblie and ratifeit by Act of Parliament of a christian prince and estait and of that same estait quhairin the kirk was establaichit, quhilk is not in this:

Secundlie, that both pastors and people, altho that thay war pressit with the hiest authority may well sum of thame be inducit to practize the forsaid buik, it is impossible that ever in this kingdome thair can be a lyking of it, be reasone that thair is into the buik sindrie poyntis that tuitcheth the fundamentall poyntis of our reformed professione quhairunto we have been all sworne of all estaits in sindrie actes of Parliament. . . . And that we do not speik of particulars it is becaus the remonstrance thairof is onlie competent to be disputit in a Nationall Assemblie.

The Presbytery's petition, conciliatory yet firm, displays clear-sighted perception of the issues involved, and very properly states that the General Assembly is the only competent body to decide the attitude of Presbyterian Scotland in the matter of the Service Book. Furthermore, there still exists a document which places beyond all doubt the ecclesiastical position of the great majority of the people of Haddington and neighbourhood during this grievous time. The descendants of the East Lothian historic family of Sydserff retain to this day a copy of the National Covenant which for the most part was signed locally. This parchment is crowded with the signatures of those who pledged themselves to stand by the Kirk at all costs. Sir Archibald Sydserff's name is there, so are those of such prominent defenders of the existing state of things in the Church of Scotland as the Earls of Wemyss, Cassillis, and Rothes, and Lords Balmerino and Balcarres.

It is a far cry from the imposing ritual of the Roman Church to the Secession movement with its insistence on evangelism and the right of congregations to a determining voice in the settlement of their ministers. Yet it represents the general trend of the ecclesiastical history of Haddington in a period of divided loyalties and throughout the greater part of the eighteenth century. Broadly speaking, if it was with considerable hesitancy that the townsfolk adopted the principles of the Reformation, once they had done so the essentials of the new religion were countenanced with sincerity and warmth of feeling. Religion pure and undefiled might almost be said to be the slogan of the town of John Knox. More than once the bulk of the community did battle for such an ideal. Haddington, as we have seen, was not behind other burghs in bearing aloft the banner of the Covenant and obstinately resisting the oppressive decrees of a hierarchical government. And when, in the first half of the eighteenth century, the Kirk became irrevocably divided over the patronage question, and "forced settlements" of ministers was the order of the day, Haddington became a stronghold of the movement led by Ebenezer and Ralph Erskine. So early as 1680 there appears to have been opposition to the Earl of Haddington's choice of a minister for the Second Charge, which had been constituted in 1635. His Lordship, however, insisted on his right as patron and won his case in the Court of Session, though Sir George Mackenzie of Rosehaugh ("Bluidy Mackenzie") pleaded eloquently in behalf of the town.

The ground therefore was prepared for the Secession, and when patronage emerged as an issue of first-class importance, the townsfolk bore warm testimony to what was strong and praiseworthy in Dissent, if also to what was weak and unedifying. Nowhere perhaps were its centrifugal tendencies more marked, nowhere did discontent with the government and procedure of the Established Church lead to a more complex situation. Those who went forth from the Church of their fathers formed themselves into small groups and clung tenaciously to certain doctrines until some fresh controversy, theological or ecclesiastical, drove them still deeper into divisive courses. Sectarianism can at least take credit for this, that it signified that those who were identified with it were awake intellectually: their thinking powers were at work, and they drew distinctions, though not always wisely. What made the Secession so conspicuous in Haddington was the fact that one of its leading representatives laboured there as pastor and teacher for nearly forty years. John Brown of Haddington, as he was called (the designation being applied to distinguish him from others of the same name who also rose to fame and influence and of whom he was the progenitor), wielded immense authority by reason of his powerful Gospel preaching, his theological and linguistic scholarship, his encyclopædic learning, and as the accredited instructor of those training for the ministry of the Secession.

In 1751 Brown was unanimously called by the Seceders of Haddington, and in 1768 added to his pastoral duties those of Professor of Divinity to the Burgher Synod. The students, usually numbering about thirty, studied at Haddington, the course lasting five years. Among them was the celebrated George Lawson of Selkirk, who succeeded Brown in his professorship. Lawson, who is supposed to be the original of Josiah Cargill in *St Ronan's Well*, is said to have known the Bible by heart, on which he wrote a ponderous commentary, which, however, was never published. In the matter of authorship Lawson was but walking in the footsteps of Brown, who wrote or compiled numerous works which gave "an impress to the Scottish mind and evoked intellectual through religious interests." Brown was a man of prodigious learning, being acquainted with many European and several Oriental tongues. He is most widely known by his *Self-interpreting Bible* which, with his *Dictionary of the Bible*, took rank with Boston's *Fourfold State* among the books that moulded the religious life of the Scottish peasantry. In one of his poems Burns speaks of "perusing Bunyan, *Brown,* and Boston." Many stories are told of casual meetings with people whom Brown persuaded to take a more serious view of life. Once David Hume heard him preach, and was so impressed that he is said to have remarked: "That old man speaks as if Christ stood at his elbow?" Another story represents Brown as awakening religious feeling in Robert Fergusson, the poet.

When John Brown began his ministry in Haddington the Secession Church was still suffering from the dire effects of the "Breach" in 1747, which gave rise to two bodies irreconcilably opposed to each other—Burghers and Anti-burghers. The former maintained that it was lawful to take the Burgess Oath, the latter that it was unlawful. The minister of the Secession congregation in Haddington in 1747 was Robert Archibald. Sympathising with the Anti-burghers, Archibald, together with seven elders and two deacons, withdrew, and formed the nucleus of the Anti-burgher congregation. But the majority of the original congregation favoured the Burghers and retained the property and funds. To the vacant pastorate they called John Brown, who accepted. In 1765 the original meeting-house, as it was styled, was demolished and a new place of worship erected on the same site, which in turn gave place in 1806 to a more modern building. There were successively two manses—the one occupied by Brown and a later one, more commodious, built on ground adjoining the church. In 1847 the Burgher congregation became the East United Presbyterian Church.

Archibald and his Anti-burgher followers met in a malt store in Newton Port, which occupied the site of the town's library. There they held services for many years but ultimately built a place of worship. In 1805 arose the Auld and New Licht controversy as to the validity of one of the questions in the formula put to ministers and elders at ordination. The Anti-burgher minister then was Robert Chalmers, who supported the Auld Lichts, and who, because of his "divisive and schismatical courses" was, along with two elders, deposed. But the bulk of the congregation upheld the views of their minister, who remained their pastor till his death in 1837. After litigation, it was arranged that those adhering to Chalmers, who were known as Original Seceders, should have the use of the meeting-house in the forenoon, while the New Lichts were to hold a service there in the afternoon or evening. Subsequently the New Lichts parted with their rights to the property for £610 with which they purchased a place of worship near the West Port, formerly belonging to the Relief Church. In the course of later developments the New Lichts became the West United Presbyterian Church and in 1900 the West United Free Church. This congregation, made stronger by a union with the old Free Church, re-entered the Church of Scotland in 1929.

The history of the Auld Lichts was also eventful. They continued to meet in Newton Port after the New Lichts had left, but in 1852 joined the Free Church and were known as the Knox Church. In 1876 the congregation became a mission charge, and in 1881 their property was acquired by the town for the public library. In 1903 an effort was made to effect a union between the East (John Brown's old congregation) and West Churches, but the former was averse. The East Church was then dissolved, a portion of the members joining the West Church and others the Free Church.

In 1831 the population of the parish was 5883, of which 3751 were resident in the town and vicinity. An ecclesiastical visitation of the burgh revealed the fact that about 1800 persons above the age of seven, and professing connection with the Established Church, could not obtain sittings in St Mary's, whose seating capacity was limited to 1200. These circumstances led to the building in Newton Port of St John's Church *quoad sacra* which was opened in 1838. Its first minister, John W. Wright, "went out" at the Disruption and was followed by many members of the congregation. He was afterwards associated with Dr Lorimer, minister of the parish, who also "came out," and together they originated the first Free Church congregation in Haddington.[1] For more than thirty years after Wright's departure, St John's *quoad sacra* was empty. In 1876 the building was re-opened. Its constitution was revived in 1897, but in 1910 was rescinded by the General Assembly. Since then this *quoad sacra* church has been used as a hall in connection with St Mary's.

To pursue our survey of the ecclesiastical divisions in Haddington, it should be explained that there was a Relief congregation consisting partly of people dissatisfied

[1] It was also called St John's and stood in Newton Port till 1890 when a new church was opened near West Port.

with the ministrations of the parish church and partly of those averse to joining either Burghers or Anti-burghers. Dating from 1791, they built the church near West Port already referred to. After 1800 the congregation declined and their building was bought by the Independents, a body established in the town by Robert and James Haldane about 1798. When the brothers Haldane became Baptists the congregation remained loyal to the tenets of the Independents, but as their place of worship was the private property of the Haldanes, they in 1815 built a chapel in Hardgate, which was in constant use till the dissolution of the congregation in 1872.

Considering the sturdiness of Presbyterianism in Haddington, it is not to be wondered at that the Episcopal communion had a precarious foothold. The present church was built in 1770, but the congregation dates from about the beginning of the eighteenth century. The old meeting-house was in Poldrate, where John Gray (whose famous library is preserved in an annexe to the Public Library) occasionally ministered after his retirement from the pastoral oversight of Aberlady parish. The church registers go far back, and are of more than ordinary interest, since English runaway marriages were sometimes solemnised in the church, it being the nearest of the Episcopal persuasion after crossing the Border from England. When couples found it inconvenient to come to Haddington, they proceeded to Blackshiels and arranged with the Haddington incumbent to officiate. Charles Hughes Terrot, afterwards Bishop of Edinburgh and Primus of the Scottish Episcopal Church, ministered at Haddington from 1814 to 1817.

Methodism, like Independency, was an exotic plant in East Lothian, as elsewhere in Scotland. John Wesley himself paid more than one visit to Haddington, but the entries in his *Journal* do not convey the impression that he was greeted with much cordiality. The controversy between Calvinists and Arminians was then at its height, and as a leading champion of the teaching of the latter, Wesley could hardly look for sympathetic understanding in a town in which lived and worked so virile and able a champion of Calvinism as John Brown. The latter was the friend and correspondent of the Countess of Huntingdon, whom he assisted in her intractable opposition to Arminianism and, of course, to the theological attitude of Wesley. On 11th May 1761 the great apostle of Methodism preached in "Provost Dickson's parlour," which makes clear that his listeners must have been few, an experience that seldom came his way. Wesley again visited Haddington in 1764 and again proclaimed his message in "Provost D——'s parlour," this time to "a very elegant congregation." He is, however, ingenuous enough to confess that he had no great expectations of good being done.

In May 1772 Wesley intended another visit and "had designed to preach at Provost Dickson's." The Provost, however, says Wesley, "had received light from the 'circular letter' and durst not receive these heretics." The "circular letter" emanated from the Countess of Huntingdon, who was so relentless as to try to dissuade people from listening to his message. Wesley had preached at Ormiston, but the parish minister, after bidding him God-speed, turned against him on being informed that Lord Hopetoun had received a letter from Lady Huntingdon praying his Lordship to discountenance Wesley, who was a "dreadful heretic." Word to this effect had evidently been sent to Provost Dickson who now gave Wesley the cold shoulder. It is interesting to add that Thomas, seventh Earl of Haddington, and his second Countess, showed Wesley every mark of friendship. In the *Journal*, under date 30th May 1786, there is this entry: "I had the happiness of conversing with the Earl of Haddington and his lady at Dunbar. I could not but observe both the easiness of his behaviour (such as we find in all the Scottish nobility) and the fineness of his appearance, greatly set off by a milk-white head of hair." Wesley visited Tyninghame in 1770. Here are his impressions: "We rode over to the Earl of Haddington's seat, finely situated between two woods. The house is exceeding large and pleasant, commanding a wide prospect both ways; and the Earl is cutting walks through the woods, smoothing the ground, and much enlarging and beautifying his garden."

Not till Wesley had been in his grave fifteen years did Methodism become part of the religious life of Haddington. In or about 1806 James M'Cullagh, a subaltern in an Irish regiment stationed in the barracks in the town, began preaching Wesleyan doctrine, and founded a congregation which for many years was well attended. In 1816 a chapel seating three hundred people was built in Sidegate at a cost of £600. Here local Methodists met till about 1850 when the chapel was sold, the congregation being too small to sustain the financial burden.

Roman Catholicism, vigorous and influential in Haddington before the Reformation, never recovered the blow it then received. For three centuries it was a proscribed religion, and if there were members of the communion in the town, they must have worshipped in secret. But in 1862 Catholic Christianity once more raised its head, when a chapel, called St Mary's, was erected from plans by E. W. Pugin, son of the great Victorian architect. On the opening day there was elaborate ceremonial, including a procession round the church, the first to be witnessed in the town since the Reformation.

The ecclesiastical history of Haddington has been traced in outline. It is a strange and not uninstructive story. Perhaps its chief characteristic is a tendency to veer in the direction of extremes. The *via media* has never been attractive. The Pauline injunction: "Let your moderation be known unto all men" is a counsel more honoured in the breach than in the observance. And through what religious vicissitudes has Haddington not passed? In the beginning the town was only less important than St Andrews as an outpost of Catholicism. At the Reformation the pendulum swung in the direction of Protestantism, though the early stages were a gradual process. In the days of the Covenant the inhabitants were champions of the Kirk and of the divine right of Presbytery, and were in full sympathy with the brethren immured on the Bass. Finally, in the eighteenth century, when the Established Church was under fire, and because of its tepid preaching of the Word and its system of placing ministers in vacant parishes, there arose a formidable body of Dissent which, if it kept alive the flame of evangelical religion, also perpetuated features of church life less commendable. Throughout the centuries Haddington has pursued the policy of "Thorough" in matters of religion.

CHAPTER IV

Under the Stuarts

In the middle of the sixteenth century, and indeed for some time before, the Bothwell family were suspiciously prominent in the affairs of Haddington. Nor need this cause surprise, considering that the Hepburns were not only possessors of property in the town but owned the strong fortress of Hailes, a few miles to the east. With the return of Mary Queen of Scots in 1561, the family became more important than ever. James Hepburn, the fourth Earl, was the most exalted personage at court and became the affianced husband of the Queen. But if the Hepburns had immense influence, they did little that was worthy to uphold it, being for the most part arrogant, incorrigibly ambitious, and daringly unscrupulous. A Bothwell was at the bottom of nearly all the evil designs with which Scotland was then plagued.

Characteristically one of the early encounters between a member of this family and the burgh relates to what had the appearance of an extortionate demand for money. In 1531 Master John Hepburn, parson of Dalry, came before the town council in behalf of "my Lord erll Bothwell" (the third Earl), requesting £40 "of usuell mone of ye realm" to be delivered to Lord Seton, but "not hurtand yair fredome and comon weill of ye toune." The civic reply was that the demand could not be complied with. None the less the magistrates gave assurance of their goodwill towards my Lord Bothwell's service provided freedom of action was not compromised. When next the Hepburns are in contact with Haddington, it is again in the person of Patrick, the third Earl, against whom, on 27th May 1550, a summons for treason was executed at the Cross. Three years before, he had embarked on a tortuous and despicable course. Along with other Scottish nobles, Bothwell had secretly come to terms with the English king, the reward being a yearly allowance of one thousand crowns and one hundred horsemen for his protection. Bothwell's perfidy notwithstanding, the Queen-Regent not only pardoned him but made him Lieutenant on the Borders. So the summons proclaimed at the Cross of Haddington was rendered nugatory.

Not less ignoble was the career of his son James, the fourth Earl, whose part in the national story is too well known to need recapitulation. His connection with Haddington exhibits him in no more favourable light than that of his father. In 1559 Bothwell, who was hereditary Sheriff of Haddington, apprehended Cockburn of Ormiston near Dunpender Law (Traprain) while conveying from Berwick £3000 with which to assist the Lords of the Congregation in their opposition to the Queen-Regent. Bothwell took possession of the hoard, and as a reprisal Arran and Lord James Stuart (afterwards the Regent Moray) arrived in Haddington with two hundred horsemen, one hundred footmen, and two pieces of artillery, the intention being to capture Bothwell. But the latter, apprised of what was in store for him, escaped from his house, says Sadler, the English ambassador, by "a lane called the Gowl" to the river Tyne. The house, though known as Bothwell Castle, did not belong to the Earl but (as pointed out in a later chapter) to Cockburn of Sandybed. On taking refuge there, Bothwell is said to have changed clothes with a menial whose duties he performed till his escape. In return for protection Bothwell assigned to the owner of the mansion a perpetual ground annual out of the lands of Mainshill, one of his few acts that it is pleasant to record.

Still another Bothwell figures outstandingly in the annals of Haddington. This was Francis, the fifth Earl, a nephew of the third husband of Mary Queen of Scots. In October 1584 the magistrates received a letter from the Secret Council charging them to choose a town council in accordance with their (the Secret Council's) wishes, of which Francis, Earl of Bothwell, was to be provost. The civic fathers complied, and Bothwell was chief magistrate till 1590 or 1591. The duties, as was to be expected, were discharged perfunctorily. At any rate, there is no mention of him in the minutes after March 1588, though it has been inferred that he remained provost for at least other two years. When Bothwell assumed the provostship he was made a burgess, and on 31st August 1585 the council advanced him one hundred crowns in order that "ye puir man be sustenit in case this present plague of pestilence continues."

This Bothwell was the stormy petrel of Scottish politics. Whether there was foundation for it or not, James VI was obsessed with the idea that the Earl aimed at kingly power. From 1591 Bothwell was a thorn in the flesh of the monarch. Not only did he roundly abuse his sovereign but attacked Holyroodhouse when their Majesties were residing there. In danger of his life, James VI gave letters of fire and sword to suppress Bothwell. This, however, was not so easy as it looked, the king having no armed force at his disposal. Still, action of some kind had to be taken against so dangerous and relentless an enemy. Accordingly, on 10th January 1591-92, a proclamation, "thought to be penned by the king himself," says Calderwood, was issued against Bothwell. It announced a reward to any person who would kill the rebellious Earl. Calderwood refers to James VI as taking part personally in the hunt for the fugitive, and that, in riding eastward from Edinburgh, his Majesty "had almost beene drowned in a poole of water, if he had not been rescued and pulled furth by the necke by a yeoman, where the courteors durst not venture." [1] It is unfortunate that the historian of the Kirk is vague as to where this incident occurred. Happily, in a letter written by Robert Bowes to Burghley, we have a more circumstantial account. The epistle is dated 26th January 1591-92, and contains this passage:—

The King trusting to have entrapped Bothwell by means of Davy Edmonston of Barnhouse, an old familiar of Bothwell, passed to Samerson [Samuelston?] and Haddington, but the success did not fall out to the King's contentment. He was at once purposed, as I am certified, to have sought Bothwell and Niddrie in place adjoining the border of Scotland, and whereof some trial was given to Bothwell's abode there, but by advice and doubt of the truth of this tale he changed his purpose. In this journey to surprise Bothwell, *the King and his horse fell into the Water of Tyne near to Haddington, where he was speedily rescued, and yet not before he was sore wet and troubled with the water.* [2]

It would therefore appear that James VI, in his pursuit of Francis, Earl of Bothwell, narrowly escaped drowning at Haddington, an event which, had it come to pass, would have changed the whole course of British history.

In view of the fact that her third husband was closely linked with East Lothian, it might be expected that Queen Mary's connection with Haddington would have been closer. Yet the only time she probably was there was on 17th March 1565–66 when she and Darnley saw a force of eight thousand men assembled in response to a royal proclamation issued from Dunbar calling upon the inhabitants of certain districts in the Lothians and neighbouring counties to meet her, "in feir of war," at Haddington. In those hectic days Mary was intent on revenge for the murder of Riccio, and with the force she had summoned she rode to Edinburgh. Though her stay in Haddington must have been short, the Queen found time to sign the pardon of Moray who had, on her marriage to Darnley, appealed to arms. The Queen also granted an interview to

[1] *History of Kirk of Scotland*, v, 144.   [2] *C.S.P.*, x, 627. The italics are mine.

Sir James Melville of Halhill, who had been employed by her to win over Queen Elizabeth to her marriage. In his *Memoirs* Melville gives a detailed account of what passed between the Queen and himself. Mary, we are told, received him "very favourably" and expressed "great thanks for my care of her honour and welfare." Then he goes on:—

> That night in Haddington she subscribed divers remissions for my lord Murray and his dependers [Moray had been privy to Riccio's murder], lamenting unto me the king's [Darnley's] folly, ingratitude and misbehaviour. I excused the same the best I could, imputing it to his youth, which occasioned him easily to be led way by pernicious counsel . . .; praying her Majesty for many necessary considerations, to remove out of her mind any prejudice against him, seeing that she had chosen him herself against the opinion of many of her subjects.

Melville also had an interview with Darnley.

> That night in Haddington the King enquired of me, if the lord of Murray had written to him. I answered, That his letter to the Queen was written in haste, and that he esteemed the Queen and him [Darnley] but one. He said, he might also have written to me. Then he enquired what was become of Morton, Ruthven, and the rest of that company [the murderers]. I told him I believed they were fled, but I know not whither. As they have brewed, says he, so let them drink. It appeared to me that he was troubled he had deserted them, finding the Queen's favour but cold.[1]

Mary's flight into England was followed by the coronation of the infant James VI and the appointment of Moray to the Regency. Both measures were approved of by the burgesses of Haddington at a meeting convened in the Tolbooth on 1st September 1567. Towards the close of 1573, Morton, who in the previous year had been appointed Lieutenant and Justice within the Constabulary of Haddington, was entertained by the civic authorities. In January 1574–75 he made a lengthened stay, judging by the fact that no fewer than six meetings of the Privy Council were held in the town, all of which Morton attended. At Haddington also he held justice courts and wrote two letters to Burghley.

The contacts of James VI with the burgh were as unimportant as those of his mother. Occasional visits were paid to Haddington during the twenty years before his departure to England, but there is no record of this king ever having resided in the town. His interest in the community seems to have been slight. Doubtless James VI never forgot the episode of his falling into the Tyne at Haddington and being rescued from a watery grave. There is mention, however, of his granting a charter on 31st January 1605–06 in favour of David Forrest of Gymmersmylnes [2] [Gimmersmills], burgess of Haddington, and Isabell Sympsone, his spouse, of the corn mills called Gymmersmylnes and mansion with the hauch and a number of acres. The superiority of this property had formerly belonged to the prioress and convent of the monastery of Haddington.

When James left Scotland to ascend the English throne the town was by-passed, the royal cavalcade journeying to the Borders by the old road that ran along the top of the Garleton Hills. Nor did His Majesty include Haddington in his itinerary when, in 1617, he came north to revisit his native country. But if James himself did not actually enter the town, the burgh records indicate that, at the royal request, arrangements were made for part of his retinue to be accommodated there. Nearly five months before the visit, on 8th January, the town council sent Patrick Broun to Edinburgh

---

[1] Melville of Halhill, *Memoirs* (Abbey Classics), 73.

[2] Gimmersmills, the buildings of which (in part at least) remain to this day, are frequently referred to in old deeds. On 25th April 1631 we hear of a charter being granted by Mr James Cokburne of Wester Monkrig, provost of Haddington, and the bailies and council, disponing to George Forrest, fiar of Gymmersmylnes, and Jean Lauder, his spouse, the teinds of 19½ acres, including the Hermanflat and Meadowaikers.

to learn what provision was necessary for "ye strangeris." But not till 8th May, by which time the royal progress had well begun, did the Privy Council request the magistrates to prepare "meit, drink, bedding, and stabling to strangeris of his hienes companie." The burgesses responded with alacrity, and at the same time resolved that the auspicious occasion should not be allowed to pass without regalement and merry-making on their own account. The baxters undertook to supply sufficient bread, and for an entire week the fleshers were to ply their trade without "stop or impediment" of any kind. Moreover, the town officials were to attend at the Cross to see that hoarders of "fowlis, eggis, butter, and siclyke" were punished.

Although Haddingtonians were denied a sight of their king when he revisited Scotland in 1617, they had reason to be grateful to James VI for the charter granted to them in the penultimate year of his reign. Dated 13th January 1624–25, it confirmed the town in the possession of the lands of Gladsmuir (with the exception of a portion reserved to the Earl of Haddington); likewise in Ralph Eglin's Acres and Hangman's Acres. The former skirted the post-road to Edinburgh on the south, and roughly extended from West Port to Spring Gardens or Common Loan. Subsequently this ground was exchanged with Houston of Clerkington for M'Call's Park, now covered by the Knox Institute. Hangman's Acres lay to the north of the Edinburgh road. James's charter also confirmed the burgesses in the ownership of the two corn mills together with the haughs, and the port of Aberlady, as well as in their right to hold the fairs of St Peter and St Michael.

When ratified by Charles I in 1633 this charter conferred further advantages. The inhabitants were infeft in all lands, annual rents, houses, yards, acres, wastes lying within the burgh "with all and sundry other lands, moors, lochs, meadows, acres, and others pertaining to the said burgh, as well in property as commonty in ane haill and ffrie burgh Royal to be called in all time coming . . . the burgh of Haddington." The ratification doubtless was meant to signalise the propitious circumstances under which Charles I came to Scotland to be crowned. But the king neutralised any good effects the charter might have by selecting the year of his Scottish coronation for the launching of an intensive ecclesiastical policy which was to bring him into violent opposition to his northern subjects and eventually to open conflict and his own destruction.

Even before Charles returned to England there were ominous signs that the community generally were of opinion that a course was being pursued which would injure Presbyterian feeling irretrievably. After Presbytery was restored, in November 1638, events moved rapidly. In the matter of religion Charles was intractable, and it was borne in on the Scots that if their Church polity was to be preserved armed conflict could not be averted. Haddington was one of the centres of Presbyterian resistance. In May 1639 we find Leslie, the Lord General of the Covenanting Army, along with the Earl of Rothes and Lords Yester, Lindsay, and Dalhousie, marching thither at the head of thirty thousand horse and foot, and equipped with forty-five pieces of cannon. Leslie's army was on its way to Dunse Law. Before reaching their destination, however, the Covenanting forces encamped at Dunglas, and on 29th May instructions were received in Haddington to bake and brew for the troops.

In the subsequent course of the war Haddington was not prominent, though one incident must have been learned with marked poignancy. When in 1640 Leslie marched into England, Thomas, second Earl of Haddington, who appears to have been a stout Covenanter, was given a force of ten thousand men with which to defend the Borders. At his headquarters at Dunglas a large quantity of gunpowder was stored. On 30th August the castle was blown up, and Lord Haddington, his half-brother Robert, and many others perished. This tragic event, according to Scot of Scotstarvet, was caused by an English page-boy who, annoyed by a disparaging remark concerning his countrymen, thrust a red-hot iron into a barrel of gunpowder.

When the Commonwealth was established, Cromwell was sent to Scotland at the head of a formidable army with which to bring the people of the northern kingdom into line with England. One of his main objects was to crush those Scots who had espoused the cause of Charles II. The young king had done lip-service to the Covenant, and his followers were ingenuous enough to believe that the royal action was sincere. Despite his warlike intentions, however, Cromwell was inclined to be conciliatory. But the touching devotion accorded to the new king had to be overcome, and war seemed the only way of dispelling it. On 22nd July 1650 Cromwell invaded Scotland. If Baillie is to be credited, he assured "his brethren in evil of a more easy conquest of that kingdom than all the English kings ever had." [1] Cromwell's objective was Edinburgh, but finding that the Covenanting army under David Leslie occupied a strong defensive position between the capital and Leith, he led his troops round the southern outskirts, in the hope of reaching Queensferry where, with the assistance of the English fleet, he was confident that he could bring off a battle in favour of the Commonwealth. But Cromwell was out-manœuvred by Leslie, who was posted on rising ground near Corstorphine and right in the line of march of the English army. Seeing no prospect of reaching Queensferry, Cromwell fell back on Musselburgh, and on 31st August continued his retreat by way of Haddington. There he learned that the Scots were marching in his rear with "exceeding expedition." Leslie's vanguard had in fact reached Gladsmuir and by nightfall caught up with the English army at Haddington. A skirmish took place, a detailed though one-sided account of which Cromwell embodied in a dispatch written the day after Dunbar Drove (4th September).

We marched from Musselburgh to Haddington. Where, by that time we had got the van-brigade of our horse, and our foot and train, into their quarters, the Enemy had marched with that exceeding expedition that they fell upon the rear-forlorn of our horse, and put it in some disorder; and indeed had like to have engaged our rear-brigade of horse with their whole Army,—had not the Lord by His Providence put a cloud over the Moon, thereby giving us opportunity to draw-off those horse to the rest of our Army. Which accordingly was done without any loss, save of three or four of our afore-mentioned forlorn; wherein the Enemy, as we believe, received more loss.

The Army being put into a reasonable secure posture,—towards midnight the Enemy attempted our quarters, on the west end of Haddington: but through the goodness of God we repulsed them. The next morning we drew into an open field, on the south side of Haddington; we not judging it safe for us to draw to the Enemy upon his own ground, he being prepossessed thereof;—but rather drew back, to give him way to come to us, if he had so thought fit. And having waited about the space of four or five hours, to see if he would come to us; and not finding any inclination in the Enemy so to do—we resolved to go, according to our first intendment, to Dunbar. [2]

Had the Scots fallen into Cromwell's trap, the probability is that the great trial of strength between the opposing forces would have been decided in the vicinity of the parish church of Haddington and not at Dunbar. As regards the skirmish to the west of the town, Douglas points out that Cromwell omitted to say that when the moon shone out in the interim the Scots "took their chance in the uncertain light, and charged and re-charged up to the gates, perhaps into the very streets of Haddington." [3] From the narrative in *Mercurius Politicus* one gathers that, till the first attack on his rear, Cromwell was ignorant that he was being pursued. We also glean

[1] *Letters and Journals*, iii, 68.   [2] Cromwell, *Letters and Speeches*, iii, 41.
[3] W. S. Douglas, *Cromwell's Scotch Campaigns*, p. 93.

from the same source that Fairfax's regiment bore the brunt in repulsing the night attack, and that, "on a fair and equal field," Cromwell offered battle on the Sunday morning. Douglas, too, comments on the fact that the reluctance of the Scots to engage was in all likelihood due to the ministers.[1] When it became evident that the Scots would not accept battle at Haddington, Cromwell's men in "poor, shattered, hungry, discouraged" condition marched to the scene of "The Race of Dunbar." The battle was fought on 3rd September, the Scots suffering a crippling defeat. Many fugitives sought shelter in Haddington. Moreover, the burgh records contain a number of entries of sums paid for medical attendance and drugs for the wounded. These extend over a long period. As late as 13th March 1663 the magistrates allowed Marion Forrest "ten marks Scots money in satisfaction of all fees due to Alexander Hepburn, her deceased husband, as chirurgeon to the town, and of all drugs bestowed on the hurt sojours at Dunbar fecht."

In view of the warfare that had been going on in their midst with its disastrous climax at Dunbar, it is rather surprising to learn that Haddington acquiesced in the Cromwellian union of Scotland with England. The town's decision is thus set forth:

I, George Brown, being deputed by the Brough of Haddington doe, on ye behalfe of my selfe and those represented by mee, declair our free and willing acceptance of and Consent unto ye tender made by ye Parlyam^t of England y^t Scotland bee Incorporated into and made ane Comon Wealth wth England, that thereby the same Goverm^t that is Established and Enjoyed wth out a King or House of Lords under ye free State and Comon Wealth of England, and Wee desire y^t ye people of England and Scotland may bee represented in one Parlyam^t and Governed by theire representatives therein as ye supreme authority of ye whole Iseland.

This accommodating spirit did not go unrewarded, for there was issued at Dalkeith a "Declaration by the Commissioners of the English Parliament for ordering and managing of the affairs of Scotland," to the effect that because the burgesses had undertaken "to live peaceably under, and yield obedience to the Authority of Parliament of the Commonwealth of England exercised in Scotland," they would be afforded "speciall protection." This meant that "officers and souldiers and all other persons" passing through the burgh or shire were to "offer no violence nor injury unto the person or goods of any of the Inhabitants of the same." Further, the townspeople were to receive from time to time "such testimonies of respect and favor . . . by way of benefit . . . in their libertie and Trade . . . as shall consist with the present state of affaires."

After Cromwell returned to England Monck was his Scottish representative. He had efficiently led the brigade of foot at Dunbar Drove, but it is an exaggeration to say that the victory was due to him. Cromwell left with Monck a force of between five and six thousand men to complete the conquest of the northern kingdom. Monck's army, or at least a detachment, was at Haddington in 1657 under the command of Captain Roger Legge. On 27th May the town treasurer was instructed to purchase for Legge, who had taken up his abode in "Lady Beirfoord's house," "as much linen as will make ane boord cloth" and "ane dozen servitors (table napkins), also a stouped bed (one with posts)."

On 22nd July Monck dispatched a letter to the Sheriff of East Lothian requesting him to publish "the proclamation anent his Highnes (Cromwell)" and the powers of Parliament. On the day of the ceremony the magistrates and deacons of the various crafts, "in their best equipage and apparel," walked in procession to the Cross where the reading of the proclamation was punctuated by a fanfare of trumpets furnished

---

[1] W. S. Douglas, *Cromwell's Scotch Campaigns*, p. 94.

by Legge's regiment. The occasion was also taken to make Legge and his quarter-master, Daniel Dalton, burgesses.

In the *Diary* of Andrew Hay of Craignethan, published by the Scottish History Society, we get a glimpse of Monck in Haddington. Under date 25th November 1659, Hay has this entry: "By the way to Edinburgh I met a discreet Inglishman at whom I asked newes. He told me that the General (Monck) marched to Haddington on Tuesday last, and there met a post from his Commissioners in London, showing that they had agreed with the Army." In the preceding month the general had sent a letter to the provost requesting the town council to send a representative to Edinburgh to hear from him (Monck) "some especiall business that he has to communicat . . . concerning the countrie." On 12th December the provost, William Seton, had an interview with Monck at Berwick, the council advancing "thrie scoir pounds of expenses and wage." Again, on 23rd January 1660–61, Seton consulted the Privy Council as to what action was to be taken in Parliament regarding the financial burdens of Haddington.

Another link between Monck and the burgh was forged through Sir Thomas Clarges, the general's brother-in-law. In January 1659–60 Clarges became parliamentary representative for the Haddington Burghs. The provost, it seems, had asked counsel of Monck as to a suitable candidate, and Monck had recommended his brother-in-law. Clarges, who promised to serve the constituency gratuitously, had a rather notable career. In early life he practised medicine, but, drifting into politics, was employed by Richard Cromwell, in carrying dispatches to Monck in Scotland. It was Clarges who brought to Richard Cromwell a letter expressing the general's concurrence with the new Protector's accession to power. Along with it, however, came a confidential document outlining a policy craftily designed by Monck to embroil the younger Cromwell with all parties. Clarges subsequently acted as Monck's correspondent in London, in which capacity he carried overtures to him from Fleetwood and Lambert when it became apparent that he (Monck) was about to march on London. And it was this representative of Haddington Burghs who conveyed to Charles II at Breda the message of the English Parliament inviting him to return and resume his kingly office. Charles was so overjoyed that he straightway knighted the bearer of the good news.

We have already remarked upon the composure with which the burgesses of Haddington accommodated themselves to perturbing and sometimes violent political change. As a town imbued with the Covenanting spirit, it had little reason for thinking well of Charles II, who gave piquancy to a faulty record by declaring that Presbyterianism was no religion for a gentleman. Yet the restoration of this faithless monarch to the throne of his ancestors found the community in a jubilant mood. The King's Birthday on 29th May 1660 witnessed a great outpouring of the spirit of loyalty. "For the better performing of quhat is dew be this burgh" and "upon consideratioun of the great mercie to this land be his majestie's return to his government," the town council ordered a general lighting of bonfires, while the whole population was to accompany the magistrates to the Cross "in testimonie of theyr joy." These celebrations, it was decreed, were to be a feature of each succeeding King's Birthday which, looking to the variable character of Charles II, was a dangerous precedent. But they were doubtless stimulated by the tone and temper of the sycophantic government which now ruled Scotland. When "ane solemn anniversarie thanksgiving" was arranged for in an Act passed by the Estates on 13th May 1661, the magistrates decided that the ceremony should take place on the King's Birthday "efter sermon." A company numbering "fyve or sax scoir" was to assemble under the direction of Captain James

Cockburn and to escort the civic fathers to the Cross. Here a platform was to be erected on which were to be placed two tables round which the councillors were to sit. Sweetmeats (weighing twenty pounds) with figs and raisins were to be distributed, while the king's health was to be drunk with "ane haill puncheon of wyn." And for background to this junketing there were to be a dozen flags "of whyte and blew taffateis" emblazoned with the town arms and inscribed "Haddington." Finally the soldiers, "for the better performing of the solemnitie," were to be supplied with "match and powder."

Apparently the King's Birthday celebrations did not afford sufficient outlet for the hilarious spirit, for it was resolved that the anniversary of the Gunpowder Plot should also be commemorated. On 5th November 1660, at four o'clock in the afternoon, every dweller was to "put furth a bonefyre before thyr respective housses," to signalise "that great mercie & delyverance manifested to those kingdomes be discoverie of the Gunpowder treason plotted and intended againgtst his Majestie King James the saxt of ever blessed memorie and his parliament of Ingland." A proclamation, intimated through the streets by the town drummer, announced that the Gunpowder Plot commemoration was to be a yearly event, and that those who failed to observe it in the manner prescribed would be fined £5.

Not only was the town punctilious in its fealty to the Stuart dynasty but it treated with undue respect the high officials representing its authority. When, on 1st December 1660, the King's Commissioner, the Earl of Middleton (who was no better than he ought to be), passed through Haddington, he was received by the magistrates "in their best equipage," saluted in "the tounes name," and given a banquet. On the same day John, Earl of Crawford and Lindsay, High Treasurer of Scotland, and four of his retainers, were admitted burgesses. The expense of entertaining the King's Commissioner and his retinue amounted to £203, 4s. Scots. Nor had the burgh any qualms about doing the bidding of Dalyell of Binns, who, as commander-in-chief in Scotland, had a few months before defeated the Covenanters at Rullion Green. On 30th April 1667 the "Muscovy general" wrote to the Earl of Winton to assemble the forces of East Lothian, who were to march to Musselburgh "to oppose ane pairt of the enemies navie to the number of thirty sail at least now in the water of Forth." Haddington responded to the summons without hesitation. Drums were beat in the streets, and it was made known that all fencible persons were to proceed to Gullane, and if anything happened there the magistrates were to be notified.

With the Restoration began the disastrous rule of Lauderdale. In 1667 he joined the Cabal and soon after combined insolence with power. The administration of Scotland was completely under his control, and this personage, who at the outset of his career was identified with the Covenanters, now caused them endless suffering and hardship. In East Lothian Lauderdale's influence naturally was very great. One channel for its display was the making of his retainers (many of them menials) burgesses of Haddington. In 1672 more than fifty of his dependants, including Patrick Vaus, Master of the Duke's household, and John Witherspoon, the Duke's clerk, were enrolled. A like honour was bestowed on three of Lauderdale's coachmen and a postilion. The list was augmented in 1678 by the inclusion of Robert Maitland, Deputy Governor of the Bass. Maitland, who seems to have been a kinsman of the Duke, was given his official position when the island was converted into a State prison in which the martyrs of the Covenant were immured. Maitland died in 1682 when he was succeeded in the office of Deputy Governor by his son Charles, who had served on the Bass under his father, being then known as "Ensign Maitland." The elder

Maitland's admission to the burgess-ship must have gone against the grain in the case of a Covenanting town council, but it may be presumed that the magistrates were powerless where Lauderdale was concerned.

In 1679 there was a deal of commotion in the town. The occasion was the coming to Scotland of the Duke of York (afterwards James VII) as Royal Commissioner. Lauderdale organised an East Lothian reception. On entering Haddington the Duke and Duchess were received by the magistrates with dutiful but probably not very sincere respect. From the burgh their Royal Highnesses, attended by the Marquess of Montrose and about sixty of the noblemen and gentry of the Border counties, proceeded to Lethington, where they were sumptuously entertained. The Privy Council were present and the company as a whole numbered fully two thousand.

During the latter part of the reign of Charles II the political and ecclesiastical situation steadily worsened. In June 1669 was issued the First Letter of Indulgence, which permitted such ejected ministers as had lived "peaceably and orderly" to re-occupy their pulpits, if vacant. In other words, the acceptance of the Indulgence was equivalent to a surrender to Episcopacy and the ecclesiastical supremacy of the Crown. In Haddington the oppressive enactments of the Government were strongly resented. Several town councillors refused the Test Oath, which the Duke of York was instrumental in getting passed so as to make himself secure of the Scottish Crown and at the same time able to curb (at least such was his hope) all opposition to a policy frankly Catholic.

The year which witnessed the passing of the obnoxious Test Act saw the launching, close to Nungate, of an industrial experiment second only in interest and importance to the Darien scheme. Admittedly, the topic would be dealt with more fittingly in the chapter assigned to trade and industry; but the New Mills venture was no mere local affair. It bore upon the larger issues of Scottish history, and its treatment in this place is not without justification.

The New Mills Cloth Manufactory, which reacted beneficially on the economic situation in Scotland when the paramount interests of the country were becoming commercial instead of ecclesiastical, found a competent historian in the late Professor W. R. Scott. For the Scottish History Society he narrated the whole story from authentic documents in a volume published in 1905 which, however, is caviare to the general. "Of all the undertakings established after 1681, the history of the New Mills Company is in several respects," writes Professor Scott, "the most interesting, in view of the wealth of detail afforded by its minutes, and the extensive powers conferred upon it by the state."

The New Mills concern was the very considerable fruit of a progressive movement inaugurated in 1681 when Parliament and the Privy Council enacted legislation for the encouragement of trade and manufactures in Scotland. Of the various proposals for industrial development the New Mills concern stood easily first. Factors promoting the omens of success were its situation in a wool-producing district, its proximity to Edinburgh, and its exemption from burdensome taxation. The chief promoter was Sir James Stanfield, an officer in the Cromwellian army who resided for a time in Edinburgh. A most capable business man, he had "many transactions with noblemen in giving them monetary accommodation," and was able to acquire territorial possessions near Leith. Subsequently he became the owner of New Mills, a small property immediately to the east of Haddington that had in olden times belonged to the Cistercian nunnery and in the eighteenth century was re-named Amisfield. Stanfield also had political connections, and sat in the Scots Parliament as representative for East Lothian.

The cloth manufactory was built on a site partly determined by the fact that a similar undertaking had been carried on there. Stanfield secured the old premises and granted a nineteen years' lease to a newly formed company in which he and Robert Blackwood (Master of the Merchant Company of Edinburgh and a director of the Darien Company) owned most of the shares. The tack of the cloth manufactory at New Mills, which is preserved at the Register House, refers to "that great manufactory stone house on the south side of the village of Newmylnes being one hundredth and one foot in lenth, twentie-one foot in breadth within the walls, and three storie high." Stanfield and his co-directors calculated that a capital of £5000 sterling, or £60,000 Scots, would purchase and maintain twenty looms employing 233 hands, and provide working capital as well. The annual output was reckoned at 55,823 ells, which would realise on an average £55,823 Scots. In short, the directors were optimistic enough to believe that the yearly turnover would almost equal the capital. The total expenses, including the provision of new material, were estimated at over £38,900 Scots, while the profit, subject to payments to foreign workmen, was estimated at £16,395 Scots or £1411 sterling.

At first the Company had the pleasant experience of not being able to keep pace with the demand. The articles of agreement stipulated that during the first three years there was to be no dividend. In the succeeding three years stockholders were to receive the legal rate of interest, while the balance of profit remaining at the end of the sixth year was to be added to the original capital. However satisfying the scheme looked on paper, in practice the course was strewn with obstacles of one kind or another. At the outset difficulties were experienced in inducing weavers to come from England; but once this problem was solved things for a time worked with tolerable smoothness. By October 1681 two looms were producing "coarse cloth," and in the following January fine cloth also was being turned out. In February 1683 ground for extension was needed, and in April the "Master of the Manufactory" was instructed "to take great care in improveing the spinning and dressing of the cloth." Twenty-five looms were now producing cloth and two serges. In 1684 the financial results allowed the payment of legal interest on the stock.

In response to an appeal for Government patronage as regards the supply of military uniforms, the Privy Council on 22nd February 1683–84 authorised the Company to import from England 2536 ells of stone-grey cloth for clothing the dragoons of General Dalzell of Binns. A month later, however, Dalzell was empowered to import the cloth, provided the material did not exceed five shillings per ell and bore the seal of the New Mills Company. This arrangement, however, was hardly likely to benefit the Company, who gave an undertaking to the Privy Council to furnish enough cloth as quickly as it could be imported and at the same rates. The Company also promised to dye the cloth any colour. Nevertheless licences for the importation of English cloth continued to be issued. The blow, as serious as it was unexpected, was followed by grave discontent among the workpeople, of whom there were over seven hundred. The root of the trouble was the importation of weavers from England and from abroad. In one of the disputes the provost of Haddington intervened, which led to two discharged weavers being expelled from the town. Besides internal conflict, business was not improving. Cloth in large quantities was being imported, and the Privy Council, at the request of the Company, took measures to deal with the situation. Imported cloth was to be seized and burned, and the offenders fined. But even this was not enough, and in 1685 the Company was in danger of being "utterly ruined and broke." A general meeting of shareholders actually discussed the matter of dissolution. Again the Privy Council took action. No more licences were to be granted for the importation of English cloth to supply the army. The Company entered on a new lease of life but it was short-lived. At the Revolution we hear of the garrison on the Bass being rigged out in uniforms manufactured at New Mills. In 1690, however, Parliament granted the magistrates of Edinburgh an impost of twelve shillings Scots per ell on imported English or foreign cloth, and there was another set-back.

By this time Stanfield was financially embarrassed and proposed to sell his interest in the land and buildings at New Mills to the Company. Intent on driving a hard bargain, his suggestion was that cloth for the army should be divided between the existing Company and a new venture of which he was to be the leading spirit. But his death put an end to the project for a rival company, and his interests at New Mills were acquired by his old co-directors. In 1693 the rejuvenated Company was incorporated under the title of the "Incorporation of the Woollen Manufactory at New Mills in the shire of Haddington." Considerable profits were made and the capital was increased. Then came the Treaty of Union, providing for free trade between England and Scotland, with the result that imported cloth was sold at much lower rates than the home product. The Company, unable to adapt itself to changing circumstances, fell behind, and in 1711 preparations were made for winding up the concern. The machinery was sold, and in 1713 the lands were purchased by Colonel Francis Charteris.

Stanfield, who is said to have been knighted for making the Company a thriving concern, which indeed it really never was, had a tragic end. His pecuniary troubles were due to the extravagance of his son Philip, who had plunged into evil courses and caused no end of anxiety to his father. Their relations went from bad to worse, and one day the elder Stanfield was found drowned in the Tyne. It was at first thought he had committed suicide. Suspicions, however, were aroused by a hurried funeral, coupled with the fact that Sir James's lady had prepared grave clothes shortly before. Consequently the Privy Council had the body exhumed and examined by two surgeons. The inspection, which took place in Morham Church, led the surgeons to report that death had been caused by strangulation. They also stated that the body bled on being touched by Philip Stanfield, which testimony was actually accepted as an indication of his guilt. Accordingly the young man was tried, convicted, and hanged at the Cross of Edinburgh. Furthermore, barbarity was practised on his remains. His tongue was cut out, his right hand struck off, his head exposed on the east port of Haddington, and his body hung in chains at the Gallowlee between Edinburgh and Leith.

The short reign of James VII was, as regards Haddington, marked by several arbitrary acts of royal power. One was the packing of the town council with men who, in their attitude to the policy of the Crown, could be relied on. In September 1686 instructions were received from the Earl of Perth, Lord High Chancellor of Scotland, that no new members were to be elected: the present councillors were to remain till the King's further pleasure was signified. This command, however, did not apply to the provost-ship, Sir William Paterson of Granton being appointed to the office by the Lords of Session. In 1687 there was no election of magistrates, but in 1688 the Privy Council, at Sir William Paterson's instigation, acquiesced in a "free and regular election." Although the royal nominee, and, it may be presumed, discharging the duties of provost perfunctorily, Paterson seems to have ingratiated himself with the councillors. At any rate, they were unduly deferential to a provost who could have been little more than a figurehead. Sir William was praised for his services, "and speciallie in several occasions and pursuits of law which the town had depending before the Lords of Exchequer and the Lords of Council and Session, wherein the town had verrie good success throw the said Sir William, his pains, diligence, and concurrence." In addition to according Paterson "heartie thanks," the magistrates sent him a letter approving of "all acts and deeds" done by him, "they being all for the profeit of the burgh."

Eldest son of John Paterson, Bishop of Ross, and brother of the last Archbishop of Glasgow, this provost of Haddington was at one time Regent of Philosophy in Edinburgh University, but exchanged the position for that of Clerk of the Privy Council. Wood, in his *History of Cramond*, says Paterson, "distinguished himself by uncommon asperity against the Covenanters, a conduct certainly not proceeding from purity of principle, the Session Records of Cramond bearing ample testimony to the scandalousness of his carriage." Paterson's intervention in the affairs of Haddington is a curious episode. How a community impregnated with ideals of political and religious freedom conducted itself in the face of municipal administration carried on by pliant instruments of an unscrupulous central authority, we cannot tell. Apparently there was no overt act of rebellion, but the presence of Claverhouse's dragoons in the town shows that such a contingency was not ruled out. In 1688 there is record of the town council ordering payment of "ane accompt for coall and candle . . . to Claverhous, his troupe, when they keeped guaird." Yet we are confronted with the perplexing circumstance that the birth of Prince James Francis Edward (the Old Pretender) was celebrated with the ringing of bells and the lighting of bonfires, though when the Revolution was an accomplished fact and the Crown had been transferred to William and Mary, there were signs of equal joy. With the political upheaval Sir William Paterson relinquished the provostship as a matter of course. He was succeeded by John Sleich, who on 14th March 1689 attended the Convention of Parliament in Edinburgh as representative for Haddington. The council, "being sensible of his honesty and faithfulness for this burgh in the last Parliament," instructed Sleich to vote "for the preserving of the Protestant religioun."

The establishment of William and Mary as joint sovereigns was by no means certain. A strong Jacobite party existed, who conducted a secret correspondence with the exiled James VII, the ostensible purpose of which was to restore him to his throne. The political situation therefore lacked permanency, and measures had to be adopted for imparting stability to the new regime. An appeal for military assistance was made throughout Scotland, to which Haddington promptly responded. On 3rd February 1694 the town council ordained "drums to be beat . . . for taking on volunteers," the magistrates being empowered "to give them such encouragement as they shall think fit." Again, in March 1696, when invasion seemed imminent, there was a muster on Beanston-moor by the militia of East Lothian, each soldier being supplied with accoutrements and ten days' pay. For the purpose of this levy Haddington was divided into four quarters, lists of the young men liable were made up, and the magistrates were instructed to see that those on the list "throwe the dyce or draw lots who should go out."

When the Darien scheme was projected Haddington subscribed £400 sterling, a large sum for a burgh which was none too prosperous. Consequently, when the failure of the Darien enterprise was fully known, the community was seething with discontent. In the riots that took place in Edinburgh (for the discontent was national) the hangman of Haddington was of all persons unduly prominent. The corresponding functionary in Edinburgh was his brother. The latter, however, was remiss in his duty, scourging the law-breakers "most gently," an offence which led to his imprisonment. At this juncture, as we learn from the *Carstares State Papers*, the town council of Edinburgh sent for his brother at Haddington "to scourge him (the Edinburgh hangman) for not doing his duty."

The poor executioner pled strongly for himself—that the king's privy council had taken no notice of the [lord] advocate, who, being concussed by a few of the mob, signed an order for making open the prison doors, and that he [the Edinburgh hangman] was threatened by many hundreds with death if he laid on but one stroke. The magistrates, notwithstanding, repelled his defence, and ordered him to be scourged. The hangman of Haddington, seeing a great multitude in the streets . . . makes his escape. . . . The magistrates of Haddington (some say) find themselves concerned to represent their hangman.

With the arrival of the eighteenth century Haddington was deeply concerned over the disastrous effects on local trade consequent upon the destructive wars on the Continent. On 8th May 1701 the town council forwarded a memorial embodying their grievances to the Estates. The petition, which was presented by the provost, Alexander Edgar, sheds an interesting sidelight on the state of local feeling at a critical period of the national history. After "a long and expensive war" the community expected "to have enjoyed the blessing of a happily concluded peace by the re-establishment of our foreign trade, encouraging of home manufactures, employing of the poor in the improvement of our native product, and the less'ning of our publict burdens." But such hopes had been bitterly disappointed. Instead

Wee find our trade abroad sensibly decayed, and our coin carried out by the importation of commodities from places where ours are prohibited, our Woollen and other manufactures at home by the same means, and, the remissness of magistrates in putting of the law in dew (*sic*) execution, received not that encouragement which the interest of the country requires, whereby our poor are neither maintained nor employed as they might otherwise be.

The civic authorities also deplored that "our Company trading to Affrick and the Indies meets with so much opposition from abroad, and gets so little support from home, that after so great a loss of men and expence of treasure, their settlement in Caledonia may now too, probably, a second time fall under the same unlucky circumstances as at first, if not prevented." Another grievance was that the military were not paying the current rates for corn and straw, and thereby impoverishing the agricultural interest. Having pointed out that the army commissioners are obliged by law "to keep magazines of corn and straw for the dragoons, or else to pay the current rates of the countrie," the Haddington memorial proceeds:—

Yet these thrie years bygane so great and heavie have our burdens been that when the said dragoons were marching throw this burgh . . . the said commissioners neither keeped ony magazines of corne and straw, nor payed our people the current rates of the countrie. Therefore our people were necessitate to furnish the saids troops of dragoons at the saids commissioners' rates, which was only fyve shillings Scots for each horse per night . . . whereas our burgesses and inhabitants could not furnish ilk dragoon's horse a night's corn and straw under sixteen shillings Scots. . . .

And yet after all these hardships . . . numerous forces are still kept on foot while our much wealthier neighbours are disbanding, which occasions in time of peace heavy and unnecessary taxes. All which misfortunes and other calamities . . . wee cannot but look upon as the effects of the displeasure of Almighty God for the great immoralities that every where abounds . . . to the dishonour of God and our holy religion.

The memorial winds up by requesting Parliament "to take some effectual course for the curbing of vice and putting in execution the many laudable laws for the maintaining and employing the poor . . . and for encouragement of our own manufactures at home, and carrying on our trade abroad with advantage, and to lay on such impositions on the branches of our import as may overbalance our export, particularly that of France, and to assist the Indian and African Companies' right to their Colony of Caledonia, which has been and still is unjustly called in question, and to give such support to it as may encourage the Adventurers to go on with ane undertaking which, if vigorously pursued, may so much tend in the future to the wealth, honour, and interest of the nation." [1] Finally, the curtailment of the army is urged, likewise the seeking of some means for establishing peace, and the laying down of "courses how our people may be reimbursed be the commissioners of the Army for furnishing corne and straw to the said dragoons."

Little of general interest happened within the burgh during Anne's reign with the exception of a demonstration of loyalty to the throne when, in the spring of 1708, a Jacobite invasion seemed likely. The town then voted an address expressing their zeal for and attachment to the Government.

[1] In the "List of the several persons residenters in Scotland, who have subscribed as adventurers in the joynt-stock of the Company of Scotland trading in Africa and the Indies" occur the following Haddington names: George Cockburn, younger, merchant, £200; John Hay of Alderston, £200; Robert Miller, bailie, £100; William Johnston, postmaster, £100; George Anderson, merchant, £100; Isabel Yeaman, relict of Robert Robertson, merchant, £100; Sir John Baird of Newbyth and Sir William Baird, younger, of Newbyth, each £500.

CHAPTER V

Before the Forty-Five—and After (1714-60)

THE fact has been stressed that loyalty to the throne was a characteristic of the people of Haddington. The whirligig of time brings in his revenge, but whatever the nature of it might be they generally managed to accommodate themselves to circumstance and to remain, at least outwardly, contented and law-abiding. Usually Haddington was on the side of authority, accepting almost complacently the yoke of the powers that be. The accession of a new monarch, even the coming of a new dynasty, made no perceptible difference in the dutiful respect of a town that had been a royal burgh since the time of David I. No doubt there were occasions when the burghers resented the arbitrariness and oppression of the Stuart government, as indeed they had ample reason to do, but their customary attitude enforced the duty of true citizenship—the upholding of king and country. So when, in 1714, the Hanoverian succession became an accomplished fact, and the protracted though hardly beneficent rule of the early Georges had begun, Haddington adjusted itself to the new conditions. On 19th October 1714 the town council resolved that the coronation of George I should be celebrated.

Nor had the townsfolk long to wait for a test of their devotion to the House of Hanover. Within a twelvemonth the first Jacobite rebellion broke out. Having learned that demonstrations in behalf of the exiled Stuarts had taken place in England and on the Borders, John, Earl of Mar, the Jacobite commander in Scotland, ordered a strong force to cross the Forth from Fife. It was to link up with the Border contingent and march on Glasgow. Thus would Argyle, who was then commanding a Hanoverian army at Stirling, find himself, as Mar expressed it, "in a hose-net." The army in Fife numbered 2500 men and was under the command of Mackintosh of Borlum, a capable officer. On the nights of 11th and 12th October 1715 considerably more than half of Borlum's men were ferried across the Forth and landed at Aberlady, Gullane, and North Berwick. This daring feat was accomplished with the loss of only forty men, who were captured. From the Lothian coast Borlum marched his men to Haddington. Here he fixed his camp, but only for a few hours. He found time, however, to proceed to the Cross and there proclaim the Chevalier de St George as James VIII. Borlum now altered his plan of campaign and ruined his chances of success. Instead of effecting a junction with the Jacobite troops in the Border country, he was beguiled into marching on Edinburgh in the hope of capturing the Scottish capital. This project, however, was frustrated by Argyle with 1100 men, and the Highland army was forced hastily to retreat from Leith. Haddington played no further part in the rebellion and had resumed its ordinary life before the affair ended.

On 24th November 1717 there died the Rev. John Gray, who bequeathed to Haddington (of which he was a native) a noble collection of early printed books. It was an embarrassing gift. For one thing, the inhabitants were hardly in a position to appreciate it; and for another, they had no suitable place in which to accommodate the volumes. In the burgh records the donor is referred to as the son of Robert Gray, a former bailie of Haddington, but other accounts state that his father's Christian name was Andrew. Graduating at Edinburgh University in 1664, Gray entered the ministry of the Church of Scotland, then under Episcopal domination. Passing his trials before the Presbytery of Haddington, he was licensed in 1667. His first charge was at Tulliallan, where he laboured for five years, after which he accepted an invitation from the town council of Glasgow to preach in "ony of the toune's kirkis as he sall be appoynted." In Glasgow Gray became acquainted with Gilbert Burnet, formerly minister of Saltoun and in later years Bishop of Salisbury and chaplain to William III. Both were ardent admirers of Archbishop Leighton. Reliable testimony to the personality and theological standing of Gray is furnished by a score of manuscript volumes in his handwriting. He appears to have been of resolute purpose, self-assertive, and striving for the fulfilment of clear-cut convictions. On the other hand, his wonderful library, or as much of it as remains, is the visible embodiment of his portentous learning and of his mastery of various languages, both ancient and modern.

In 1684 Gray was translated from Glasgow to Aberlady parish, but in 1689 was deprived of his charge for refusing to read a proclamation of the Scots Parliament and to pray for William III and Queen Mary. He became a non-juror, though he continued to describe himself as "minister of Aberlady." For the rest of his days he resided in Haddington, where, in the Episcopal meeting-house in Poldrate, he occasionally preached. Under a flat ornamental stone, elaborately inscribed, in the ruined choir of St Mary's, lie the remains of this most erudite minister. Gray's will is mainly concerned with his valuable library. A thousand merks were to be spent in lighting the apartment in which the books were preserved, while an equal sum was to be expended in remunerating the librarian and in buying and binding books. The provost, three bailies, the dean of guild, and the town clerk were named as trustees, in which capacity they were to meet annually on 28th February (the donor's birthday) to discuss the affairs of the library.

Gray's Library [1] has now been in the possession of Haddington for more than two hundred years. For a period it was accommodated in a room specially set apart in the English School building in Church Street, but more than sixty years ago the books were removed to the building in Newton Port now occupied by the Public Library. Here they suffered great neglect. Indeed the very existence of the Gray Collection was known to few, and fewer still showed any desire to become acquainted with its singular contents. Eventually the town council realised that they had in their keeping what is probably the finest private library of early printed books in Scotland, and in 1929 they built an annexe to the Public Library where Gray's magnificent collection, besides being preserved from further deterioration, can be inspected by all interested. As a collection of books of rare quality, Gray's Library attracts the antiquary and the bibliographer, the man skilled in the early productions of the printing press, and he who delights in rummaging for ancient lore, in studying quaint woodcuts, and appreciates splendid bindings. Sadly must it be confessed that many volumes have disappeared, but there still remain close on a thousand items, representing a varied assortment of specimens of early printing and early binding—the handiwork of the most renowned craftsmen in Europe in the sixteenth and seventeenth centuries. The books—ponderous tomes some of them—are largely works of divinity. Gray must have been a man of prodigious learning, for the venerable folios and quartos are in all languages. Further, many have marginal notes in Gray's handwriting, together with the inscription: "Ex libris. Jo. Gray, Aberladie. *Summa religionis imitari quem colis*" —a motto, it is noteworthy, similar to one which Archbishop Leighton placed on his books, now preserved at Dunblane.

But to pass from John Gray and his learned library to more commonplace topics. What, it may be asked, were the conditions prevailing in Haddington during the first

[1] See *Catalogue of Gray Library*, with introduction and descriptive notes by W. Forbes Gray (1929).

54

quarter of the eighteenth century? For answer we turn to Defoe's *Tour through Great Britain*. The author of *Robinson Crusoe* was a most accomplished journalist, who, in keeping with some followers of his profession, mingled truth with fiction. Still, Defoe was a close and shrewd observer, and it is astonishing how accurate and circumstantial he is in what he relates of the East Lothian burgh at this period, for his statements can be verified from other contemporary sources. True, his impressions are those of one who made no lengthened stay; yet he furnishes perhaps the most realistic account of Haddington which any English traveller has recorded in print.

Haddington is pictured as "an old, half-ruined Town" in contradistinction to what was formerly a "large, handsome, and well-built" place—one "reckoned very strong" because of the "Walls of Stone, which were in those times esteemed very good." Quite truthfully, Defoe says that the English in 1548–49 fortified the town "with Lines and Bastions," though if he means that the walls dated from then (as may reasonably be supposed) he is in error, as will be demonstrated in a later chapter. It is interesting, however, to learn that four of the bastions still remained and were "very large." Defoe also notes having seen "the Remains of an old Nunnery," not a stone of which has rested upon another within living memory. Nungate Bridge also attracted him— "a good Stone Bridge . . . over the Tyne, though the River is but small." The parish church is described, rather meagrely, as "large," and, though partly in ruins, is "big enough for the Number of Inhabitants." The general appearance of the town, with "some good Houses" and "well-paved" streets, took his fancy, while the Post-house (which must have been either the George or Blue Bell hostelries) is characterised flatteringly—"the best Inn I have seen in Scotland, and inferior to none I have seen on the London Road." Although the economic state of Haddington is reserved for a future chapter, Defoe is so enlightening as regards this aspect of our subject that we insert here the relevant passage which, among other matters, deals with the causes of the failure of the New Mills Cloth Manufactory.

Particularly, here was a Woolen Manufacture, erected by a Company or Corporation for making Broad-cloth, which they call *English* Cloth; and as they had *English* Workmen and *English* Wool, they really made it very good; but I cannot say they could bring it so cheap to the Market, as they do in England. This was the Reason, that though, before the Union, the *English Cloth* being prohibited upon severe Penalties, their own Cloth supported them very well; yet as soon as the Union was made, by which the *English* trade was opened, the Clothiers from Worcester, Gloucester, Wilts, Somerset, and Devonshire brought in their goods and, underselling the Scots, those Manufacturers [the Scots] were not able to stand it. However, the People turn their Hands to other things, are still employed in Spinning, Dyeing, Weaving, etc., and carry on a good deal of that Sort of Business.

As we have seen, Haddington, owing to its strategic importance, was seldom without an effective display of the military. This involved the supply of food and accommodation for the troops, a burden which fell upon the community and was at times almost unendurable. Again and again protests were made to the town council, against billeting in private houses and the service of coal and candle. So far back as 1657 this grievance had been ventilated, when the magistrates seriously attempted to rid the townsfolk of the obligation, but failed. Billeting, however, was not the whole problem. The troops, though stationed for defence and to maintain order, were not themselves always law-abiding. Large companies of soldiers quartered in or near the town frequently got out of hand and led to collisions with the civilian population. Occasionally, too, serious crime was committed. In 1721 the presence of Major-General Evans's dragoons was insufferable. In 1736 there were complaints regarding the quartering of troops and its vexatious accompaniments, which did not go unheeded, some improvement being brought about in 1739 by the erection of barracks at Lennoxlove and Bara.

Haddington played a more prominent part in the second Jacobite rebellion than in the first. In March 1744 the town council, aware of the trend of events and wishing to give undeniable proof of their Hanoverian sympathies, forwarded, through Sir Hew Dalrymple, the parliamentary representative, an address to George II, which was received "very gratiously." The civic fathers begged leave "in this critical juncture when those kingdoms are threatened with a forraign Invasion in favour of a Popish Pretender, to express our highest Resentment and indignation at so insolent and daring ane Attempt which threatens to deprive us of all that is Valuable to ourselves and all that is Worth transmitting to our Posterity. The lively and just sense of the many great and valueable Blessings which we enjoy under Your Majestie's Mild and Gentle Government awakens in us the Warmest Sentiments of Gratitude and at the same time engages us with the greatest Cheerfulness to embrace this Opportunity of assuring Your Majesty That we will in our different stations exert our utmost endeavours in defence of Your Sacred person and Government and for the Security of the protestant Succession in Your Royall family, on which the lasting happiness of those Kingdoms do under God solely depend."

Andrew Dickson, who, as provost, signed the address, had early intimation of the Jacobite menace. On 5th September 1745 he received a letter from Archibald Stewart, Lord Provost of Edinburgh, requesting him to be on the watch for "any body of armed men . . . marching towards Edinburgh," and, "by express on horseback," to notify him of any such happening. All expense incurred in complying with this request would be duly paid. Provost Dickson submitted the letter to the town council, and it was resolved, with a view to obtaining intelligence of any sign of enemy movements in the coastal area of East Lothian, to communicate with the magistrates of Dunbar and North Berwick as well as with the ministers of Tyninghame, Dirleton, and Aberlady.

It was not the rebels, however, but the Hanoverian forces that appeared on the Lothian coast. On 17th September Sir John Cope landed with his army at Dunbar, having been transported thither from the north. After disembarkation had been completed on the following day, Cope wrote to Lord Tweeddale: "I march to-morrow morning, and will do the best I can for his Majesty's service." The Hanoverian troops, exclusive of a small band of Highlanders whose loyalty was doubtful, consisted of about six hundred horse and fourteen hundred foot soldiers. Their equipment comprised six galloper guns and as many small mortars. During the forenoon of Thursday, 19th September, Cope's army marched out of Dunbar. They took the hill-road by "Charteris's Dykes" (the wall enclosing Amisfield), and on reaching Haddington encamped on rising ground to the west of the town. Throughout the ten miles' march Cope rode among the ranks, and so cheered his men "that even the dragoons breathed nothing but revenge, and threatened the rebels with nothing but distruction." Unfortunately, Colonel Gardiner, who commanded the dragoons, was unwell, and had to be conveyed in a chaise.

It was not an orderly nor disciplined force that Cope led from Dunbar to Haddington. John Home, afterwards minister of Athelstaneford, and his friend Alexander Carlyle, who became minister of Inveresk, were of the youthful band of volunteers who followed in the wake of the Hanoverian army. Both have left on record what they saw and heard during the historic march. Home tells us that "the people of the country, long unaccustomed to war and arms, flocked from all quarters, to see an army going to fight a battle in East Lothian; and, with infinite concern and anxiety for the event, beheld this uncommon spectacle." However that may be, one may suspect Home's statement that the cavalry, infantry, cannon, and baggage extended for "several miles along the road." [1] Carlyle, again, was astonished to see the country folk fraternising with the troops, and dreaded the infiltration of Jacobite influence which, he says, was rather vigorous in the neighbourhood. The force that marched by "Charteris's Dykes" looked more like a mob than armed troops under authority. "It appeared to me," Carlyle writes, "to be very imprudent to allow all the common people to converse with the soldiers on their march . . . by which means their panic was kept up, and perhaps their principles corrupted. Many people in East Lothian at that time were Jacobites, and they were most forward to mix with the soldiers." [2]

From the evidence led at Cope's trial, it would seem that the original intention of the Hanoverian general was to march straight to Edinburgh unless hindered by the rebels. He was compelled, however, to make a halt at Haddington, there being a scarcity of water farther on. Accordingly the troops encamped in the afternoon in an open field on the west side of the town and close to the post-road to Edinburgh. While there a false alarm was raised that the Jacobite army was about to attack, and Cope's men immediately formed in order of battle. For a description of the tumult in Haddington that Thursday afternoon we turn again to Carlyle of Inveresk, who sketches a colourful picture of the whole affair. Carlyle and his comrades forgathered at what appears to have been the Blue Bell Inn, where they purposed dining along with "sundry officers of dragoons," when news arrived that put the whole company in a flurry.

While our dinner was preparing an alarm was beat in the camp, which occasioned a great hurry-scurry in the courtyard with the officers taking their horses, which some of them did with no small reluctance, either through love of their dinner or aversion to the enemy. I saw Colonel Gardiner passing very slowly, and ran to him to ask what was the matter. He said it could be nothing but a false alarm, and would soon be over. The army however was drawn out immediately, and it was found to be a false alarm. [3]

The affair had an amusing explanation.

It had happened that the Hon. Francis Charteris had been married the day before at Prestonhall to Lady Frances Gordon, a daughter of the Duchess of Gordon. The bridal party, escorted by a little cavalcade, was proceeding to New Amisfield. Alarming news of an approaching foe somehow accompanied their coach, and as their Jacobite sympathies were well known, the apprehension caused was believed to have been not altogether unintentional. Cope made the best of the awkward situation by thanking his troops for their alertness, and they, Colonel Whiteford mentions, "returned him a huzza."

While the Hanoverian army lay at Haddington, George Drummond, who was six times Lord Provost of Edinburgh, arrived in Haddington, where Carlyle and other volunteers besought him to use his good offices with Cope in order that they might be allotted a position with the infantry. Drummond complied, but Cope rather deprecated the idea. Cope's view was, that as most of the volunteers were well acquainted with the district they could do more efficient service as scouts or patrols. This being agreed to, eight mounted volunteers, of whom Carlyle was one, left the camp at Haddington at nine o'clock on Thursday evening in pairs and reconnoitred the roads and byways between the town and Duddingston. No sign of the enemy being discovered, they returned to camp at midnight. Then other eight volunteers sallied forth on a similar errand. Two of the scouting party, Robert Cunningham, son of Major Cunningham of Stirling Castle, and Francis Garden (afterwards Lord Gardenstone,

[1] Home's *Works*, iii, 77.   [2] *Autobiography*, 1910 ed., p. 143.   [3] *Ibid*.

a Court of Session judge) were in danger of being hanged as spies. Entering a tavern at Musselburgh, they found the best room occupied by Colonel Roy Stuart and Captain George Hamilton of the Highland army. They, too, were engaged in scouting. The unsuspecting volunteers questioned the Jacobite officers regarding the position and strength of the Prince's army. Roy Stuart's suspicions were aroused, and hoping to throw Cunningham and Garden off the scent, charged them with being rebels. This they indignantly denied, and as tangible proof of their *bona fides*, produced Cope's pass. Both men were at once disarmed and conveyed prisoners to the Jacobite camp at Duddingston. Ignorant of the fate of his patrol, Cope and his army left Haddington on the morning of Friday, 20th September. His intention was to form a strong camp at Musselburgh from whence he could, without the fatigue of a long march, attack the Highlanders wherever they made a stand. But to Carlyle's disappointment, Cope altered his plan. "Instead of keeping the post-road through Tranent Muir, which was high ground and commanded the country south for several miles, as it did that to the north for two or three miles towards the sea, they [Cope's army] turned to the right by Elvingston and the village of Trabroun, till they passed Longniddry on the north, and St Germains on the south." [1]

After the victory at Prestonpans, a portion of the Highland army proceeded to Haddington where it caused considerable stir, the presence of the rebels being harmful to merchants and others intent on pursuing their peaceful business. As much may be gathered from a petition to the magistrates forwarded by William Field, tacksman of the West Port, who requested to be indemnified for loss sustained by him. Field represented that the Highlanders had prevented people from outlying districts attending the Michaelmas Fair, to his detriment, he being unable to meet his financial obligations. The town council agreed that there was substance in the petition and granted Field's request. In 1746, as we learn from the same source, an official was remunerated for having gone to Edinburgh concerning certain Jacobite prisoners in Haddington jail.

When the rebellion was at an end, Haddington revealed its Hanoverian proclivities by honouring the victor of Culloden. Even before this decisive battle the town council had decided (11th February 1746), somewhat precipitately, not only to congratulate the Duke of Cumberland on the success of his arms up to that time but to send an address to George II, expressing the loyal sentiments of the burgh. It is doubtful, however, if the resolution was carried out. Indeed it would appear that the civic authority on further reflection were inclined to view the whole matter as premature. Anyhow it was not till 4th July, nearly four months after Culloden, and while the victorious general was still carrying out those reprisals against the insurgents which earned him the opprobrious title of "Butcher Cumberland," that the Haddington magistrates and council voted a congratulatory address to the Duke "upon the Happy Success of His Majesty's Arms" under his command. Cumberland, in the obsequious and untruthful words of the address, was "the darling of the army" and "a protector of the oppressed." The Duke was also voted the freedom of the burgh, which was to be presented when he passed through Haddington on his way south. But this hope was not realised: Cumberland never visited the town. So the congratulatory address and the silver casket containing the burgess ticket were sent after him.

Carlyle of Inveresk, as we have seen, declared that Jacobite sentiment was strong in East Lothian, but there is little indication that this was so as regards Haddington. In obedience to instructions issued on 7th May 1746, the supervisors of excise in Scot-

---

[1] *Autobiography*, p. 146.

land drew up lists of persons concerned in the rebellion, together with a brief note of the circumstances in each case. The list for East Lothian was compiled by George Fairholm, and contained the names of thirteen persons belonging to Haddington. What strikes one most is not the numerical insignificance of the Jacobites as the fact that some of the disaffected were persons holding official positions—persons who would hardly have been suspected of Jacobite leanings in a community predominantly favourable to the reigning dynasty. Among them we find Thomas Donaldson, the schoolmaster, who, it seems, uplifted the duty for the rebels. And along with Donaldson may be placed Charles Lauder, the procurator fiscal, who was with the Highland army before it marched on Edinburgh. He further embroiled himself by assisting Donaldson.

On the other hand, there need be less wonder that Joseph Robertson and Bower Barthol figure in the list. Robertson was a nonjuring minister and preached in the Episcopal meeting-house in Poldrate. He was active in trying to obtain recruits for the Prince's army from among the townsfolk. It was further laid to Robertson's charge that after the Preston skirmish he "solicited the Pretender's son" for permission to preach in the parish church of Haddington. But the reply was: "That was going too fast." It may be added that Robertson's nephew, Joseph Forbes, journeyman wright in Haddington, joined the rebels about the time of the battle of Preston and continued to serve till the final defeat at Culloden. Barthol, again, is classed with Robertson, he being precentor in the Episcopal meeting-house. He carried messages and undertook commissions for the Highlanders. Barthol also insulted those well affected to the Hanoverian government—an equally serious charge.

Other Haddingtonians on Fairholm's ignominious list were George Anderson, junior, a tanner to trade, who joined the Jacobites in their march into England and, obtaining a captaincy, served under Prince Charles Edward till the cause was lost; John Anderson, journeyman saddler, who also marched to Derby; Alexander Bouglass, a millwright, who fought for the Prince at Preston, though he deserted when the Highlanders invaded England; Patrick Crombie, vaguely described as a "workman," who joined after Preston and gave information regarding prominent Hanoverians; John Denham, a gardener, who carried arms at Preston but dissociated himself from the Pretender's cause when it was decided to cross the Border; James Hay, "residenter," who rallied to the Jacobites at Edinburgh and continued with them till after the battle of Falkirk; Alexander Lilly, journeyman wright, who was "supposed to be a Spye" (he carried arms with the rebels, and came to Haddington "well-mounted"); and Robert Lindsay, weaver, who was a comrade in arms with the Jacobites at Preston but deserted when they crossed the Border.

Despite their adherence to the Hanoverian dynasty, more especially the sending of an address to the King on Cumberland's victory, there were some queer transactions in Haddington during the Forty-Five. After Prestonpans, and when the Jacobite court was installed at Holyrood, the magistrates of Haddington in common with those of other Scottish burghs received a communication from John Murray of Broughton, the Prince's secretary, commanding them "upon receipt, to repair to the Secretary's office in the palace of Holyrood-house, there to have the contribution to be paid by the town, for his highness's use, ascertained: to be done according and in proportion to the duties of excise arising out of the said town of Haddington." This they were ordered, "upon pain of rebellion, forthwith to obey, by his highness's command." Haddington's assessment was £50 sterling. To this intimidation the magistrates appear to have tamely submitted. The rebels temporarily were in command, and the town was not neglectful of the maxim that discretion is the better part of valour.

The same principle governed the action of the town council in the case of George Vert, "meatseller." Vert had complied with a demand by the Highlanders for two horses, one of which was valued at £7 sterling. Yet for this he was duly rewarded, being admitted "a burgess and guild-brother gratis." Against this rather dubious conduct may be placed the pleasant fact that the town council in 1746 authorised the payment of £6 Scots each to Janet Cockburn and Margaret Irvine "in respect of the dammages the petitioners have sustained by the Rebells being in this Burgh whereby the mercates, and particularly Michaelmas Fair, was in some measure altogether neglected."

The Seven Years' War, which lasted from 1756 to 1763 and brought Great Britain such splendid gains in Canada and India, nevertheless entailed heavy sacrifices. The drain on our resources, both in men and equipment, was enormous; at least it was so reckoned then. The navy as well as the army were far behind full strength, and repeated and insistent appeals for more men for the fighting forces were made. Haddington did not escape the attentions of the recruiting sergeant. On 28th March 1759 the provost was notified that he must search the burgh for able-bodied seamen who were trying to evade the press-gang, and to see to their impressment. To this appeal the town council loyally responded, offering a premium of two guineas, exclusive of the Government bounty, to induce suitable men to join the navy. How far these efforts were successful, it is impossible to say, but there can be no doubt that the Seven Years' War seriously affected the town from an economic standpoint. It can therefore be imagined with what transports of joy the town council on 18th May 1763 voted an address to the King on the conclusion of a "successful and advantageous peace."

"At no period since the Union of the Crowns," writes John Ramsay of Ochtertyre in *Scotland and Scotsmen*, "was the political horizon of Scotland more calm and unclouded than from 1754 to 1760." Yet during this comparatively tranquil period at least one piece of legislation roused patriotic susceptibilities north of Tweed. In 1757 Parliament passed a law establishing a militia in England. Why, Scotsmen argued, should not this enactment be extended to their country, which was as open to attack as England? The matter was much canvassed and even the Presbyterian ministers did not fail to be actively interested. Carlyle of Inveresk wrote a pamphlet on the subject entitled: "The Question relating to a Scots Militia considered, in a Letter to the Lords and Gentlemen who have concerted the form of law for that establishment." The pamphlet, which was signed "By a Freeholder," was, according to the author, praised in influential quarters. Eventually, as the result of intensive propaganda, Sir Gilbert Elliot of Minto introduced into Parliament a measure intended to safeguard the interests of Scotland by organising a militia on similar lines to that already established in England. Most of the Scottish members warmly supported the bill, but the Whig government of Newcastle declined to pass it on the entirely inadmissible ground that it had emanated from a Tory source.

The reaction to the failure of the Militia Bill was one of widespread and deep-rooted dissatisfaction, the public resentment being likened to the ebullitions of popular fury that followed the incident of the Porteous Mob. The town council of Edinburgh resolved to raise the matter at the Convention of Royal Burghs, and sent a letter to every town entitled to be represented there, recommending local agitations in favour of setting up a militia in Scotland on the same footing as that in England. Edinburgh's lead was supported in East Lothian. Andrew Fletcher of Saltoun, who represented the county at Westminster, was requested to support a new bill. It was duly introduced, but failing to gain adequate backing, the militia question remained in abeyance till 1762 when, on a proposal being submitted to amend the English Militia law, an effort was made to include Scotland within its ambit. Lord Haddington was appointed chairman of a national committee, in which capacity he sent a letter to all the counties and royal burghs of Scotland announcing the urgent need for "a numerous and well-disciplined militia" for Scotland, the "exposed and defenceless state" of that country being well known. On 18th February 1762 Dr James Lundie, who was then provost of Haddington, ventilated the matter in the town council, which, however, "declined giving in an application to Parliament for a national militia under the present circumstances of the country." The Jacobite rebellion was too recent a memory, and Haddington hesitated to bring into being a force that conceivably might be used should there be another upheaval. The farmers and manufacturers in the county even went the length of holding a meeting in Haddington at which resolutions were passed indicating, very decidedly, the drift of industrial feeling.

The present is a most improper time to make application to Parliament for a militia-law on account of the great scarcity of hands over the whole country for carrying on the necessary work of agriculture, manufactures, and other valuable branches of trade. Who can dispute the numerous draughts of men made by the army and the navy within these few years from the plough, the loom, and other mechanic employments? It is, in fact, to so great a degree, that these arts of peace cannot be cultivated and carried on, although the employer be willing even to pay that extravagant rate to which labour hath already advanced. The young men, the idle, and the profligate of our nation are already swept off by the army and navy. If then a militia-law should be extended to Scotland and carried into execution, who are left to serve? None else but the honest laborious husbandmen; the industrious manufacturer and busy tradesman, many of whose wives and young children must fall a burden upon the parishes. What a melancholy scene from hence opens on our country!

This somewhat doleful picture might have been sketched at the present hour. The problems that confronted the "laborious husbandmen" and the "industrious manufacturer" in East Lothian nearly two centuries ago are again engaging the attention of their descendants in circumstances far more stupendous and fateful, and in forms incomparably more aggravated.

CHAPTER VI

Under the Later Hanoverians

WHEN, towards the close of 1760, George III mounted the throne in succession to his grandfather, the town council of Haddington voted a dutiful address to His Majesty. Signed by Provost Robert Thomson, it was presented by Andrew Fletcher, younger, of Saltoun, who was then parliamentary representative. And when, in the following year, the King married Charlotte Sophia, Princess of Mecklenburg-Strelitz, the civic fathers promptly dispatched another congratulatory address. During the long reign of George III the contacts of the county town with national affairs were definitely fewer. With the changing times Haddington was no longer the important place it once was. The townsfolk, rarely distracted by war or rumours of war, became absorbed in internal affairs, and sought to improve their position economically by garnering the fruits of local industry. At the same time there was no slackening of interest in progressive movements: the voice of Haddington was always heard on controverted public questions like Roman Catholic disabilities or parliamentary and burgh reform. Nor was the town behind in bearing a share in defence against the menace of a French invasion.

At the opening of George III's reign there was renewed trouble over the quartering of soldiers in the town. Barracks erected at Lennoxlove and Bara had alleviated to some extent the inconveniences of promiscuous billeting, while Robert Reid, a local mason, had built stables to contain "a full troop of horses besides a magazine for their forage." The magistrates declared that they were "often straitened for stabling for the horses of dragoons by reason that many buildings formerly used as stables were now used as dwelling houses." But for this state of matters they were themselves partly to blame, since they bargained with Reid that the barracks and stables erected by him should be used as ordinary houses when not required by the military. At first there does not appear to have been sufficient animals to occupy the stables, and the magistrates arranged that dragoons should be billeted in the surplus accommodation.

Despite the fact that the troops were now kept together, the townsfolk were still dissatisfied, and altercations between them and the soldiers were not uncommon. On 10th March 1761 an announcement in the newspapers accused the inhabitants of wounding several horses of Colonel Hales's regiment so severely that they were unfit for service. A reward of ten guineas was offered for the discovery of the perpetrators of the outrage. But an investigation by the magistrates proved the charge to be false, and the calumny was refuted in the Edinburgh newspapers on three successive days. That such a charge should ever have been made is a matter difficult to explain, for, so far from injuring the horses of the military, the inhabitants were anxious that the animals should be billeted upon them in the hope that market prices for fodder would be paid. Long after this incident there were complaints concerning the billeting of soldiers in private houses, and the magistrates were forced to deal with the problem. They took action on 5th April 1794 when Lord Adam Gordon, Commander of the Forces in Scotland, was informed that the two Gallowgreen parks were at his disposal for the erection of additional barracks. But the offer was declined on the score that the cavalry barracks then being erected at Piershill, near Edinburgh, would provide all the accommodation that was required.

UNDER THE LATER HANOVERIANS

Throughout the centuries Haddington had suffered much havoc and privation from periodic inundations of the river Tyne, but the one which occurred on 4th October 1775 seems to have eclipsed all others and was much talked of throughout Scotland. Indeed to this day one is reminded of this dire calamity by an inscribed panel affixed to a tenement at the corner of High Street and Sidegate. When all danger was passed, the town council decreed "that a stone should be put up at the end of John Hume's house, near the Custom Stone, describing the height of the flood, and the day and year of God thereon." The inscription reads: On the fourth day of October MDCCLXXV the River Tyne at three o'clock Afternoon rose to this Plate. *Quod non noctu Deo gratias nemo enim periit.*

The significance of the inscription will be appreciated when it is stated that the river suddenly rose eight feet nine inches. All accounts of this enormous flood that have appeared since the publication of Dr Barclay's *Account of the Parish of Haddington*, written in 1785, are in error in declaring the rise of the Tyne to have been seventeen feet. There is, however, evidence to show that the river became swollen eight feet nine inches—an appreciable difference, though certainly very alarming at the time. Barclay is accountable for the former dimensions, and modern writers have accepted his statement, excusably however, since Barclay was an eye-witness of the deluge. He attributes the portentous overflow of the Tyne "to the bursting of a waterspout to the southward, amongst the ridge of mountains called Lammer-muir, for the day was not very rainy." Barclay's description is as follows:

The main branch of the river Tyne . . . was not remarkably increased; it was from the rivulet called Gifford water that the immense flood poured into the river Tyne which, about two o'clock afternoon, began suddenly to increase to an uncommon height, and in less than an hour rose seventeen feet perpendicular above the ordinary bed of the river. It continued in this state for several hours, and then gradually subsided. The mansion house of Clerkington and the beautiful Chinese bridge over the river, near the woollen manufactory, were immediately swept away. The whole suburb called Nungate and more than half of the town were laid under water. The inhabitants were obliged to abandon their houses and take sanctuary in the fields. Had it happened in the night many must have perished, but happily no lives were lost, though several of the aged and infirm were saved with great difficulty.

An even more realistic account of what happened is contained in a letter, dated 5th October 1775, addressed to John Douglas, session clerk, Bolton parish. Here is an extract:

The whole town is now in the utmost confusion. On Tuesday a heavy rain came on and continued without intermission till this morning. [This statement conflicts with Barclay's, who says "the day was not very rainy."] The river Tyne swelled prodigiously, so that about two o'clock yesterday morning it overflowed the whole east end of the town, and continued so impetuous for two hours that it rose six or eight feet during that period, and seemed to threaten destruction to the whole town. For three or four hours there was nothing to be seen but every one trying to save themselves. Numbers of carts came floating west . . . with fowls sitting on them where they had roosted for shelter, some of the people who lived in the lower end of the town coming west wading in water up to the armpits, and the cries of women and children, formed a picture of the most shocking nature. On the other side of the town numbers of people were seen sitting on the tops of their houses, and dead cattle, furniture, etc., were floating on the surface of the water. About four o'clock the waters took a turn and began to decrease gradually.

Not a very grammatical description, but sufficiently clear to be faintly suggestive of the conditions that prevailed when the Ark, containing Noah and his very miscellaneous company, rested on Mount Ararat.

As has been already stated, the deluge of 1775 was merely one of a series, though probably the most alarming and devastating that had ever visited the town. In 1358 the very existence of Haddington (then a very small place) was threatened. Again, in 1421, many houses were destroyed and the inhabitants forced to take refuge in the parish church, making their way thither, it is said, in a "great boat." On this occasion, according to Spottiswoode, many of the church's treasures, including a fine library, were swept away. Another watery visitation took place on 5th September 1659 when, the burgh records tell us, the "Tyne ran in the gutters at the Cross." Again, on 19th July 1673, the magistrates decreed that the school be cleansed, having been "spoiled with the last great flood." And there have been inundations since the memorable one of 1775—inundations which on more than one occasion have partially submerged the town.

But to resume the chronicling of normal happenings. The year 1778 witnessed a signal illustration of the fact that a nation aroused can make its will felt under any form of government. Parliament then passed a measure for relieving Roman Catholics from the disabilities imposed by the Act of William III "for the further preventing of the growth of Popery." This measure applied to England only, but when it was rumoured that a bill was about to be introduced freeing Scottish Roman Catholics also, there was a violent outburst of national feeling, dread and hatred of the ancient religion being intense north of Tweed. "It was the spectre of Rome," says Hume Brown, "that had been the main cause of the Covenants and of the final rejection of the House of Stuart." [1] People of every religious and political persuasion declaimed against the proposed legislation as a making of terms with a dangerous and insidious superstition. And condemnation was reinforced by aggressive action. Under the designation of "Friends of the Protestant Religion" a society was formed to avert what was regarded as a threatened calamity. This organisation had representatives in all parts of the country whose duty was to obtain subscriptions to a general petition against the bill. Everywhere there was an eager response.

On 18th January 1779 the magistrates of Haddington received a petition affirming relentless opposition on behalf of a great number of burgesses and inhabitants, likewise a resolution of the nine incorporated trades requesting that the impending legislation should be opposed. After long and earnest deliberation, the provost was requested by the council to insert in the newspapers the following rather wordy and confused resolution:—

That being fully convinced that such a step would be attended with bad consequences, which every friend of the Constitution, both in Church and State, must wish to prevent, [the Council] have resolved, and do hereby publish their resolution, that they are ready to join with the Convention of Royal Burghs, with the Correspondence of the Committee-meeting, Society-hall, Edinburgh, or with any other society meeting, in a peaceable and legal manner, in opposing the repeal by every method warranted by the Constitution, and further recommend to the Provost to correspond with the Provost of Edinburgh, to obtain a meeting of a committee of the burghs for the same purpose.

The approach to the Lord Provost of Edinburgh was unsuccessful. So anxious, however, were the magistrates to make known their uncompromising attitude, that they not only petitioned Parliament but consulted Fletcher of Saltoun as to whether or not counsel should be employed to plead their cause at the Bar of the House of Commons. But this was declared to be unnecessary. Eventually the petition was presented by William Nisbet, younger, of Dirleton, the local M.P. In the end the people of Haddington were heartened on learning that the *status quo* was to be maintained, Henry Dundas having no alternative but to withdraw the bill.

[1] *History of Scotland*, iii, 350.

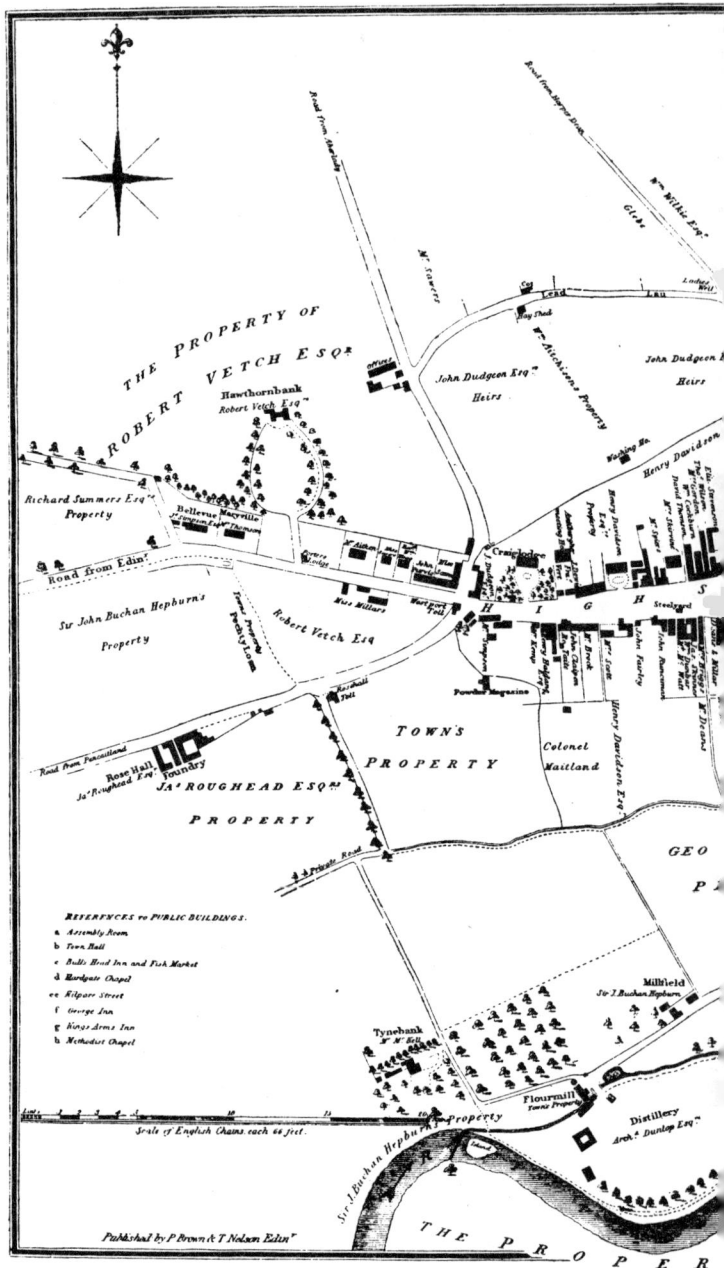

Plan of the Town in 1819, s

PLAN OF HADDINGTON and NUNGATE

SURVEYED

JOHN WOOD, 1819.

Road to Dunbar

PROPERTY OF THE EARL OF WEMYSS AND MARCH

Nungate

James Wilkie Esqr Property

The Haugh

Road from West Salton

LORD BLANTYRE

In the midst of the Catholic controversy came the perturbing news that France and Spain had linked themselves in a confederation against Britain, and that hostilities of a grimmer sort lay ahead. To Dundas's appeal for a larger and stronger navy, the town council of Haddington responded patriotically by offering (not for the first time) over and above the royal bounty of three guineas to every able-bodied seaman, two guineas to ordinary seamen and one guinea to every fit landsman, residing in the burgh or the port of Aberlady, who voluntarily came forward to serve on one of His Majesty's ships. Mindful, too, of the interests of trade, the magistrates instructed their Parliamentary representative, the Hon. Francis Charteris, younger, of Amisfield, to oppose the proposed commercial treaty between Great Britain and Ireland. Nothing, it was felt, could be more injurious to local industries.

As the eighteenth century drew to a close the strenuous labours of Wilberforce and others drew attention to the iniquities of the African slave trade, and humanitarian feeling throughout the country was stirred as it had never been before. Haddington was not behind in letting its voice be heard on this question, the town council passing a resolution in support of the abolition of the African slave trade "as being contrary to the principles of humanity and religion." Sometimes, however, the town's participation in public affairs was not to be commended as, for example, in February 1789, when the magistrates, somewhat tactlessly, voted an address to the Prince of Wales on his appointment as Regent during the mental illness of his royal father. Happily the King's derangement on this occasion was brief, and on 14th March the magistrates, with a trifle more sense of the fitness of things, congratulated His Majesty on his restoration to health.

In 1792 the town council disapproved of proposed legislation empowering the road trustees to erect additional toll-bars on turnpike roads in order to defray the expense of constructing certain new roads. The chief ground of their opposition was that a toll-bar recently removed fron the suburb of St Laurence had been set up at the west end of the town in such a position that toll had to be paid by persons entering the burgh from the Aberlady road, a highway exempt by charter from any imposts. The magistrates were of opinion that no toll should be exacted on any side road within a mile of Haddington without the consent of the community, and petitioned the House of Commons to the effect that the toll-bar at the west end was "in direct violation both of the town's charter and the Act of Parliament." Moreover, the erection had increased the price of coal and had interfered with the free entry of grain. So strongly did the community feel regarding this matter that they held a public meeting to ventilate their grievance.

When the French Revolution broke out the magistrates were tardy in expressing sentiments of loyalty to the throne. But when they did declare them, which was not till January 1793, by which time the worst features of the upheaval had manifested themselves, they took care to give them wide publicity by publishing a series of resolutions in the Edinburgh newspapers. Perhaps the magistrates were a little conscious of being chargeable with procrastination and wished to wipe out any reproach.

Periodically the town council scanned the political horizon and did not scruple to criticise the existing Government. The younger Pitt might be at the head of "a Ministry of peace and reconstruction." No matter: he was the pet aversion of the Haddington bailies. On 19th April 1797 they voted "that a petition should be presented to the King, requesting him to remove his present Ministry, by which means it was supposed that the blessings of peace might be restored." But the problem was not so simple. Although striving at other times for amity, the Napoleonic menace had forced Pitt to become a War Minister: in other words, he had to subdue himself to the material in which he worked. But before a year had passed the logic of events drove the Haddington magistrates to adopt a different line. On 18th March 1798, after reflecting on the possibilities of invasion by their "mortal and daring enemy the French," they agreed to contribute £100 sterling for purposes of defence. Wisely, too, they resolved that "a subdued and sober spirit" should be imparted for the time being by the eschewing of public entertainments, though this did not apply to drinking "a few glasses of wine" at the Cross in honour of the King's birthday.

Haddington was no more apprehensive than other municipalities that the Treaty of Amiens was only a feint of Napoleon to gain time to prepare for an attack on Britain. Accordingly there were the usual congratulations to the King upon the apparently fortunate turn of events. But hard upon the Treaty of Amiens came a declaration of war with rapid deterioration of the vision of peace. Every precaution had now to be taken to guard against invasion. An incursion from the North Sea was well within the bounds of possibility, and the East Lothian coast was regarded as particularly vulnerable. Consequently military preparations in and near Haddington were extensive and thoroughgoing. A signal station was erected on East Garleton Hill. Then, in June 1803, the Haddington Volunteers, consisting of two companies under Captain William Wilkie and Captain William Cunningham, with Lieut.-Colonel Hay Mackenzie of Newhall as commander, were embodied. The Government allowed the usual rate for uniform, which was augmented by £21 voted by the town council. The local Volunteers wore a scarlet uniform faced with green. The trousers were grey, and for head covering there was a round hat with black cockade and tuft. Each man carried a musket and haversack. As for the officers, they were decked out in the uniform of a militia commander. Drills took place on the East Haugh twice a week.

The recruiting made serious inroads on agricultural labour, and several farmers, rather than allow their men to be withdrawn from the land, paid as much as £65 to persons who would serve in the forces as substitutes. This led to the formation by John Croumbie, a Haddington ironmonger, of the Militia Insurance Society whereby those paying three guineas for an insurance were protected from military service in the event of their being drawn at the ballot. Local accommodation for so large a body of troops was another problem. The infantry barracks, consisting of 104 huts accommodating 74 officers and 1084 non-commissioned officers and privates, occupied the whole of the policies of Templedean, Gourlay Bank, Goatfield, and Vetch Park. There was also stabling for 40 horses, and close to the infantry barracks was a military hospital for 96 patients.

The large field on the farm of Amisfield Mains just outside the north-east port was set apart for artillerymen. Here, in what is still known as Artillery Park, were erected 34 huts. These accommodated 13 officers and 288 non-commissioned officers and privates. In addition, there were stables for 140 horses, also a gun shed and workshops for smiths, farriers, saddlers, and wheelers. The cavalry barracks were erected in Hope Park, situated between Lydgate and the footpath now known as the "Blackpaling road," and having the Aberlady road at its western extremity. The buildings consisted of 44 huts which accommodated 22 officers and 304 of other ranks, while stabling was provided for 320 horses.

With nearly two thousand troops accommodated in the three camps, Haddington had its share of the "pomp and circumstance of war." Patriotic fervour rose to an unwonted height. Then, as at the present hour, almost every able-bodied man donned a military uniform and enlisted in one or other of the Volunteer companies, for it was widely believed that an enemy landing would be attempted at Aberlady and Gullane. Each recruit carried sixty rounds of ball cartridge and two days' provisions. Intensive drilling took place at the Haugh and at Lennoxlove, Amisfield, and Clerkington, while Gladsmuir and Teuchit Muir were the rendezvous for field exercises. On 7th July 1803 all supplies of corn, meal, and flour, as well as live stock, were removed as a precautionary measure. In November instructions were issued which were to be acted on in the event of invasion. On the alarm being given, three companies of the East Lothian Yeomanry were to assemble in Haddington and act with the other troops stationed there. No untoward incident occurred during the winter, but, as the danger still existed, troops were constantly on guard. On 7th May 1804 the Haddington Volunteers took duty at Dunbar for a fortnight, and on the 19th the whole of the military stationed there were reviewed on West Barns Links by the Earl of Moira, Commander-in-Chief of the Forces in Scotland. The local Volunteers, numbering nearly seven hundred, remained on duty till 1808, when they were embodied as the Haddington Militia. They were commanded by Lord Sinclair of Herdmanston, with Lord Binning as Lieutenant-Colonel.

Martine points out that while the Napoleonic menace lasted there was a "glorious harvest" for Haddington shopkeepers. The presence of such a formidable body of military gave an impetus to trade, and certain businesses profited on an unprecedented scale. Nor were the farmers behind in participating in this run of good luck. Hundreds of horses meant a large consumption of grain and straw. Haddington also benefited in other respects. Many officers were accommodated in private houses, and imparted both colour and gaiety to the social life of the town. Yet the predominance of the military, while it resulted in material gain, was not wholly advantageous. The harvest of plenty brought attendant evils. The inhabitants complained of "nightly depredations on the part of soldiers wandering from the barracks" under cover of darkness. Considerable damage was done to property, and even robberies were reported. John Hay, tenant in Duncanlaw, was attacked by two soldiers on the Gifford road. Happily the offenders were secured, apparently by Hay himself, since he was presented by his farm workers with a piece of silver plate in recognition of his resolution and bravery. Such delinquencies compelled the town council to take action. Their remedy was embodied in a suggestion that the "nightly forays" would cease if the barracks were enclosed instead of being left entirely open. This, at any rate, was the recommendation they forwarded to the Lord Advocate.

When the fiftieth anniversary of the accession of George III came round, Haddington, punctilious as ever in honouring royal events, arranged a programme of public functions, and at night there were fireworks and illuminations. Besides sending a congratulatory address, which was presented by Sir George Warrender, Bart., the town council resolved that "the King's birthday should be celebrated as formerly," and that the burgesses should be regaled with "wine and toddy at the Cross . . . at the town's expense." In 1814 another congratulatory address was dispatched—this time to the Prince Regent, on the occasion of the entry of the Allied Army into Paris and the deposition of Napoleon. At the same time the Prince Regent was entreated to use his influence so that the approaching congress of the Continental Powers would ordain the total abolition of the slave trade.

Between 1817 and 1819 quite a spate of royal addresses emanated from Haddington. There were congratulations to the Prince Regent on escaping from a dastardly attempt on his life. Another address condoled with him and Prince Leopold of Saxe-Coburg on the death of the Princess Charlotte of Wales, to whom Prince Leopold had been married a short time before. A third, couched in similar terms, was sent on the death of Queen Charlotte, mother of the Prince Regent, and a fourth, on 28th October 1819, drawing attention to the disaffected state of the country and assuring the Prince Regent that "amidst the frantic clamours of faction under the specious pretext of reform" he would find the royal burgh of Haddington true and faithful. In 1822 George IV paid his memorable visit to the Scottish capital where, and in the vicinity of Edinburgh, he was the centre of attraction in numerous functions. In this connection it is interesting to recall that the East Lothian Yeomanry took part in the review of the troops by the King on Portobello sands. Nor ought it to be forgotten that the town subscribed ten guineas towards Chantrey's statue of George IV, which was erected in Edinburgh.

Despite that East Lothian had long been a preserve of Toryism, the people of Haddington, or at least a majority of them, warmly supported the movement for Parliamentary Reform. Electoral arrangements in Scotland under the old system were even more anomalous than in England, and the battle for political freedom was fought in circumstances that brought both parties into personal and professional rivalry. Representatives for the Haddington Burghs were returned by self-elected town councils—a state of matters quite unimaginable nowadays. The rejection of the second English Reform Bill caused indignation among the middle and artisan classes, and it was firmly believed that a similar fate would overtake the Scottish measure. "For God's sake," wrote Lord Advocate Jeffrey to Solicitor-General Cockburn, "keep the people quiet in Scotland." This, however, was more easily said than done. The people would not be kept quiet, and the military had to be quartered in places where there were opposing factions.

In Haddington matters did not assume a violent form. Nevertheless agitation ran high, and it was clear that the will of the people would eventually carry the day, cost what it might. The era of public meetings had now arrived, and on 4th May 1832 one was held in the town, which had for its object the hastening of Parliamentary Reform. The hustings were set up on the East Mill Haugh, and in front gathered a crowd that is said to have been unprecedented. Before the meeting there was a procession through the streets in which the crafts took part. From a newspaper report we learn that the Skinners carried two large horns on a pole, also a stuffed sheep. The Shoemakers wore black aprons and bore aloft a banner inscribed: "We stand to the *last.*" The Carters, again, carried the model of a plough from which a harrow was suspended, while the Bakers were represented by a sheaf of wheat and a box of biscuits. On their banner was emblazoned the couplet

Our oven now is just in trim
We'll push the Borough-mongers in.

At the hustings rousing speeches were delivered by William Dods, late provost, George Tait, bookseller and founder of the *East Lothian Magazine,* and Patrick Shirreff, the pioneer of cereal seed-breeding in Scotland. The last-mentioned was one of the leading champions locally of political and social reform. In later years Shirreff identified himself with the Anti-Corn Law League and the Free Trade movement, and was brought into contact with Cobden and Bright. At the East Mill Haugh meeting a series of resolutions were passed which played their part in bringing the movement to a successful issue. Seven weeks later the Scottish Reform Bill was read a third time and on 17th July received the royal assent.

From the Union of 1707 Haddington Burghs (comprising Haddington, Dunbar, North Berwick, Jedburgh, and Lauder) returned one member to Parliament. For the greater part of two centuries the constituency was represented by members of notable East Lothian families. During the reign of Anne and the opening years of that of George I, Haddington Burghs had for its representative Sir David Dalrymple of Hailes, Bart. On his death in 1721 he was succeeded by Sir James Dalrymple of Hailes, who in 1734 gave place to Captain Fall, one of the Dunbar merchant princes. Other members for Haddington Burghs in pre-Reform days included Sir Hew Dalrymple of North Berwick, Bart., the Hon. Francis Charteris, Robert Baird of Newbyth, the Hon. Thomas Maitland, the Hon. William Lamb (afterwards Viscount Melbourne, Queen Victoria's first Prime Minister), and Sir George Warrender of Lochend, Bart.

The last member for Haddington Burghs under the old regime was Sir Adolphus Dalrymple. In 1831 there was a sharp contest between Dalrymple and Robert Stewart of Alderston. The result was disputed, but the House of Commons decided in favour of Dalrymple. In December of the following year Stewart, who was very popular in the constituency, wrested the seat from Dalrymple and became the first post-Reform member. He resigned in April 1837 on being appointed a Lord of the Treasury but was afterwards re-elected member for the constituency. Stewart held the seat till 1841 when James Maitland Balfour of Whittingehame, father of the first Earl of Balfour, was elected.

Robert Ferguson of Raith was the first county representative under the new conditions. Ferguson, who had previously been M.P. for Kirkcaldy Burghs, was a strong Whig, and after a vigorous fight won the seat from John Thomas Hope, younger, of Luffness, who had opposed the Reform Bill. Ferguson's majority was only 34. But in view of the smallness of the electorate the Whigs were satisfied with their victory, since at the first opportunity under the Reform Act they had won a seat that had long been regarded as a Tory preserve. The Whigs therefore saw to it that their triumph was fitly celebrated. On 6th February 1835 about three hundred of them entertained Ferguson to dinner in the Assembly Room, Haddington, which, says the *Scotsman*, was "elegantly and tastefully decorated with buff and blue, and with wreaths and festoons of laurel." Two galleries were erected at the far end of the hall, in which about sixty ladies—"the beauty and fashion of East Lothian"—were seated. Sir David Baird of Newbyth presided, and the victorious candidate delivered an eloquent and inspiring speech. Ferguson's success, however, was short-lived. Within two years he was ousted by Lord Ramsay, afterwards Marquess of Dalhousie. None the less the personal character as well as the public services of the laird of Raith were considered so outstanding that a striking monument was erected in his honour at the west end of Haddington. An inscription below Ferguson's statue mentions that the memorial, which was unveiled on 2nd June 1843, was erected by the "tenantry of East Lothian" to "a kind landlord, a liberal dispenser of wealth, a generous patron of literature, science, and art."

In September 1835 Earl Grey, whose Ministry was responsible for the Reform legislation, was given a warm welcome in passing through Haddington on his way to Howard Hall. The town bells were rung, the trades mustered with their banners, and at a meeting in the George Inn, Samuel Brown, representing the magistrates, presented the Earl with an address of congratulation. The Whig tide was flowing strong. A public meeting was held in the town in the same year the object of which was the political discomfiture of Wellington. The hero of Waterloo was looked upon as the principal reactionary in British politics—the head and front of an effete system. The Duke, it is true, supported Catholic Emancipation, but he had opposed Parliamentary Reform. As a result, his unpopularity had become markedly evident.

Haddington was prominent among the Scottish burghs in petitioning for Wellington's removal. But he was not without a small group of supporters in East Lothian. In June 1835 these followers of the lost leader met in Haddington with a view to bringing about Wellington's political rehabilitation. In the *Scotsman* appeared a characteristically Whiggish account of the proceedings.

> A full muster of the admirers of the late Dictator, the hero of Waterloo, and his worthy coadjutors in the short but glorious reign of the late Conservative Parliament, took place in the Bell Inn, Haddington, this afternoon. Town and county were alive with the din of preparation for the *fête*. A numerous committee was organised, and consequently, as was to be expected, a "tremendous rush" took place on the opening of the banqueting hall doors. Seats were quickly taken, and the band struck up: "We conquer or we die!" Twenty-five sat down, the band playing at a late hour, "The duk's dang o'er my daddie." The ulterior object of this *great* meeting is understood to be the establishment of a Conservative Association and the returning of a Tory M.P. at the next election.

Such facetiousness, more clumsy than corrosive, did not stay the hand of the Haddington supporters of Wellington: they fulfilled to the letter what they set out to do. Two years later Ferguson, the Whig representative of the county, was supplanted by Lord Ramsay.

While the struggle for Parliamentary and Burgh reform was proceeding, a large and not uninfluential section of church-going people was turning its attention to the amendment of the law of patronage which had been a crying abuse in Scotland since the days of Ebenezer and Ralph Erskine and the Secession. Under the sturdy personality, preaching ability, and theological scholarship of John Brown of Haddington, the town had become a citadel of aggressive Dissent. The forced settlement of ministers was not, however, the main grievance in the early decades of the nineteenth century, the policy being now conducted on milder lines. The question being agitated was whether any good could come out of a church allied with the State. In short, Voluntaryism had become the goal for many who were much concerned about religious freedom, and forces were being marshalled that were to render effective service in ventilating a grievance that had for long disturbed the peace of Zion. In March 1833 a public meeting was held in the Assembly Room, at which it was all but unanimously agreed to petition Parliament for the abolition of lay patronage. Of the five hundred persons present no fewer than 347 belonged to the Established Church. A resolution on similar lines was passed at a public meeting in April 1834. Opposition, however, was anticipated to another resolution supporting Sir Andrew Agnew's Sabbath Protection Bill (which was carried), and the organisers of the meeting deemed it prudent to issue handbills announcing that "no discussion" would be allowed, while sheriff-officers with drawn batons were posted at the door of the place of meeting to prevent "disqualified persons" from entering.

Writes a *Scotsman* correspondent:—

> Every arrangement was made for an overflowing audience. But whether the people were affronted at the presumption of those who got up the meeting in thus skulking from free and open discussion, and at the same time demanding signatures, or whether they felt indignant at the bare-faced attempt to palm the crude absurdities of Sir Andrew Agnew upon the public in the present age of enlightenment, or whether it was that they had no relish for an appeal to bludgeon argument on any question, we cannot well say. Yet so it happened that at ten minutes past the hour only six persons had assembled, four of whom were elders of the Kirk, and at twenty minutes past the hour the number amounted to ten. In short, the meeting turned out to be a miserable failure, and the party resolved, like their betters in Edinburgh, to hawk the petition from door to door.

The precautions taken by the promoters of the meeting seem to have been due to fear lest the question of the separation of Church and State should be raised, an eventuality not unlikely in view of the circumstance that the Haddington Whigs had already, at the previous Church meeting in 1833, managed to carry by an overwhelming majority a resolution for the dissolution of the connection between Church and State. The rather malevolent paragraph which appeared in the Press seems to have been written by a person who was piqued at the measures taken to prevent a discussion on the question of the separation of Church and State. But the whole affair is rather obscure, and it would be foolish to dogmatise. Apparently the meeting was arranged by members of the Established Church, who, while they wished lay patronage abolished, were not prepared to advocate, indeed were opposed to any interference with the relations between Church and State. As regards Sir Andrew Agnew's Sabbath Protection Bill, it received not only the general support of the meeting but of the Presbytery, though the ecclesiastical court objected to its details.

The minister of Haddington Second Charge at this time was John Cook, who was able and resourceful in his whole-hearted defence of lay patronage and of the Establishment generally. Cook, who was minister of the First Charge from the Disruption till his death in 1874, belonged to an ecclesiastical family that had consistently upheld the Moderate party in the Church of Scotland, and he showed no disposition to dissent from the views of his forebears. Cook stood out uncompromisingly for the old order of things. The mainstay of the Establishment in Haddington, Cook organised the opposition to Voluntaryism. He was the chief speaker at a meeting of noblemen, landed proprietors, and other notables held in the Assembly Room on 28th February 1840, and presided over by the Marquess of Tweeddale. What is known in Scottish ecclesiastical history as the "Ten Years' Conflict" was then in progress, and Cook, in a forceful speech, gave reasons for approving of the Church of Scotland as by law established and annihilating the party bent on resistance to the decisions of the Court of Session in ecclesiastical cases. Cook also took a leading part in securing nearly two hundred signatures to a petition for maintaining the *status quo* in Church affairs.

In the years immediately preceding the Victorian era Haddington therefore had its full share of acrimonious controversy—political, municipal, ecclesiastical—but gradually matters were straightened out, and though a truce was never in sight, a more harmonious period was ushered in.

CHAPTER VII

The Victorian Era—and Later (1837–1918)

It is the merest truism to say that loyalty is an inestimable quality: without it the human lot would indeed be vexatious. But loyalty should be tempered with discrimination, otherwise it is a worthless thing and apt to make suspect a show of devotion that is thoroughly deserved. So far as Haddington is concerned, there have been times when it would have been well had loyalty been more restrained, had there been less haste in presenting effusive addresses to monarchs who were hardly exemplars of regal worth—monarchs who were entitled to dutiful respect but not to the affection of their subjects.

But with the accession of Victoria such criticism became effete. By her the conception of the British monarchy was heightened immeasurably, and never were the people of Haddington more justified in evincing their devotion to the throne, as they did in addresses presented at appropriate intervals throughout an unusually protracted reign. On the day on which Victoria began her rule the town council drafted a congratulatory address which was duly presented to the youthful sovereign. Then on 28th June 1838 the coronation was celebrated with great enthusiasm. At nine o'clock in the morning the bells of Haddington rang out a merry peal, while a band playing popular melodies paraded the streets. At four o'clock shops were closed, and two hours later the magistrates and the town council with a number of the townsmen met in the Assembly Room and celebrated the auspicious occasion. "We have not for a long time past," wrote a *Scotsman* correspondent, "seen a demonstration of so much happiness in our little town. Men, women, and children—rich and poor, high and low, young and old—were to be seen rejoicing in a general merriment. There was a great display of fireworks in the evening, and shortly after midnight the streets were again as quiet as on ordinary occasions."

There were further rejoicings on the occasion of the Queen's marriage, in February 1840, to Prince Albert of Saxe-Coburg and Gotha, Haddington displaying "its ancient liberality in a propine to the burgesses." The birth of the Princess Royal followed by that of Albert Edward (afterwards Edward VII) afforded the inhabitants further opportunities of demonstrating that Her Majesty had no more loyal subjects than those in East Lothian. On the latter occasion there was a procession, headed by the magistrates, from the Assembly Room to the Cross, where "glasses of wine" were warmly pledged to the Queen's health and that of the infant heir. The remainder of the day was spent, reports Miller, who was probably an eye-witness, "with that joy and hilarity which such an uncommon and happy occurrence was calculated to inspire." Furthermore, when Victoria paid her first State visit to Scotland in September 1842, Thomas Lea, the provost, attended a levee at Dalkeith Palace (where Her Majesty and the Prince were the guests of the Duke and Duchess of Buccleuch) and presented an address in behalf of the community. The provost, we learn, "was arrayed in a black silk tabby gown, faced and trimmed with crimson silk velvet, a cocked hat, and a set of court-dress knee and shoe buckles."

Reference has already been made to a facetious article in the *Scotsman* which told how, on 20th June 1835, the Haddington admirers of "the late Dictator, the hero of Waterloo, and his worthy coadjutors in the short but glorious reign of the late Con-

72

servative Parliament," met in the Blue Bell Inn to establish a local Conservative Association and return a Tory representative at the next election.   In 1840 a movement was inaugurated to erect a national monument in Scotland as a tangible token of Wellington's military genius.   Haddington was invited to contribute, and on 10th January a meeting of those in sympathy was held in the Assembly Room.   Wellington's military greatness was extolled, while the political rancour of the previous occasion was conspicuous by its absence.   At any rate, so it seemed, judging by the newspaper reports.   The meeting was attended by "men of every shade of political party" who "mingled in unison to carry the object of this lasting testimonial of a country's gratitude into effect."   The Marquess of Tweeddale, who had served under Wellington in the Peninsula, was chairman, while Sir George Warrender of Lochend, Bart., another of the Peninsular veterans, as well as a friend of the Duke, moved the principal resolution, which was unanimously adopted.   In closing the proceedings, Lord Tweeddale declared that East Lothian would show "to the whole of Scotland that there is not a county in it that feels more sincerely than we do the debt of gratitude which the country owes to the Duke of Wellington."

Nor did East Lothian's effort belie these words, since its total contribution amounted to £1153, 8s. 6d., a considerable portion of which was raised by ladies.   And when it is remembered that the total cost of the equestrian statue of Wellington, which was unveiled in Edinburgh in 1852, was £10,000, it will be seen that more than a tenth of the total amount was raised in East Lothian.   No doubt the substantial sum was to some extent accounted for by Wellington's son and heir having married, in 1839, Lady Elizabeth Hay, daughter of George, eighth Marquess of Tweeddale.   In due time Lady Elizabeth became Duchess of Wellington.   Lord Tweeddale, her father, was Lord-Lieutenant of East Lothian for twenty years.   This long tenure of office came to a close in 1842, when he was appointed Governor of Madras and Commander-in-Chief of the military forces there.   On the eve of his departure, 20th May, he was entertained at a public dinner by the East Lothian Agricultural Society, of which his Lordship had always been a warm supporter, being himself a practical farmer.   The function, which was held in the Assembly Room, was attended by upwards of one hundred and fifty gentlemen.   Lord Elcho, who presided, proposed the health of the guest.   He extolled Lord Tweeddale's services in the Peninsular War (he was wounded at Busaco and Vittoria) and mentioned that Wellington had "repeatedly placed the Marquess in offices of trust and responsibility"—a "just exordium" which was received "with the loudest expressions of applause."   Lord Tweeddale, in his reply, explained that his going to India was the direct result of a command from Queen Victoria.

In the late autumn of 1843 there was considerable political commotion in Haddington when Richard Cobden and John Bright addressed a Free Trade demonstration.   That the two foremost leaders of the Anti-Corn Law propaganda, who were untiring in their efforts to expedite the importation of foreign foodstuffs and thereby lower prices for home-grown grain, should have ventured into a region so conspicuously agricultural as East Lothian was assuredly an act of courage.   Nor did it go altogether unrewarded, for the meeting brought crowds of people from all parts of the county, whether from sympathy with the object or from the sole desire of hearing the two most influential orators of the day, who shall say?   Anyhow the proceedings were entirely harmonious, and the speeches of Cobden and Bright were attentively listened to and frequently applauded.   Both statesmen were the guests of George Hope of Fenton Barns, who, though himself a distinguished and extensive farmer, was strongly in favour of free trade and cheaper food.   At the Haddington meeting, which was held on 27th October,

Mr Davie, a local merchant, presided. Cobden spoke first. He began with a prediction that the present generation, by tolerating a law to diminish the supply of food, would a century hence be thought as wise as their forefathers who had burnt witches —an apt allusion, considering how prominent East Lothian was in the days of witchcraft. Proceeding, Cobden, in an effort to demonstrate what free trade meant, drew upon local topography in a manner which must have arrested the attention of his audience. Here is the passage in full:—

Let us suppose an island rather larger than the Isle of May, and let us suppose that some strong-fisted fellows, clad in mail, sallied out of Tantallon Castle and took possession of this island and divided it among themselves, and held the people as tenants to till the land and pay them for the use of it. In process of time the people increased so much that they could not find corn to feed them with, but underneath the surface they found that Providence had been sufficiently bountiful, and had endowed the island with a quantity of coal, lead, copper, and every species of mineral wealth, such as no other island in the world possessed; suppose this people industrious, and, not having a sufficiency of bread, had delved into the surface and brought up the coal, iron, lead, and copper, and by dint of industry and skill had fabricated this iron and other materials into beautiful machines for spinning and producing a great variety of those articles which people on the Continental coast wanted. They gladly give the islanders corn and every article of food in exchange, with which the industrious mariners return to their island; but there they are met on the shore by a number of those strong fellows who intercept the ship and tell them that they have corn enough at home. Now what would be the consequence to this little island where there was not enough corn grown on the soil? That is the condition to which you find Great Britain fast approaching.

Cobden's sentences are exasperatingly long and involved, but to those who wrestle with them the meaning is not in doubt. At a later stage, Cobden deplored the fact that the Free Trade movement was making slow progress in Scotland. "How is it," he asked, "that the people of Haddington and the Scotch people generally have been so quiet about this [matter], considering the heads they have in Scotland?" Towards the close, the Free Trade orator crossed swords with Sir David Baird for having, at a meeting in Haddington earlier in the day, advocated a fixed tax on corn. Cobden concluded a lengthy speech by adjuring the people of Haddington to give the matter "deliberate consideration," and to co-operate in endeavouring to establish the principle of free trade. "We shall look to Haddington as a stronghold whence we can derive powerful assistance in our exertions."

Cobden was followed by George Hope of Fenton Barns, who, in the course of a fighting speech, called on all present to put an end to the "unjust legislation" under which they were groaning. Samuel Smiles, father of the author of *Self-Help*, having congratulated the meeting on the spontaneous movement by the farmers, John Bright delivered the concluding speech. He apologised for the lateness of the hour (it was then ten o'clock) but nevertheless spoke for nearly sixty minutes. Bright's was a fine platform performance, being full of limpid expression, but, unlike Cobden's, contained no local allusions. At the close a vote was taken when only one person registered against free trade. It may be of interest to add that some twenty years later Cobden paid another visit to East Lothian, when he was present at a demonstration of a ploughing machine invented by Saddler of Ferrygate. The Free Trade leader, who was accompanied by Duncan Maclaren, a former Lord Provost of Edinburgh and brother-in-law of John Bright, afterwards spoke at a luncheon given by Mr Nisbet Hamilton of Archerfield in a large marquee erected in the grounds of Dirleton Castle. There were one hundred and fifty guests.

When the Rifle Volunteer movement began in 1859, and army reform and national service were in the forefront of domestic politics, Haddington took decided action.

An excellent lead was given by Francis, ninth Earl of Wemyss, who from 1847 till the death of his father represented the constituency in the House of Commons. In his opinion the strengthening of the defence forces of the country was an urgent necessity, and both inside and outside Parliament he made frequent appeals for placing Britain on a war footing, so that it could meet the attack of the most powerful enemy. His Lordship, who threw himself into the movement with unquenchable ardour, had much to do with the creation of the London Scottish regiment, of which he was lieutenant-colonel. He also was the first chairman of the National Rifle Association, an organisation to which he presented the Elcho Challenge Shield, which is competed for yearly.

Lord Wemyss's exertions in behalf of the Rifle Volunteer movement also inspired local efforts, though these were mainly directed by Provost Roughead and Lieutenant-Colonel Vetch of Caponflat. At a public meeting convened by them on 25th October 1859, it was resolved to raise a volunteer corps in Haddington, for clothing, equipping, and maintaining which a subscription list was opened. So successful was the project that in little more than a fortnight sixty-seven riflemen belonging to the burgh were enrolled for "Defence, not Defiance." Known as the First Company, they comprised well-to-do folk, and were commanded by George Gaukroger. A Second Company was also formed and mainly consisted of artisans. The numerical strength of the corps increased. In 1863 the Haddington Volunteers adopted a uniform consisting of "dark green, nearly black, with scarlet facings, cuffs, and neck, and a thin scarlet braiding down the outside seam of the trousers." Each tunic had a bronze star enclosing a St Andrew cross of white metal, and the lettering, "Haddington Rifle Volunteers." Every member of the rank and file wore a white belt.

When Queen Victoria held the first large review of Scottish Rifle Volunteers in Edinburgh, on 7th August 1860, the Haddington contingent attended in full force. There were between two and three hundred riflemen, comprising five companies, all connected with East Lothian. The county men were under the command of Captain Kinloch of Gilmerton, and those of the burgh under Captain Roughead. East Lothian was also well represented in the other memorable Edinburgh review on 25th August 1881, known as the "Wet Review" because of the torrential rain which marred the proceedings and caused the death of not a few of the riflemen who took part. The number of officers and men present from East Lothian was 360 out of a total of 430. Lieutenant-Colonel Scott commanded, and other officers included Colonel Charles S. Dods, bank agent and seedsman in Haddington, son of William Dods, the friend of Jane Welsh Carlyle; Rev. Dr Sprott, North Berwick, Regimental Chaplain; Dr J. R. Ronaldson, Haddington, Regimental Surgeon; Dr Crombie, North Berwick, Assistant Regimental Surgeon; and Captains W. Hadden and W. T. Ferme of the A and B (Haddington) Companies. The East Lothian regiment was complimented in the *Times* as being "remarkable for keeping correct distances" and "marching past well in every respect." The contingent constituted part of the second of the three divisions of the whole force reviewed, and was brigaded along with three Edinburgh regiments and the 2nd Northumberland. It was under the command of Colonel Davidson, son of a former sheriff-clerk of Haddington and the intimate friend of the Carlyles.

Haddington once more testified its devotion to the Crown when, on 10th March 1863, the Prince of Wales (afterwards Edward VII) married the Princess Alexandra, daughter of Christian IX of Denmark. The town was gaily bedecked. Bunting in great variety was displayed in the principal streets, and there were triumphal arches at the west end of High Street and at Custom Stone Corner. The town bells were rung at nine o'clock in the morning, and an hour later shops were closed and all business suspended. In the forenoon the local Volunteer companies paraded, and, uniting with the Ancient Order of Free Gardeners, marched to the Haugh, where an oak sapling from the woods at Letham was planted in honour of the occasion. Later on, the Rifle Volunteers were entertained to cake and wine at the Corn Exchange, when the healths of Queen Victoria and the Prince and Princess of Wales were drunk. About three hundred people, mostly artisans and their wives, were given a public dinner in the Corn Exchange. This was followed by a banquet in the Assembly Room, to which prominent townsfolk, all of whom wore wedding favours, were invited. The day's rejoicings closed with a display of fireworks. By way of illumination a transparency figuring the Prince and Princess of Wales and encircled with a floral wreath was exhibited at the George Hotel. Chinese lanterns were suspended from the two triumphal arches while a large bonfire blazed at the Cross.

In the sixties of last century political forces were again unusually active. Parliamentary reform as represented by the Act of 1832 was recognised as a step in the right direction, but only a step. Salutary so far as it went, that measure was no more than a piece of class legislation: it enfranchised the middle class—they and they alone. The working man had still to come to his own; and from the Chartist movement onwards for nearly twenty years determined agitations were proceeding for the extension of the franchise, so that industrialists might be given the vote. Haddington's reaction towards the movement left no room for doubt. The community as a whole was not, it is true, closely identified with industry, but the formidable agricultural population had as yet no voice in the government of the country. Accordingly, the extension of the Reform Act of 1832 was a matter that had a wide and pressing application, and its advocacy was gone about in no half-hearted fashion. In December 1865 a local Parliamentary Reform Association was formed at a meeting attended by fifteen hundred people. Provost Farquharson presided, and was supported by the bailies and councillors. The farm workers had a strong representative in George Hope of Fenton Barns, who, in a trenchant speech, gave interesting particulars regarding the history of the franchise in East Lothian. Before 1832 there were about one hundred and sixty freeholders, but most of them had no interest in the land of which they were the nominal superiors. In the burgh, on the other hand, the town council were reasonably free, though the time-honoured system whereby the members elected each other still prevailed. Hope of Fenton Barns also retailed some of his political experiences in pre-Reform days. "To a meeting in Haddington we marched to the hustings with the beating of muffled drums and with black flags and skull and crossbones, for had the Tories not yielded, our freedom would have been achieved with blood."

Another speaker, William Brodie of Dunbar, said that in all the political struggles in which he had engaged since when, as a boy, he drove the Reform candidate's coach through the streets of Haddington, their plans had usually been destroyed by the want of unity amongst the working classes. Therefore, in the hope that this handicap would be got rid of, he moved a resolution to the effect that in order to secure a further extension of the franchise, "the reformers of the county of Haddington and the district of burghs sending a member to Parliament should unite in political action." The resolution was adopted, together with another expressing the opinion that the time had arrived "for the admission of a great body of the unenfranchised . . . which would be the means of strengthening the Government and giving stability to the political institutions of the kingdom."

The second Reform Act passed by Disraeli in 1867 undoubtedly admitted "a great body of the unenfranchised," but it had reference exclusively to the industrial classes in towns. To East Lothian therefore it was only a partial benefit, and the agricultural labourer had to wait other seventeen years before he was placed on a footing of equality with the town worker—till Gladstone in 1884 brought about the third extension of the franchise. Haddington, more especially the county, had reason to be grateful to Gladstone, and when, in 1874, the great Victorian statesman spent a few days at Whittingehame, he was invited to accept the freedom of the burgh. He, however, was unable to do so owing to the multiplicity of his engagements.

The direct effect of the enfranchisement of the labouring class in Haddington was to strengthen the Liberal vote. This was strikingly exemplified at the General Election in February 1879 when Sir J. H. A. Macdonald (better known by his judicial title of Lord Kingsburgh), who was then Solicitor-General, contested Haddington Burghs in the Conservative interest. The Liberal candidate was Sir David Wedderburn. Political feeling ran high, and when Macdonald addressed a public meeting in Haddington, he was subjected to continual interruption—was, in fact, literally howled down. He lost the seat, but because of his gallant fight his supporters entertained him to a banquet in the Corn Exchange on 21st April 1879. The Hon. R. Bourke of Coalstoun (afterwards Lord Connemara) presided, and local speakers included Captain W. T. Ferme, the Rev. William Ross of Haddington Parish Church, Rev. W. B. Turnbull of Gladsmuir, and Rev. Dr Caesar of Tranent.

Another step in Parliamentary reform was taken in 1885, which had a purely local interest. As has been already indicated, there existed from the Union of 1707, and to some extent before, a constituency known as the Haddington Burghs, comprising, in addition to the county town, the burghs of Dunbar, North Berwick, Jedburgh, and Lauder. This anomalous state of matters was ended in the year above-mentioned, when Jedburgh and Lauder were disjoined, while Haddington, Dunbar, and North Berwick were amalgamated with the county to form a single constituency—East Lothian. The arrangement was opposed by the Conservatives, the county having always returned a member of their way of thinking. Indeed, the constituency had come to be regarded "almost as a pocket burgh of the Wemyss family." But Gladstone's Franchise Act had now given the vote to the rural labourer, and it was not difficult to predict how an election would result under the new conditions. The incorporation of the three East Lothian burghs with the county favoured the Liberals. This was clearly demonstrated at the first election under the new regime when Richard B. Haldane (afterwards Viscount Haldane of Cloan) defeated Lord Elcho, the Conservative candidate, by 1528 votes. Not only so, but Haldane retained the seat in the Liberal interest for upwards of a quarter of a century. In his *Autobiography* his Lordship writes: "I threw myself with all the energy I had into a prolonged contest, and in December 1885 ejected the sitting member, Lord Elcho, by a large majority. Having turned him out from a seat which by tradition had long been a Conservative one, I had of course to fight hard afterwards to keep the constituency. But it became a splendid Liberal seat."

Queen Victoria's jubilee in the summer of 1887 afforded the royal burgh still another opportunity of displaying its appreciation of Her Majesty personally as well as commemorating her long and beneficent reign. On Sunday, 19th June, a thanksgiving service was held in the parish church. The building was completely filled. The Rev. R. Nimmo Smith preached an eloquent sermon in the course of which he extolled the Queen's exemplary character and her long and glorious reign. On the following Tuesday a peal of bells wakened "not a few late sleepers." At noon three hundred people belonging to the town and parish sat down to a public dinner in the Corn Exchange. The Queen's health was drunk, and a telegram dispatched to the Duchess of Roxburghe, who was in attendance on Her Majesty as a Lady-in-Waiting. The Duchess replied: "I have told the Queen of the loyal message from Haddington, and am desired to express Her Majesty's thanks and appreciation of the congratulations sent." In the afternoon there was a revival of the Tyneside Games in Amisfield Park. But the central feature of the rejoicings was a banquet in the Assembly Room attended by about one hundred and fifty guests and presided over by Dr Thomas Howden, an ex-provost.

Ten years later, almost to a day, Queen Victoria's Diamond Jubilee was celebrated. The occasion was marked by a series of functions on similar lines to those that took place in June 1887. As usual, the festive mood was prominent and the town was gay with flags and other decorations. In the forenoon a procession, headed by the band of the 7th Battalion of the Royal Scots Volunteers, marched from the Cross to the West End Park, when Provost A. Mathieson Main planted a Californian tree (*Wellingtonia gigantica*) in commemoration of the Queen having occupied the British throne for sixty years. At the conclusion of the ceremony the procession made its way to a row of new houses to which Mrs Main, wife of the provost, formally gave the name of "Victoria Park." A bonfire on the Garleton Hills ended the proceedings of a memorable day.

In October 1888 a banquet was held in the Corn Exchange in recognition of the outstanding political services of Mr Arthur James Balfour (as he was then). The laird of Whittingehame was Chief Secretary for Ireland, had attained Cabinet rank, and was looked upon as a future Prime Minister. The banquet, however, was not so much a party affair as a tribute to Balfour's public services by those of his own country-side. His speech, in acknowledgment, was acclaimed one of the best that he had yet made.

The consequences of the second Boer War, with its unexpected reverses and long duration by reason of the vigorous and skilful resistance of the Dutch farmers in South Africa, were only slightly felt in Haddington. Recruiting for the army was then voluntary, and the conflict did not necessitate the enormous forces that were requisitioned in the War of 1914–18 and, to a very much greater extent, in the War now being waged. When military operations ended with the fall of Pretoria (June 1900) the news was greeted locally with the liveliest satisfaction. "Flags flew out," writes one, recalling the occasion in the *Haddingtonshire Courier* in 1938—"Flags flew out as if at the touch of a magician's wand, crowds gathered, and everybody seemed to be congratulating everybody else." There was a torchlight procession and a bonfire (roughly calculated to be 15 feet high and 60 feet in circumference) at Ball Alley. Provost Main and the town council were present. Congratulatory telegrams were dispatched to the Queen, the Prime Minister (Lord Salisbury), Joseph Chamberlain (the Colonial Secretary), and Lord Roberts at Pretoria. The six surviving Haddington volunteers were given the freedom of the burgh in May 1901.

The War of 1914–18 produced in Haddington a very different state of matters. Its repercussions were distinctly felt and before long were of tragic significance. Immediately hostilities were declared the town assumed the aspect of an armed camp. Troops estimated at about 3000 were quartered in the Corn Exchange, in the various maltings, in most of the public buildings, and in not a few private houses. Nor was this all. Wooden huts occupied practically the whole of Amisfield Park, which provided accommodation for the Lothians and Border Horse and latterly for other regiments.

The mansion of Amisfield was reserved for the officers.[1] Finally, the old *quoad sacra* church in Newton Port was transformed into a military hospital.

On the evening of Sunday, 1st November 1914, the "first offering" of the "Territorial manhood" of East Lothian was got ready. In the *Courier* we read of how, in the gloaming of a stormy day, considerable commotion was caused in the town by the news that the fateful summons had come for the men of Haddington and district to bear their share in subduing the military might of Germany. The summons had been eagerly awaited, and now that it had arrived, brought a measure of relief inasmuch as the long suspense had definitely ended. The die was cast, it being decreed that the local contingent must leave within twenty-four hours. When Monday morning came the appearance of Haddington had wonderfully altered: Khaki-clad men fully armed were everywhere. The time of departure was fixed for the evening, so farewells had to be quickly spoken. A drizzling rain was falling when Mr Arthur James Balfour, at half-past five o'clock, mounted an improvised platform in front of the County Buildings and wished "God-speed in the name of friends and neighbours." Accompanying the statesman were the provost (George Young) and town council, likewise Major (later Colonel) Alexander Brook, the Commanding-Officer of the 8th Royal Scots, the regiment of which the Haddington Territorials formed part. At the close of Mr Balfour's address, the men, preceded by the pipe band, marched to the railway station, where they entrained in two detachments, the one preceding the other by an hour and a half.

The Haddington contingent saw severe fighting in the early stages of the War, and its losses were particularly heavy. At the battle of Festubert, which lasted from 15th to 18th May 1915, the 8th Royal Scots took a prominent part. In addition to the greatly lamented loss of Colonel Brook, who died from a wound in the head caused by a shell splinter, 31 of other ranks were killed, while 11 officers and 148 rank and file were wounded. Colonel Brook's name was mentioned in a dispatch by Field-Marshal Sir John French, while those under his command were specially commended by John Buchan (afterwards Lord Tweedsmuir) in a communication from the front to the *Times*. "The 8th Royal Scots," he wrote, "was brought into the firing line after the first hour and kept its place to the end in the thick of the fighting. Its heroic Commanding-Officer was killed."

On the first anniversary of the opening of the War a public meeting was held in Haddington mainly for recruiting purposes. The principal speaker was the Earl of Wemyss, who alluded to the existence of an "orgy of pessimism," doubtless fostered by the severe losses that had been sustained locally. Before the War was a month old Lord Arthur Hay, heir presumptive to the Marquisate of Tweeddale, was killed in action. Then followed the death of Colonel Brook, and in the closing year of the War, on 25th March 1918, that of Lieutenant-Colonel William Gemmill, who had been awarded the D.S.O. for his splendid services at Festubert. Colonel Gemmill, who in civil life farmed Greendykes, was by the side of Brook when the latter fell. He himself narrowly escaped being struck by a splinter. Gemmill succeeded to the command of the 8th Royal Scots, and in that capacity acquitted himself well.

After Christmas 1918 demobilisation proceeded steadily, and by the beginning of March 1919 the 8th Royal Scots was down to cadre strength. The regiment, or rather the local contingent, which was under the command of Major T. B. Mitchell, M.C., reached Haddington on 30th April, and, it need hardly be stated, was warmly welcomed.

---

[1] Built of excellent red sandstone, this building was pulled down after the War, the stones being utilised in the erection of a large secondary school at Prestonpans, also the Vert Hospital at Haddington.

THE VICTORIAN ERA—AND LATER (1837–1918)

The men, who were met at the railway station by the provost (Thomas Ross) and town council, were entertained to lunch, Sir Archibald Buchan Hepburn, Bt., Convener of East Lothian, being present. Two regimental flags brought back from France were given into the custody of the Town Council. Eventually they were hung in the nave of the parish church of St Mary.

Of the band that left Haddington for the War front on that dismal November day in 1914 but a fraction returned. The mournful tale of those belonging to the town and parish who gave their lives for their country is recorded on the War Memorial which stands by the west gate of Haddington Churchyard. On it are inscribed the names of 130 men of all ranks. This of course includes not merely 48 men who served with the 8th Royal Scots but those enlisted in other Scottish and English regiments, likewise those who served in the Royal Navy, of which there were 82.

With the War of 1914–18 this narrative of the far-stretching and in many respects distinguished history of the royal burgh of Haddington in relation to national events may fitly close. What has been chronicled in the preceding chapters will have been purposeless unless it has demonstrated the nature of the contribution of the county town of East Lothian towards the development of Scotland, both ecclesiastically and from the point of view of secular affairs. This contribution has been anything but negligible. Indeed few communities of equal size have been swept into the stream of Scottish history so often and with such arresting results. Not seldom has the harvest been garnered at critical junctures as, for example, in the siege of 1548–49. Altogether it is a colourful story, shot through with the lights and shadows of Scottish life, sometimes of tragic import but on other occasions invested with a touch of pageantry and splendour and romance.

PART II

CHAPTER VIII

Town and Parish

THE royal and ancient burgh of Haddington is noteworthy for its situation. It lies in the valley of the Tyne with uplands extending southwards to the Lammermoors, while on the north the nearer range of the Garleton Hills stands sentinel over the town. Although it may be considered low-lying, it is actually 150 feet above sea-level, at the very heart of East Lothian, and in the midst of a far-stretching and remarkably fertile plain. Through this agricultural landscape, embodying what in Wordsworthian phrase may be called the very "pomp of cultivated nature," the river Tyne threads its way, and, making a graceful curve as it passes the town, enhances a scene of great pastoral beauty.

Haddington, it has been remarked, preserves more of the character of a mediæval burgh than any other in Scotland. Certainly its general outline has not altered much with the passing of the centuries. Apart from a modern housing scheme, north and south-east of the ancient boundaries, there is nothing brand-new. True, most of its ancient buildings, if they have not been swept away, have undergone structural alteration more than once. Still, in the matter of lay-out the broad features are pretty much as they were. Could we transport ourselves into the eighteenth century, or even into the seventeenth, we should be surprised to find how little has been changed. The hand of Time has dealt gently with Haddington: the atmosphere of the old world can still be felt. As for the existing buildings, there are a number whose obtrusively classical design speak too plainly of the nineteenth century, but alongside of them are not a few that are unquestionably ancient.

Nothing is definitely known of the origin of the town, nor how it assumed the rather peculiar shape it has retained from early times. The *Auld Register of Haddington*, which dates from 1423, furnishes the first glimpse of the burgh, but it is shadowy at best. Hardgate, Sidegate, and Poldrate—thoroughfares still existing—are however mentioned.

When David I granted a charter to Haddington (as seems to have been the case) he was imbued with the laudable idea that spaciousness comports with the dignity of a royal burgh. Indeed this is a characteristic of most of the burghs associated with King David. Every visitor to Haddington is impressed with the uncommon width of High Street. But it was probably much wider when the town came into being, for the island group of buildings separating High Street from Market Street did not exist till a later date, so at least some authorities contend. Be that as it may, a fairly ancient origin can be claimed for the island group, since Kilpair (Caleperys) is referred to in 1426. If the conjecture that the Middle Raw (as it was called) was non-existent in far-off times be correct, we are to conjure up a vision of the market-place of Haddington as stretching at one time from the north side of Market Street to the south side of High Street. This immense space would then be grass-grown, and serve partly as pasturage and partly as a place where local merchandise was disposed of at stalls or booths. Not only would this be the centre of the town's economic life but of its social life as well, the accustomed meeting-place of the community on important occasions, the scene of what pageantry there was in rude times, the common on which games and pastimes were engaged in. But of this period little that is informative can be said, for the history of Haddington is speculation more or less till the second decade of the fifteenth century when the town's records begin.

Dr George Barclay of Middleton, one of the ministers of Haddington in the latter half of the eighteenth century, contributed a long and, in parts, valuable account of his parish to the first volume of *Archæologia Scotica* (1792). His topographical description, not wholly accurate however, contains the following: "The town consists of four streets which intersect each other nearly at right angles, and though the buildings are not very elegant, yet they are at least equal in appearance to those of most other Scots burghs." If, as seems likely, Barclay's four streets were High Street, Market Street, Hardgate, and Sidegate, he was taking a somewhat circumscribed view of the town, even as it was in his day. Barclay takes no account of thoroughfares beyond, nor of the numerous wynds and closes. The latter were a notable feature. Narrow and often dark, they were lined with buildings, quaint and picturesque, but huddled together and in various stages of dilapidation. The streets, of which the wynds and closes were appendages, did not lack width and contained structures some of whose frontages rested on pillars while others had outside stairs—the whole presenting an agreeable effect. Originally the houses were of two storeys and had thatched roofs.

John Wood's plan of Haddington (1819) shows the town in general outline as it is now, with the exception of streets outside the ancient boundaries.[1] The most bustling part is, of course, High Street (Croce Gait) and Market Street (Tolbooth Gait). On the south side of the former there remain to this day a row of houses forming as fine a street façade of the kind as is to be found in Scotland. Perhaps nowhere else is there so long an unspoilt elevation in the traditional Scottish style. Some of the houses have foundations of earlier periods and have been reconstructed and modernised time and again, but the majority of the frontages are reminiscent of the eighteenth and earlier part of the nineteenth century, at the end of which period the outside stairs and bow-fronted windows were removed.

The parallel thoroughfares of High Street and Market Street run from east to west and are divided by a group of buildings which long ago bore the not inappropriate name of the Middle Raw. These blocks were broken up by wynds linking up the two parallel streets. At the east end was George Inn Wynd (now Brown Street), half-way down which is a narrow passage that still goes by the name of Birlie's (or Burley's) Walls. Opposite this vennel is Kilpair Street containing some eighteenth-century houses. Farther west is Cross Lane, formerly known as Fishmarket Wynd. Beyond was Britannia Wynd, in which was a tavern bearing that name (now the Commercial Hotel). Then came the Broad Wynd (sometime known as Pirie's and then as Neilson's, both names being derived from local traders). Finally, the most westerly passage for long bore the name of the Jail Wynd because alongside stood the house of correction.

Market Street formerly terminated at the east end in Tolbooth Wynd, an outlet to Hardgate, which runs at right angles with a prolongation due south called Sidegate and Poldrate. Situated on slightly elevated ground, Hardgate, roughly speaking, formed the eastern boundary of the old town. Industry early established itself here, several tanneries lining the east side. A portion of Sidegate was formerly known as St John Street, a reminder of the tenement of the Knights of St John which stood at the junction of Hardgate and High Street.

[1] From the burgh records it would appear that a plan of the town was executed by John Adair in 1682, but no trace of it can be found.

TOWN AND PARISH

In pre-Reformation times most of the south-east part of Haddington was occupied with ecclesiastical buildings of one kind or another, all of which have been referred to in a previous chapter. At the Sands there is a piece of ground surrounded by a wall (recently lowered) known as "Lady Kitty's Garden." In the eighteenth century the site was occupied by a group of buildings, and earlier still was reserved for archery and bowling. In 1771 Lady Catherine Charteris, the owner of this property, successfully petitioned the town council for leave to alter the enclosing wall, thereby necessitating the removal of the Churchyard gate farther east. At what precise time the buildings occupying the site of "Lady Kitty's Garden" were removed and the place converted into greensward has not been ascertained.

Close to the far end of Church Street, and reached by the picturesque three-arched bridge across the Tyne (described in a later chapter), are the suburbs of Nungate and Giffordgate which, though beyond the ancient boundary, are now incorporated with Haddington. Alexander de Martin is said to have gifted certain lands and tenements, together with the mills, to the nuns of the Abbey of Haddington under whose jurisdiction Nungate remained till the Reformation. Created a burgh of barony at an unknown date, the right to appoint a bailie of Nungate passed, with the alienation of the lands, to the Hepburns of Nunraw, with which family it remained till 2nd October 1708 when the provost and magistrates, "considering that they have [been] adjudged the heritable office of the baillerie of the Nungate from the Lairds of Nunraw," appointed James Dods, "one of the present bailies," to that office. The custom of electing a baron bailie continues to this day. South of the town, and skirting the river, are the East and West Mill haughs which, notwithstanding their being outside the ancient boundary, are town property. Formerly the haughs were let for grazing but are now exclusively devoted to recreation purposes.

Till about the middle of the eighteenth century Haddington in general appearance as well as in administration was mediæval. Subsequently there was a breakaway from conditions which in the main had persisted for centuries. Ruinous buildings gave place to others that in design and internal economy approximated to modern standards of communal living. Altogether a progressive and enlightened spirit was abroad, and the Haddington of to-day slowly emerged.

It is customary to speak of the town wall and to point to certain fragments of stonework as authentic remains. Doubts, however, have been expressed as to whether Haddington ever was a walled town in the ordinary sense. Till the sixteenth century the scheme of defence was primitive, a haphazard affair at best. At that time the town was encircled, not by a continuous wall of sufficient height and breadth to withstand the assaults of the "auld enemy," but by a system of earthworks—a hastily improvised plan of obstruction intended more to keep out beggars, vagabonds, and especially persons from plague-stricken areas, than to oppose the armed might of England. Owners of property at the circumference of the town were then obliged to maintain for purposes of defence their "heid roumes," or, in modern phrase, that portion of their retaining wall that faced the open country. These "yaird dykes" (to borrow another expression from the burgh records) were to be kept in good repair for a double purpose. They were to be so built that no one outside the town could use them as a means of entrance. Secondly, the "yaird dykes" must not assist accused persons trying to escape from the town. In October 1543 proprietors of outlying property were enjoined to be mindful of their "heid roumes." They were again warned in 1568, and in cases of non-compliance it was ordained that repairs be carried out by the public authority at the owner's expense.

It will therefore be seen that no town wall existed in the sixteenth century, though there seems to have been one at a later period. The rude scheme of defence relied on the "heid roumes" of tenements on the outskirts. These were joined up, and where no buildings existed the gap appears to have been filled with a rubble wall erected at the expense of the town. The siege of Haddington in 1548–49 caused the first serious attempt to put the town in a proper state of defence, and this, be it noted, was done by the English when they captured it. Up to this time the fortifications were rudimentary. Even the ports, as we are reminded by an act of the town council in September 1538, were "hung and clad with burdis (boards)," which means that nothing more than a flimsy wooden barricade existed. Outside there was a fosse or ditch of sufficient depth to make the scaling of the barriers more difficult. In December 1541 a "fowsy" was constructed on the north, and in April 1545 the provost was requested to ascertain the depth of the south stanks or ditches.

What the English garrison did to strengthen the defences has already been indicated. But the burghers were slow to learn the lesson. Not till 1597 did the civic authority decide to get rid of the "heid roume" plan and build something in the nature of a town wall. For "lack of wallis or fowsayis" there had been much lawlessness in the form of "steilling furth of nolt, horses and uyer [other] geir thereof." And, to make matters worse, there was the old nightmare of the plague. "In tyme of pest na part" of the existing structure was strong enough "to kep out suspect folks and uyer evils." Such were the circumstances which impelled the town council at long last to consider the erection of "ane substantious wall."

But it is problematic if the scheme was ever given effect to. In January 1604, six years after the scheme had been unanimously approved, estimates were obtained for the construction of "ye common wall on ye north syde of the town beginning at the West port and fra yat north-west to east." Yet after building operations had made some progress the sense of security was still lacking. Undesirable persons from the open country could surmount the obstacles placed in their way, and so late as 1618 there were complaints about gaps in the town wall and of ditches being filled up. It seems fairly clear that reliance was still being placed on the efficiency of the "heid roumes," the owners of which were, in 1609, to be "unlawit, poindit, and wairdit" if their enclosing dykes were not "biggit up." Again, in 1619, those possessing "dykes or yaird heides" were to maintain them, as well as all "yetts or passages to and from their own yairds that no swine pass out or through the dykes, yetts or sloppes (slopes) either to their awne or thair neighbour's corn or skaith." From a study of the burgh records the inference to be drawn is that wherever there were no "heid roumes" the gaps were filled by the erection of a *common* wall, the adjective being used to distinguish such portions from *private* walls or "heid roumes."

While the entire line of the so-called wall of the early seventeenth century is not precisely known, its general direction can be described with tolerable accuracy. Beginning at the West Port, situated close to the junction of the roads leading to Edinburgh, Aberlady, and Pencaitland, the wall ran alongside the West Church, and proceeded north as far as the "Black Paling" footpath. Here it turned due east and was parallel with the footpath till it reached the building formerly known as St John's Church. This wall evidently was substituted for the fosse constructed in 1541. Immediately south of the fosse and the wall of 1604 were the town's crofts where the fairs were held, and beyond these the "heid roumes" of the properties west of Market Street and Court Street. The line of these "heid roumes" was connected with the port near the Public Library, known variously as the North, North-West, and

Newton.[1] The town wall then continued behind the gardens of the east part of Market Street, and eventually reached the North-East Port in Hardgate. A portion of the wall can still be seen in the lane leading to Old Bank House.

Soon after the erection of the wall, Newton Port, as the burgh records testify, was removed higher up the loan, to a site adjoining St John's Church. At the same time a deviation was made in the line of the north wall, which, according to Dr Wallace-James, was carried from this point straight across to Tenterfield and then to the North-East Port. It then took a southerly direction, skirting the left bank of the Tyne and forming the eastern boundary of the Franciscan friary. Much of the old wall still remains, also a built-up red sandstone doorway which may have given the Franciscans access to the riverside.

The east sides of the Episcopal Church and Elm House abut on the town wall. Between the garden of the latter and the English School building in Church Street stood the East Port. From this point the course is not very clear. Dr Wallace-James hazarded the view that the wall bore south-west, past the site of the King's Yaird, and traversed obliquely the newer portion of the churchyard. On reaching Sidegate opposite Maitlandfield, it joined the South Port. It then proceeded up Mill Wynd, and bending round behind Maitlandfield, pursued its course north and then west on the line of the Butts footpath to the S.E. corner of Victoria Road. From here to the West Port the wall, Dr Wallace-James suggests, crossed the eastern part of the bowling green in Wemyss Place to the West Port. Thus the town was completely encircled.

The four original ports (or entrances) to the burgh were of no great strength. The magistrates seem to have thought that all ends were met if the ports were constantly and closely watched. This duty devolved on the burgesses, the penalty for default being a fine of eight shillings. Punishment also was inflicted in the case of a watchman who fell asleep, or was drunk, or absented himself without leave. The vigil must have been a long one, since the ports were open from five o'clock in the morning till nine at night. Special precautions were taken when the plague was rampant. No stranger was allowed to enter unless he could produce a certificate from some reputable person that he was free from infection. If the watchman were remiss in this matter, he was placed in the stocks for fifteen days.

The burghal lands lay principally to the west of the town and bordered the post-road to Edinburgh. At one time they were extensive, stretching as far as Gladsmuir, and comprising Clay Barns, Teuchit Muir (as far west as Hodges), Gladshot, Barberfield, Liberty Hall, Coalburn, and Heathery Hall. Outside the West Port were two strips of land which belonged to the town. On the north side of the post-road was Hangman's Acres or Gallow Green which extended to Bellevue. The land on the south side stretched to Letham Mains, and was known as the Loanings. It is supposed originally to have included Ralph Eglyn's Acres. The boundary of the Loanings was marked by a large boulder known as the Haddington Stone.

Most interest attaches to the commonty lands of Gladsmuir. In a notarial instrument in the Douglas Collection, preserved in the Register House and dated 19th March 1427-28, reference is made to the perambulation of the common muir of Haddington. The Gladsmuir property, which covers hundreds of acres, is frequently mentioned in the records of the sixteenth and seventeenth centuries. These lands were granted to the town by David I and were confirmed by charters of James VI

[1] The North-West Port constituted an additional entrance to the town. In 1617 it was decided "to mak ane yet (gate) or port of tymer (timber) to hing upoune ye *new* north-west port."

and Charles I. For a long time the means for their development were not available, and they were a burden on the community. So early as 1543 we find the town council reporting that Gladsmuir "is and has been these many ages bygane not only hurtfull and expensive . . . but also unprofitable, the same not being teillet (tilled), labourit, or manurit." The real difficulty was that the burghal lands lay too far off when communication and facilities of transport were of the most primitive character. None the less the magistrates felt that they must do something to ease the financial strain. Various means were tried to make Gladsmuir valuable commercially. The burgh records of 1531 contain a long entry concerning the "wynning of a coal pit" there. In 1543 the possibilities of feuing were investigated. Then we hear of one George Simpson offering £100 for permission to sink a mine, but history is silent as to whether the offer was accepted. In 1572, however, a nineteen years' lease was granted for this purpose, though it does not seem to have fared better than previous attempts. Still the hope persisted that Gladsmuir was a potential coal-mining district, and from time to time there were efforts at realisation. In 1749 an experiment was abandoned after a year's trial, and so late as 1826 the town spent £1800 in boring operations and in erecting cottages for the miners. But optimism was again quenched: the seam was not of sufficient thickness to make its working profitable.

There were other attempts to place Gladsmuir on a remunerative basis. In 1687 a somewhat pretentious feuing scheme was launched. Two hundred acres of the moor known as Robswells was offered on a nineteen years' lease or for longer. At the same time the town, with the aid of William M'Call and James Lauder, merchants, also William Lillie, Deacon Convener of the Trades, effected certain improvements on the moor itself. Then in 1692 the parish of Gladsmuir was constituted, being carved out of the parishes of Haddington and Tranent. A fresh building period was inaugurated in 1728 when feus were given off at nominal rents to various persons, who enclosed their properties and improved them by judicious planting. But the land was only moderately productive, and in 1752 part of the rents and feu-duties went to pay the town's debts. The final stage was reached in the earlier half of the nineteenth century when the greater part of Gladsmuir was acquired by John Buchan of Letham. Buchan paid off the debt incurred by the coal-mining experiment of 1826, and ten years later was given the lands of Liberty Hall, likewise a row of dwellings and fifteen acres at Samuelston Loanhead.

The "Riding of the Marches" at Gladsmuir was carried out annually till well into last century. The magistrates, together with some of the burgesses, were mounted, while others made the journey in coaches. The town's officers always formed part of the cavalcade. Besides Gladsmuir, the "Riding of the Marches" included Aberlady, the port of Haddington, where the party rode to a large rock at the mouth of the Peffer Water known as the "King's Kist."

At Aberlady the town had a harbour, or rather an anchorage, from the fourteenth century, if not earlier. In a charter of Robert II mention is made of "free transit to our said harbour." Aberlady, it is true, is not specifically named, but from information derived from other sources there can be hardly any doubt that the harbour was there. In 1475 David Hepburn of Waughton was interdicted from interfering with the carting of goods dispatched from Haddington to the haven at the mouth of the Peffer, and from availing himself of the anchorage there. In 1535 reference is made to the "biggin of ye haiffen of Aberlady," the expense being defrayed out of the Common Good. Sasine both of the harbour and the town's house at Aberlady was given in 1543 by Henry Cockburn, Sheriff-Depute of Edinburgh. The town's property was known as Haddington House, and in it shipping business was transacted. Most of the ships, all of average size, had to be "entered" before using the anchorage. They usually brought cargoes of timber from the Fife coast. At one time two small craft, the *Perseverance* and the *Eliza*, plied between the port of Haddington and Leith. Their cargoes consisted, of manure for the farmers, bark for the tanners, and linseed cake for the merchants. The shore dues were rouped annually. In 1548–49 the English, when in possession of Haddington, landed troops and equipment at Aberlady, which they fortified. The road to the town's port passed through lands belonging to the Earl of Haddington, Lord Elibank, and the laird of Alderston, who in 1659 were requested to keep the highway in good repair. Originally forty feet wide, it was an inalienable right of the town, as was demonstrated in 1761 when encroachments were attempted. The doom of Aberlady as a port was sealed when the railway was extended to Haddington. In April 1848 the anchorage and Haddington House were purchased by the Earl of Wemyss for £375.

Like most Scottish towns Haddington in early times was forced to concern itself with matters of public health by reason of frequent visitations of the plague. It goes without saying that in a benighted age, when not even an elementary knowledge of hygiene existed, the toll of human life was appalling. To the civic authority especially, the plague was a nightmare, so persistent and ravaging were its inroads. Many of the records of the fifteenth and sixteenth centuries are explanatory of what was being done to combat the deadly scourge. The means devised were haphazard. Water drawn from the public wells, even when supplemented by private sources, was none too plentiful. The situation was, of course, aggravated by dwellings being built so closely as to exclude all but a minimum of light and fresh air, while insanitary conditions provided an admirable breeding ground for every form of disease. The frequency with which the community was assailed by this terrifying enemy makes it a topic that cannot be overlooked, unpleasant though it be.

What perhaps impresses most is the almost ludicrous means adopted to avert the pest or, if it had got a hold, to stamp it out. In 1530 it was decided that "the mercat . . . be cryit doun for yis contagious pestilins fra ye toune west, and yat na stuff come to yis mercat but victuals, fisch and flesch; and yat nane of Edinburgh, Leith na (nor) otheris suspic place be latten in ye toune . . . without special licens of ye baillies and yat na man travel to Edinburgh or Leith under ye payne of banysching off ye toune." Besides keeping a watchful eye on food-stuffs and a surveillance of persons entering or leaving the town, a "burgess or indweller" having "ony sickness within his house" had to notify the bailies under "paynes of tynsall of lands and gudes and banysching of ye toun." And by a decree of 1539 candlemakers were not to pursue their calling "in ony forgait of the toun" but in "quiet bak rawes." Instructions were also issued to "seik and unclengit persons" not to leave their dwellings on market days under "payne of deid." Nor were they to "cum on the Friday to the kirk," though apparently it was permissible to hear Mass in St Catherine's Chapel. But in spite of these stringent regulations for "eschewing of infection of air" and the threat of the death penalty, the pest could not be kept out of Haddington, and further precautions became necessary. These were put in force in 1545. Infected persons and those "not able to be clengit" were to be removed "to the south quarter outwith Sanct John's Port," and to remain there till certified by the "principal clenger" whose duties must surely have exposed him to extreme peril. Infringement of this regulation incurred the death penalty.

From all accounts the scourge was particularly severe in 1545. Nearly twenty years later the memory of it was still in the minds of the magistrates, who, dreading another visitation, attempted to devise fresh preventive measures. In 1568 their worst fears were confirmed. Again there was intensive activity. Officials were appointed to go through the town to discover the dead and dying. All beggars except natives were ordered to leave, and the old regulations, that no strangers be admitted at the ports and no inhabitants to go to Edinburgh without licence, were strictly enforced. In 1584 a fair was forbidden because of the pest, and in the following year the ports were closed and watchmen posted at each. Four masters were also appointed, each to supervise a quarter of the burgh, which meant that they were to visit every house in their district daily to ascertain if there were any fresh victims.

During the first quarter of the seventeenth century the plague lost none of its virulence. The burgesses had not been careful to keep their retaining walls, or "heid roumes," in repair, with the result that strangers were furtively entering the town. A stern warning was issued in 1602, and not before time, for in the next year the plague again broke out. On 6th September the town council, "understanding that the suspicion of pest daylie increases in divers parts" of the burgh, ordained that "no person shall enter any house where any sick person is." Nor were they to have "any dealing with them until the Magistrates be forseen thereof, and gif (if) ony person dies . . . discharges ony lykwake to be used; and that no person resort to the house . . . except the persons of the house." Disobedience was to be visited by fifteen days' imprisonment, and banishment for those who lodged or entertained persons from suspected areas. It was surely common sense, too, to make a rule whereby no member of the community should be allowed to bring merchandise from an infected district, "especially apples, pears, plums, onions, or carrots." An infraction of this regulation was to be visited with the death penalty.

The poor among the afflicted were supported by the town. Victims who appeared to be recovering were removed to Gladsmuir where they were accommodated in tents and regaled with "ane pund of bread and ane chopin of ale" daily. William Wilson was instructed to bake for "the poor folks put out on the Muir, or other parts within the town inclosit [for] the pest," while the brewer was to give "twentie gallons reasonable ale for every boll of malt." It is hardly necessary to add that the outbreak of 1607 which raged for six years, put a strain on the financial resources. The poor were supported with the utmost difficulty, even with the aid of borrowed money. Hence the regulation that strangers must give security that they would not become a public charge in case of sickness or from any other cause. Late in the seventeenth century the plague again made itself felt but was less harmful. So late as 1721 contagious disease was raging in the town, and preventive measures were announced in the *Edinburgh Evening Courant*. Haddington had also the unenviable distinction of being the first place in Scotland to be visited by the cholera epidemic of 1832. During the three months it lasted there were 125 cases and 57 persons succumbed.

The care of the healthy poor was a problem almost as baffling as that of plague-stricken persons of this class. Haddington, being on the direct route from England, was constantly invaded by swarms of beggars and nondescripts of all sorts, and it was often impossible to discriminate between those "undesirables" and the genuine poor. The magistrates, anxious to do well by the latter class, were frustrated by itinerant beggars and "gangrel" bodies who, during a temporary sojourn, preyed on the charitably-minded, and not seldom were recipients of food and clothing which ought to have been bestowed on the local poor. The magistrates were fertile in proposals for dealing with the problem but in most cases the measures proved ineffectual. In 1532 "ony vacabondis within the toune" were ordered to be expelled. The town's poor were sometimes fed and clothed at the public expense. For example, in 1539 two bailies were instructed to pass through the town with John Fleming "to get alms for him from the good folks" while the town treasurer was to furnish him with clothing. But this was mere tinkering with the problem, as the "uncouth beggars" from other parts deprived the genuine poor. In 1606 the influx was abnormal, and the whole question of mendicancy was seriously canvassed. Once the roving beggar got into the burgh it was not easy to get him out. And the situation was made worse by the fact that the incomers preferred begging to honest work. Even in harvest time, when the need for unskilled labour was great, the professional beggar would not lend a helping hand. After the plague of 1603–1609 persons who were not natives and were without visible means of subsistence were ordered to leave the town. This may have eased the problem but did not remove it. Vagrancy in its worst form continued to flourish.

In the *Register of the Privy Council* a curious local case is reported in the year 1689. Robert Whyt, sometime tenant in Laverocklaw, was confined in the tolbooth at the instance of William Hepburn of Beanston, one of his creditors. Being on the verge of starvation, Whyt offered to make a free disposition of all his goods to those to whom he was indebted. The Court of Session ordered his release, but Robert Hepburn, brother to Beanston, expressed his willingness to aliment Whyt if he were not released. While the other creditors favoured the view that Whyt should be given his freedom, Robert Hepburn appears to have had his way, though he failed to implement his promise. In the circumstances Whyt was forced "to make use of the common method of a poor begging prisoner by hanging over a purse quhilk is far from preserving him from famine iff he had not been supplied by the charitable support of the honourable magistrates of Haddington, quhilk is a great burden to them, as appears by a declaration under their hands." Fortunately the Court of Session relieved them of the "great burden" by ordaining Whyt's creditors to aliment him at the rate of six shillings Scots daily, failing which, he was to be liberated.

For a long time there was no advance on the inefficient methods of the sixteenth century. Not till 1698 was an earnest attempt made to better the position. The magistrates were then empowered "to make choice of ane house within this burgh . . . to be ane hospital for the poor." The town was divided into four quarters and the names of all persons unable to support themselves were sent to the magistrates. The actual sum required for relieving their distress was then ascertained, and the burgesses were assessed proportionately. It was also decided that if a poor person kept a house and did not beg, the rent, if not exceeding £6 Scots, was to be paid out of public funds. Besides feeding the indigent, the council clothed them in very necessitous cases. Attention has been drawn to the case of John Fleming, but more peculiar was that of "Mr Henry Cockburn, *late Provost*, now distressed." The town treasurer was instructed to purchase "shirts, cravats, hats, stockings, and shoes" for this quondam head of the community of Haddington, and to allow "threttie shillings Scots weekly" for his support. It comes as a shock to learn that a former provost had fallen so low as to require his wardrobe to be replenished out of public funds. But Cockburn did not stand alone. The council also resolved "to give in charitie to Margaret Mitchell, relict of umquhill Andrew Malloch, procurator-fiscall of this burgh, and her children ten shillings Scots weekly . . . during the Counsell's pleasure."

So far as the civic fathers were concerned, the enrolment of a former provost, likewise the widow of a town official, among public beneficiaries may have been to soften the blow to offended dignity. At the same time the town council were generally well disposed towards "natives in needy circumstances." While the hospital for the poor was being got ready, begging was permitted on Tuesdays and Saturdays, provided each of the fraternity had the town's authority in the shape of a card bearing the recipient's name and the seal of Haddington—in short, an official licence. Obviously the privileged beggars were natives, and were differentiated from "vagabonds and sturdy beggars," who were to be dealt with unmercifully. They infested the town and begged to such an extent that, in the language of the burgh records, "if not prevented will undoubtedly render the . . . inhabitants . . . almost if not altogether unable to keep their dwelling houses." The punishment meted out to such odious people was confinement in the tolbooth, where they were kept on bread and water for eight days. Thereafter they were conveyed out of the burgh "be the hand of the hangman." In 1764 a later poorhouse was opened. It carried on for ten years, after which the boarding out of paupers was considered the better plan.

In view of the fact that outbreaks of fire were frequent and destructive, as was almost to be looked for in a closely built town, it is surprising that no serious effort was made to combat these till the eighteenth century had almost run its course. Only then did municipalities begin to take precautions against fire. In 1770 Haddington purchased a fire engine, and, significantly, a whole page of the council minutes is taken up with directions how the engine was to be used. Thirteen firemen were appointed, their remuneration being five shillings per annum. One must of course distinguish between what may be termed local fires and the conflagrations that overtook Haddington periodically in olden times. As has been stressed in an earlier chapter, probably no Scottish town suffered more from the wholesale burnings of the English. From the visit of King John in 1216 Haddington was again and again subjected to a baptism of fire by the "auld enemy." Henry III burnt the town in 1244, Edward III in 1355, and Somerset's army in 1547. These burnings were devastating in the extreme, both as regards human life and property, and must have entailed extensive rebuilding more than once. But the most disastrous fire of all cannot be laid at the door of the English. It occurred on 18th May 1598. One side of High Street was almost completely destroyed. Great distress and privation ensued, to relieve which and to provide means whereby inhabitants who had lost their all could rebuild their houses, a general appeal for help was made throughout Scotland. To aid the effort, "Mr James Carmichaell, Minister [of Haddington]" journeyed "with ye Kings Majesties Officers to ye burrows . . . for support to repairing of ye faithfull burgh, presentlie burnt and destroyed," Thomas Spottiswood and Paul Lyle being deputed "to ride with the Provost and Minister." Contributions, some of them liberal, were made by various Scottish burghs, while private persons swelled the total amount. "As their voluntar collection for support of the most indigent persons that had their houses and gear brunt," Edinburgh sent £1027 Scots. The minister of Dunbar subscribed £10 Scots, and Carmichael received £10, 5s. Scots from the minister of Gullane. But doubt prevails as to whether the sums promised were paid in full. Prevention being better than cure, the council enacted that every "heritor within the burgh" provide himself with "ane ladder and ane bucket, for fear of fyre, ilk ladder to be of the height of his house, and to have the same in reddynes under the pane of four pounds."

Another result of the fire of 1598 was the "Coal and Candle" proclamation, which was an instruction to the burghers to acquaint themselves with every device for fire prevention. The proclamation was announced by the town crier nightly except Sunday from Martinmas to Candlemas. Martine records that this functionary, having rung his bell at eight o'clock, went through the streets drawling out in a sing-song manner the "Coal and Candle" proclamation, the words of which were first recorded in Miller's *Lamp of Lothian*. The doleful rhymes are as follows:—

> A' gude men-servants where'er ye be,
> Keep coal and can'le for charitie,
> In bakehouse, brewhouse, barn, and byres,
> It's for your sakes, keep weel your fires:
> Baith in your kitchen and your ha',
> Keep weel your fires, whate'er befa';
> For oftentimes a little spark
> Brings mony hands to meikle wark;
> Ye nourices that hae bairns to keep,
> Tak' care ye fa' na o'er sound asleep:
> For losing o' your gude renown,
> And banishing o' this burrow town.
> It's for your sakes that I do cry,
> Tak' warning by your neighbours by.

Whenever "Coal and Candle" was heard it was the signal for children to go to bed. The crying of this proclamation continued into the middle of last century. Samuel Smiles, author of *Self-Help*, often heard the weird strains of "Coal and Candle" and in his *Autobiography* actually produces the music. The town-crier was rewarded for his services with a pair of shoes and a few trifles. William Souness appears to have been the last to make known the "Coal and Candle" proclamation.

Till 1874 the town depended for its water supply upon a number of public wells (two were in High Street and two in Hardgate). There also were numerous private wells. In 1869 a water company was formed, and at a public meeting it was urged that pipes should be laid for conveyance of the water. But the year 1874 was outstanding in this respect, for then the town acquired a supply of more than one hundred thousand gallons per day of pure spring water from the reservoir at Chesters on the estate of the Earl of Wemyss, constructed at a cost of about £5000. In 1893 a supplementary supply was introduced, involving an outlay of between £6000 and £7000, while in the present century the inhabitants were enabled to draw upon the abundant resources of the reservoir at West Hopes.

In early times Haddington was permitted to hold two fairs annually, at which commercial bargaining was combined with general festivity. According to a charter of James V, dated 1542, the fairs were held on the feast-days of St Peter (29th June) and St John the Baptist (Midsummer Day). It is difficult to say why the two fairs were held with such a brief interval. James VI granted what seemed to be a third fair known as Michaelmas. The alteration from old to new style in the reckoning of time, which took place in the middle of the eighteenth century, led to the custom of holding the fairs early in July and October. At one time the fairs caused a deal of commotion, perhaps it would be more correct to say an upheaval. In 1687 we hear of sixteen men being appointed to keep guard at Michaelmas Fair. Gradually the popularity of these functions waned, so much so that Dr Barclay, the parish minister, writing near the end of the eighteenth century, comments on the fact that neither fair was much frequented. The old-time importance attaching to the fairs was, it appears, over-shadowed by the markets which by and by laid greater stress on trade and less on what was merely spectacular and festive.

James V sanctioned a weekly market, which was held on Saturdays. This arrange-ment continued till 1633 when Charles I granted an additional market which took place on Wednesdays. Later on, the latter market was discontinued, while the Saturday one was changed to Friday. Barclay notes that the Haddington weekly markets of his time were reckoned the greatest in Scotland for all kinds of grain, and that the prices obtained were for many years quoted in the newspapers. Grain, however, was not the only commodity. From remote times there were markets for fish, flesh, meal, and other produce. Most of the markets were held in the High Street. Butter, eggs, and poultry, likewise vegetables, were sold near the Cross. The Flesh market originally was also in the High Street but was removed to Newton Port. East of the tolbooth in Market Street was the site of the Fish market, and to the west of that ancient build-ing wheat was sold. Not till the Corn Exchange was erected was the traditional site of the latter departed from. Oats and barley were in early times disposed of on ground now occupied by the Assembly Room. In 1748 a new Meal market was set up. Numerous bye-laws existed for the regulation of the markets, the general object being that all articles exposed for sale should not be prejudiced economically. For instance, in 1580, it was made obligatory that no staple goods be placed on the causeway on market days, the intention presumably being that business on the part of those who had a right to be there should not be hindered.

The breakaway from the past and the introduction of new and enlightened ideas which eventually led to the conditions that prevail to-day came, so far as Haddington is concerned, near the close of the eighteenth century. Obsolete ways and means which, with but slight modification, had held sway for centuries, gradually fell into the background, their place being taken by progressive ideas. Trade and the means of communication and transport rapidly improved, and before the nineteenth century was well advanced there was no comparison between the old Haddington and the new. Progress in almost every direction was noted—in higher standards of domestic comfort, in the lapsing of antiquated customs and out-of-date methods, in the modernisation of buildings, both public and private. More money was in circulation, trade and industry having become more prosperous, and the whole atmosphere of the town was sweeter and more salutary.

Among the important changes of this period was the introduction of the railway. There was much dissatisfaction, however, and with some reason, that it was not brought nearer the centre of the burgh. When, in 1846, the North British Railway Company fixed the site of the station on the post-road to Edinburgh, and almost beyond the precincts of the town, the inhabitants presented a memorial suggesting that the railway station should be placed behind Maitlandfield, in what is now the Neilson Park; but the Company were adamant, and so it remains where it always has been. The coming of the railway was not altogether an unmixed blessing for Haddington. Being the terminus of a branch line, most of the traffic which had formerly passed through the town was diverted, while travellers to and from the south journeyed by the direct east coast route. The result was that Dunbar became more prominent, while Had-dington found itself to some extent in the backwater. The trade of the burgh was materially reduced, while the carriers' carts, which in the old days were such a picturesque feature, almost disappeared. Jane Welsh Carlyle, revisiting Haddington in 1849, just

Haddington House. Sidegate.

The building with roundel (now demolished) was the home of the Hay Donaldsons.

after the opening of the branch railway, remarks on the change. Much of the life and animation which characterised the town in the days of her youth had gone, the streets, except on market days, were comparatively empty, hotels and inns languished, stage coaches no longer rumbled over the causeway, while a rather sombre air seemed to brood over the place. Admittedly the railway brought some advantages, but these, it is feared, were outweighed by disadvantages.

CHAPTER IX

Municipal Affairs

IT has been acutely remarked that history is an approximation to the truth rather than the truth itself. Nowhere perhaps is this more strikingly displayed than in the study of the early government of the royal burghs of Scotland. The internecine wars led to the disappearance of the records, with the result that it is impossible to furnish a wholly authentic view of the subject. And so far as internal administration is concerned, Haddington is in the same category as any other royal burgh. Much that is stated must therefore be regarded as provisional, since the matter is full of pitfalls.

Take the provostship as an example. It has been confidently asserted and widely believed that the office was a creation of the sixteenth century, whereas in the Ragman Rolls of 1296 one may read the name of "Alisaundre le Barker, provost of the burgh of Hadingtone." At the same time it seems safe to affirm that when, on 9th October 1543, the whole community, being assembled in the tolbooth by handbell, elected, "all with one assent," William Broun, of Stottencleuch, to be provost, a new chapter in the municipal life of Haddington had begun. Two features of Broun's election are noticeable. In the first place, it was democratic, he being raised to the chief magistracy by the burghers duly and regularly brought together for this specific purpose. Secondly, the provostship is referred to as a gift to Broun. Whether his successors were similarly honoured we have no means of knowing. But the important point is that Broun derived his authority, not from a clique, but from the townsfolk as a whole, a feature which gave place not long after to a state of affairs that was anything but democratic. Instead of the early form of "government by the people," there was substituted a self-elective system which existed without intermission till the advent of burgh reform in the first half of the nineteenth century—a system, it is superfluous to add, that provided excellent opportunities for those who were concerned more about their own interests than the welfare of the burgh.

When Broun was made provost, two bailies were elected to serve with him. Both provost and bailies were chosen for one year only, but when the period expired the provost was re-elected "for all ye dayis of his life." This arrangement, however, did not last long. In 1554, James Oliphant, who had already served as provost, was again chosen, but the council, in deference to his wish that "every honest man be provost in tyme cumin his zeir abowt," agreed that he should not be called upon to serve a further term. The council, however, were in doubt as to the legality of their action, and sent a bailie to Edinburgh to seek advice. The result was that Oliphant was allowed to delay acceptance for three years. From which we may conclude that the chief magistrate's chair was not always coveted. There were often burdensome duties. It fell to the provost to bring municipal grievances to the notice of the Parliament in Edinburgh, or elsewhere, which might mean several journeys and abstention from private affairs for a long period. Besides considerable expense was frequently incurred which an economical town council were slow to meet. Indeed the provost had now and then to defray his own charges. It is conceivable therefore that the office was sometimes declined through no lack of public spirit but simply because its assumption implied more time, energy, and money than was consistent with the oversight of personal affairs.

Moreover, in confused and distracted times, when local matters impinged upon national, the provost's position was doubly precarious. He might be saddled with the responsibility of leading the able-bodied townsmen in battle, or be forced to comply with distasteful royal behests. James VI, for example, capriciously interfered more than once as regards the provostship. But when all is said, the office was recognised as one of honour and distinction. At first it carried with it certain emoluments, but in 1552 it was ordained that the chief magistrate "have na mayr fee but vj merks."

In or before the year 1552 there was inaugurated the time-honoured custom of the retiring council electing its successor. The council once comprised thirty persons, seven of whom were merchants, eleven "labourers of ground" and maltmen, and twelve craftsmen. But in 1655 the Convention of Royal Burghs reduced the number of councillors to twenty-five—sixteen merchants and nine craftsmen, a figure which seems to have remained till well into last century. It will thus be seen that whereas under the old constitution the merchants were decidedly in the minority, they were now given very definite preponderance. Nor was this all. The magistracy for the most part was composed of "trafficking merchants." Only one craftsman could aspire to the office. There was also a baron-bailie for Nungate and another for the town's lands at Gladsmuir. In 1761 it was decreed that gold medals hung with blue and gold cords should be worn by magistrates; but the cords have long since been replaced with gold chains.

As there is a blank in the town's records from 30th December 1545 to 15th March 1551–52 it is problematic whether the council fulfilled its intention of having William Broun, of Stottencleugh, as provost for life. Probably he held office during the siege of Haddington. When the records are resumed, Thomas Wauss (Vass) was chief magistrate. He was the first native to be provost as well as the first bailie to be promoted. Wauss's house, only demolished in 1941, was next a vennel leading from Hardgate to the Tyne. The mansion had crow-stepped gables and a sundial. At both ends there were gates, which the Council resolved should remain open from five o'clock in the morning till nine at night. At the Court of Schillinghill, which dealt with irregularities at the mills, Wauss was accused of "grynding of yair corne fra ye commoun Mylnis of ye said burgh." Yet he was loyal, for in 1542 he "offerit his cart to ye bailies to serve the Kyng."

From 1594 to 1598 and from 1605 to 1608 the provost was Sir William Seton of Kyllismore, Sheriff of Midlothian, Postmaster for Scotland, and a commissioner to Parliament. He was, therefore, a person of some consequence. Seton seems to have been popular, but, suspected of leanings towards the Roman Church, the council sought the royal commands as to whether he could remain provost. The king's reply was in the negative, and so the council had to part with a chief magistrate whom they liked personally. Another provost of note, bearing the same patronymic, held office during the Cromwellian regime. In 1657 Provost Seton was Haddington's representative at the proclamation of "My Lord Protector" at Edinburgh. There, too, he conferred with Monck as to whom the Haddington burghs should elect commissioner to the Parliament at Westminster. Subsequently Seton himself sat in the Parliament of 1661, to which he presented a petition proposing that the reddendo of Haddington's charter should be altered as regards the money to be tendered. The council sent this provost on various missions. In 1659 Seton again interviewed Monck with the object of having the number of troops quartered in the burgh reduced by one half. Despite his usefulness, Seton was not immune from severe and well-merited criticism, and at least on one occasion was imprisoned. In 1663 he was accused of acting arbitrarily in liberating certain prisoners, including two Samuelston witches.

The following year found Seton in conflict with a group of prominent burgesses—George Forrest, John Sleich, Robert Naesmith, and William Swinton among the number—who petitioned the Convention of Royal Burghs for redress of disorders committed by the provost "to the violation of the laws of the kingdom, acts of burrowes, and eminent prejudice of the said burgh." While the action was pending, Seton, with his "friends and favourits," summoned the complainers to a meeting of the town council. The latter complied, and were "immediately put in close prison," deprived of their burgess-ships, fined £100 each, and ordered to be kept in captivity till the following June, "or longer."

Seton's provostship ended abruptly in 1667, when he was confined in the tolbooth of Edinburgh for acting illegally and tyrannically towards two East Lothian men. The circumstances are reported at length in the *Register of the Privy Council*. The complaint was at the instance of George Seton of Barns and John Hay of Aberlady. On 8th March 1667–68 they were "sitting about their owne affaires in the house of David Kyle in Haddington" when Provost Seton officiously intruded, and "after some needlesse and frivolous expostulations, without any just reason given him, did . . . comand the toune officiers, who were standing ready . . . , to enter the roume where the . . . complainers were and to take them to the . . . tolbuith." On the latter asking "by what authoritie they took upon them so to doe," Provost Seton pointed a halbert at Seton of Barns, then drew a sword, and ordered the removal of the complainers to the tolbooth where they lay for two nights until released by "ane order from the Commissioner." "Which ryotts and insolency," the petition continues, "are most odious and insufferable . . . considering the complainers are neighbours to the town of Haddington, who have always lived in a good correspondence with the inhabitants." Although the complaint was an *ex parte* statement, the Privy Council found it "sufficiently proved," and the offending provost was ordered "to crave pardon of the Councill and also of the saids persewars and to be caryd prissoner to the tolbuith of Edinburgh and ther to be keept during the Lord Commissioner his Grace's pleasur."

Provost Seton died in 1682. He is buried in the ruined portion of St Mary's, where there is an ornate monument with a long inscription in sonorous Latin which, in the manner of long ago, superlatively extols his virtues as well as sheds light on his career. He was "by birth a citizen of this town of Haddington . . . and by his pedigree descended from the most ancient and most noble family of Seton, as deriving his original in a right line from the house of Seton of Northrig." The inscription goes on to tell that Seton was provost "for the space of ten years together," that he was known for his "fidelity, prudence, and moderation," and that he was "altogether averse to covetousness, revenge, injustice, or hatred against his fellow-citizens." Apparently the provost's faults lay gently on him, or perhaps the compilers of his epitaph turned a blind eye to them. Anyhow the discrepancy between his record, as here revealed, and the testimony of his tombstone is rather glaring.

During the Revolution period municipal affairs were largely influenced by John Sleich and his son, who bore the same name. Father and son belonged to the merchant class and were well connected locally. The elder Sleich was born in 1595 and died in 1686. The inscription on his monument (now gone) in the choir of St Mary's acclaimed him "a very famous man" and said that he discharged the duties of the provostship with "the greatest commendation." The younger Sleich was also provost.

On 14th March 1689 he represented Haddington at the Convention of Estates which met in Edinburgh, and voted "for preserving the Protestant religion." It was this provost, too, who consulted the Lord Advocate regarding Elizabeth Moodie, who was charged with witchcraft and whose case is noted in Sinclair's *Satan's Invisible World Discovered*. When others were charged with this delinquency, Sleich went to Edinburgh with their "confessions and delations" and obtained "commissions for trial and assize."

In spite of his epitaph, Sleich seems to have been as human as the rest of us. Under date 6th May 1680, Fountainhall, in his *Historical Notices of Scotish Affairs*, writes: "Ther ware mutuall libells by John Sleich, provost of Hadington, and George Cockburn, bailzie ther, against one another, for verball injuries and calumnious expressions. It was referred to friends." Which is fairly clear indication that there had been wrangling in the town council. Fountainhall is also our authority for saying that in January 1687 Sleich raised an action against his (Sleich's) tenant "for breach of arrestment, convocating the leidges, and stealling away his cornes on Sunday"—another proof that the provost was not slow to assert his rights. Further light on this incident was shed a year later when, says Fountainhall, "John Sleigh, Provost of Hadington, 'prosecuted' Steill, his tenant in Greengelt, for carrieing away his cornes on the Sabbath night with ane convocation of 63 carts, to defraud him of his rent, and after ane arreistment was laid on; and for beatting and bruising him . . . Steill had a reconvention, that his master had incarcerat him after ane standing suspension intimat, and had charged him for terms he was payed of. Both were admitted to probation."

During the industrial revolution Haddington had an outstanding provost in Samuel Brown, who held office from 1834 to 1836. Brown, whom Dr Thomas Chalmers dubbed "the philanthropist," did a great deal for the social, educational, and religious welfare of the town. He was a very active member of a society for scientific study which became the Haddington School of Arts. But Provost Brown earned a reputation more than local by his "itinerating libraries." These were put in operation in 1817 and were peculiar to East Lothian. His first step was to buy 200 volumes, two-thirds of which had "a moral and religious tendency." The remainder comprised "books of travel, agriculture, mechanical arts, and popular science." The volumes, having been divided into four assorted sets of 50 each, were sent to Aberlady, Saltoun, Tyninghame, and Garvald, where they were "under the superintendence of gratuitous librarians." There they remained for two years, at the end of which period they were exchanged for another set. By 1836 no fewer than 47 libraries (or sets) were in "circulatory motion" within the county.

Two Victorian provosts who rendered conspicuous service were David Stevenson and A. Mathieson Main. The former was three times provost, and died in 1890. Proprietor of the George Hotel in its palmy days, Stevenson was closely identified with the public life of the town for more than thirty years, and the memory of his services is perpetuated in the Stevenson foot-bridge at West Haugh. He was actively interested in the Volunteer movement and took part in the first great Review in Edinburgh in 1860. His son, George H. Stevenson, was sheriff-clerk of the county and town clerk of Haddington. The latter office is now held by Provost Stevenson's grandson, Mr A. C. Stevenson. The other notable Victorian provost, A. Mathieson Main, carried on a drapery business in Hardgate for almost half a century. During his provostship the Victoria Bridge over the Tyne was erected. In the carrying out of the scheme Main rendered important service, and his name appears on the inscribed plates affixed to the bridge. He was a Justice of the Peace, a member of the local

School Board, and a Free Churchman. Nor ought there to be omitted a third Victorian provost—John Brook. A local merchant, he will be always remembered as the moving spirit in the establishment of the Knox Institute. This provost was the father of Colonel Alexander Brook, referred to in Chapter VII.

But to pass to other aspects of the municipal life of Haddington. In bygone centuries there were various town officials performing duties that have long been obsolete. Quaint, picturesque figures, most of them were, displayed against a social background which it is difficult now to visualise. The heyday of these officials was in the sixteenth and seventeenth centuries, though some, lagging superfluous on the stage, projected themselves into later times. The wheels of existence turned slowly, and as the channels of communication were few and restricted, the corporate feeling was stronger than it is to-day. Migration from one town to another was of rare occurrence. Consequently the members of a small community living constantly together and crossing each other's path daily, conduced to a familiarity that assumed the complexion of a large family.

The town officers were not always popular, some of their duties being distasteful to the inhabitants. But what perhaps brought them most disfavour was an avariciousness which took the form of extorting fees. No doubt the regular remuneration was paltry, but this did not entitle them to resort to unworthy means to augment it. Anyhow there were often bitter complaints. In 1733 protests were made against the town officers demanding "presents" from well-known inhabitants, also from "gentlemen at their houses . . . at the time of the holidays." This practice, however, was peremptorily stopped by the simple means of increasing wages by £4 Scots annually.

Of these old-world public servants the town drummer and the town piper stand in the forefront. Despite similarity of function, the two offices were distinct. The piper is mentioned so far back as 1542, but the earliest reference to the drummer that has been discovered is in 1572, when the town treasurer was instructed to buy a swasche (i.e. a drum) for the town's service. One of the drummer's chief duties was to rouse people in the morning and to see that they went to bed at a reasonable hour of night. This official paraded the streets beating his "swasche" at four o'clock in the morning and again at eight in the evening. In 1598 it was resolved that if the drummer failed to perambulate the town in fine weather he was to be fined forty shillings. Should the weather be "fowle whereby the swasches may not gang openly upon the gate (street)," the drum was to be beaten under cover of a stairhead.

Early in the seventeenth century the drummer was charged with the summoning of the inhabitants when proclamations had to be made, or on muster days, or when the Riding of the Marches was announced. In 1613 his remuneration was twenty merks, and out of this trifling sum he was expected to keep his drum in repair.

There exists a coloured drawing by R. Mabon (a local artist) of the drummer and piper in the latter half of the eighteenth century. Andrew Simpson was drummer and James Livingstone piper. Both were old soldiers and are said to have fought in the battle of Fontenoy. The drummer's uniform consisted of "ane doublet of Lyonis cameis, ane pair of blue breeks, and schone." We hear less of the town piper. In 1662 John Reid from North Berwick was appointed. He was given the same wages and wore the same livery as the drummer. Ten years later each functionary was allowed twelve shillings with which to provide the necessary uniform. The last town piper seems to have been Donald Macgregor, who was appointed in 1824. The office of town drummer also survived into last century.

The town bellman comes into the records as early as 1532. One of his duties was

Town Drummer, Andrew Simpson, and Piper, Jas. Livingstone, with Harry Barrie, a "character."

[*To face p.* 98.

to keep beggars "furth of ye kyrk and ye daggs." When he was not ringing the town bell (as he had to do several times daily), or attending to the town clock, or summoning the townsfolk by handbell, the bellman employed himself in grave-digging. If the person to be interred was an adult he received sixteen pence, but if a child half that sum. Then there was the lockman, who had the custody of prisoners in the tolbooth. He subsisted on perquisites rather than wages. In 1766 there were meagre supplies of meal and the lockman was a loser; but the town council granted him twenty shillings as compensation.

Akin to the office of lockman was that of hangman who, if all accounts be true, was assigned various jobs that had no connection with his primary duty. That the hangman's post was not coveted need cause no surprise. Indeed it often went abegging, and the town was hard driven to get a person to perform the disagreeable duty. In 1619 the problem of filling the post was ingeniously surmounted. One, William Elliot, from Hawick, was sentenced to be hanged for stealing sheep on the Letham estate but was offered a free pardon provided he agreed to be hangman for Haddington. Elliot accepted, and so instead of being hanged himself he hanged others. Although there was a Gallow Green at the west end of the town (on the site of which was found in modern times what was believed to be the stone into which the gibbet was fixed), the records are silent as to persons expiating their crimes there. Most of the hangings took place at Nungate Bridge, on a hook (still existing) below the west arch. In 1596 "the juge decernt and ordained George and John Hallis to be tane to ye cleek of the brig and yair to be hangit quhill they be deid." Again in 1617 two men, whose hands were tied behind their backs, were conveyed to "ye westmost bow of the brig" and hanged. In 1623 the hangman was dismissed because he refused to place a ladder at the "bow or pend" of Nungate Bridge in order that John Thomson might be hanged.

From a minute of 6th November 1787 we learn that a town-herd was included among the local public servants. One may guess the service he rendered. In the year mentioned his remuneration was considered "too low," and the levelling-up process took the form of allowing the town-herd to receive one pound Scots from a burgess and half a crown from a non-burgess for every "cow or other beast" looked after. Finally, there was the officer who bore the rather cryptic title of "Examiner of Goods." Even more puzzling is that the term was interchangeable with that of sergeant. This official had to do with the customs and in a secondary sense with commodities sold in open market, which it was his duty to see reached the recognised standard. In 1539 ale and wine "cunnars" and fish and flesh pressers (*i.e.* searchers) were appointed, and in the burgh records allusion is made to the "sear" of the flesh market and the "keipper" of the markets for wheat, barley, and meal.

The history of Haddington in regard to burgess-ship is uncertain. There were, of course, matters common to all the royal burghs but the practice was not always uniform, and, as frequently happens, it is the exceptions that are historically interesting. The freedom of the burgh did not belong to all the members of the community but confined to a class known as burgesses. Their admission by the magistrates was subject to conditions which varied from time to time. The term "freeman" had nothing to do with personal liberty, but was synonymous with the rights of citizenship as then understood. Burgesses were required to reside within the burgh and swear fealty to the king, the magistrates, and the community. Certain obligations attached to the distinction. A burgess had to contribute to the town's funds, attend the head courts of the burgh, take his turn in watching and warding, and accept such offices as the law imposed. But there were also privileges. Only burgesses could engage in commerce, and they alone could have business relations with foreign merchants. Moreover, the right of electing magistrates was entirely in the hands of the burgesses.

Judging by scattered references in the records, burgess-ship in Haddington deflected to some extent from the normal. At all events certain anomalies are revealed which are difficult to account for. In the seventeenth century, if not later, an undue proportion of the aristocracy and their retainers was enrolled. Some of the latter were even menials and all belonged to a shifting population. The most glaring instance of patrician influence occurred (as has been already noted) in the case of the Duke of Lauderdale. Doubtless presuming on his position as the most powerful man in Scotland, Lauderdale in 1672 contrived matters so that more than fifty members of his household (most of them ordinary servants) were made burgesses of Haddington, these appearing in armour at their creation. That the privilege should have been conferred with such open-handed liberality is understandable enough. What perplexes is that the Duke should have been anxious to have so many of his retainers created burgesses, unless it were merely a gesture to magnify his own importance. On the other hand, what did burgess-ship signify in the case of persons who had no connection with trade?

The whole episode rather suggests that the burgess-ship of Haddington had become cheap. Yet the fact that between 1669 and 1715 about seven hundred persons were given the freedom of the burgh—an average of fifteen a year—is proof that the admissions were not excessive. As the eighteenth century progressed there grew up a tendency to bestow the burgess-ship promiscuously, but steps were eventually taken to counteract the practice. While gentlemen's servants were eligible, it was made a rule that the Guildry was not to be inserted in tickets given to such. Furthermore, in 1738, it was resolved that no gratis tickets be given to any of the military except commissioned officers, or to any trader in the burgh, or to any entitled to a heritable ticket.

In the Douglas Collection preserved in the Register House there is a thin volume, labelled "Proceedings at a Poll Election of Haddington Town Council," which sheds an interesting sidelight on burgess-ship in the eighteenth century. Apparently there had been a dispute, and a poll was demanded, authority for which was obtained from Whitehall. Preliminary to a poll it was necessary to find out the persons entitled to vote, and this was ascertained by cumbrous methods worthy of the Circumlocution Office described in Dickens's *Little Dorrit*. The books of the Dean of Guild had to be consulted for persons made burgesses on and after 15th November 1669. Included in the seven hundred names recorded are those of Lauderdale's servants, likewise their particular occupations—coachman, flesher, confectioner, postilion, violer, etc. Heritable burgesses admitted subsequent to 1719, and numbering sixty, were also entitled to vote. From these two lists the Poll Register was compiled. In recording his vote each burgess had to sign an "Assurance" to the following effect:—

I do, in the sincerity of my heart, acknowledge and declare that His Majesty King George is the only lawful and undoubted Sovereign of this realm, as well *de jure*, that is of right, King, as *de facto*, that is in the possession and exercise of the Government. And therefore do sincerely and faithfully promise and engage that I will, with heart and hand, life and goods, maintain and defend his Majesty's title and government against the person pretended to be Prince of Wales during the life of the late King James, and since his decease, pretending to be and taking upon himself the style and title of King of England by the name of James the Third, or of Scotland, by the name of James the Eighth, or the style and title of King of Great Britain, and his adherents and all other enemies who either by open or secret attempts shall disturb or disquiet his Majesty in the possession and exercise thereof.

MUNICIPAL AFFAIRS

In his *Early Burgh Organisation of Scotland* Dr David Murray states that, so far as organisation, property, and government are concerned, there was originally little difference between royal burghs and burghs of barony. In the administration of justice they possessed much the same machinery, but very little can be said as to how this was exercised. Theoretically the civil and criminal jurisdiction of the burgh courts was fairly wide. It included all crimes except the four pleas of the Crown, likewise murder taken red-hand. But in practice the action of these courts was limited. Besides the ordinary jurisdiction of magistrates of royal burghs, those of Haddington had at one time the jurisdiction of sheriffs within the royalty; but this fell into desuetude. In attempting to describe the functions and powers of local courts we are treading controversial ground. Indeed the subject is surrounded with many problems, not least the inter-relation of the various tribunals, that an authoritative statement in the present state of knowledge is impossible.

In Haddington there were the Head Burgh Court, Burgh Court, Court of Council, Guild Court, Sheriff Court, Assize, and a judicial body known by the queer title of the Court of Schillinghill. The majority of these courts flourished in early times. When the *Curia Quatuor Burgorum* existed, an appeal from sentences of the burgh court was made to the royal Chamberlain at Haddington, who summoned the Assize, consisting of burgesses from the royal burghs. The executive of the burghs possessed judicial as well as magisterial functions, but if a distinction was made between the duties of the town council and the burgh court it has never been precisely stated. Meetings of the burgh court and town council were often entered in the same volume. It is therefore a rational assumption that these two bodies were closely connected. We also know that the Head Burgh Court (sometimes called the "Heid Court of Counsell") met thrice annually, and that the Assize, consisting of a score of members, usually met in the tolbooth. Both civil and criminal causes came before it. In 1425 the Assize adjudicated in a dispute over a property claim, and in 1531 the same body settled the price of butcher meat. Four years later mention is made of an Assize at the burgh court. We find the Assize, too, issuing strict orders that none "pass with the kirk brod [1] but honest men," issuing instructions as to the ringing of the town bell on occasions of mourning, ordaining the parish clerk to "uphold the lamp with oil that hangs in the choir" of St Mary's, and even deciding a claim for killing a pig. The functions of the Assize thus ranged over a wide and heterogeneous field.

A few stray facts have been gleaned about the Court of Council. In 1532 this body, consisting of twenty-two members, gave directions as to the order of the crafts in the procession on Corpus Christi Day. Evidently some importance attached to this court, for the bailies decreed that "if ony of ye Counsall (*i.e.* town council) comes not to the Court of Counsell," he having been warned by "ane officier or by the sound of the handbell," he was to be fined eight shillings.

Much investigation requires to be done concerning the history of the Sheriff Court. In terms of James V's charter (1542) the provost and bailies of Haddington had "full powers and liberty to open, fence, and hold sheriff courts." The Dean of Guild Court in Haddington was constituted in the middle of the seventeenth century. Archibald Sydserff, merchant in Edinburgh, in response to a request, submitted the views of the magistrates and council of the capital, while William Thomson, town clerk of Edinburgh, represented the merchants of Haddington, who were "suitors" for the gild. On 28th May 1659 the Decree Arbitral was accepted. The first dean was James Spottiswoode, who presided over a court comprising sixteen merchants and nine

---

[1] Collection box.

craftsmen, the latter number being made up of seven deacons, one bailie, and one councillor. The Guild Court had the oversight of trade, and adjudicated on all matters concerning neighbourhood, *i.e.* the sites of buildings in relation to others, besides their actual erection. It also saw to it that weights and measures were of legal standard. In early times there was stern supervision in this matter. In 1543 a first offence meant outlawry, the second an accusation of theft, and the third expulsion from the town. Keepers of booths were obliged to bring their firlots and pecks to the tolbooth to be tested. If found correct, they received the official stamp. Merchants were compelled to have their weights ringed with iron.

From courts of law and administration we pass by a natural transition to petty misdemeanours and their punishment. Miller in his *Lamp of Lothian* devotes considerable space to the imaginary crimes and dark superstitions which, in the sixteenth and seventeenth centuries, led to revolting scenes and relegated many a luckless wretch to the faggot. The references are chiefly to demonology and witchcraft, of which Haddington and East Lothian generally seems to have had more than a proportionate share. But there also was a substantial volume of actual wrongdoing, although what perhaps strikes one most in reviewing the shady annals of the period is the truculent, and not seldom barbaric, methods by which the civic fathers attempted to curb what in many cases were hardly serious offences. For having stolen a cow James Hume in 1555 was adjudged "to have his lug takkit (nailed) to the tron," and for cutting young trees another delinquent was, in the following year, drummed out of the town and not allowed to return. Another offender was subjected to remorseless flogging. He was ordered to be bound to a cart "and to gang through all ye strettis . . . and ye lokman (jailor) to stryke him with ane wand . . . and to haif ane fresh wand at ilk streit end." And having undergone this ferocious castigation, the victim was to "forsweir the toune," while there hung over him the prospect of hanging should he ever return. As further examples of the kind of punishment meted out to evildoers, we may cite the case of John Sharp and William Mason, who must have rued the day when they broke the town clock—whether wilfully or otherwise is not stated. Having passed "in lenyn clayths on Corpus Christi Day afore ye Sacrament, all ye tyme of ye procession," they were "to offer to ye baillies in name of ye toune ilk ane pund of walx," as well as to ask their forgiveness. They were also to pay for the repair of the clock, but if they defaulted they were to be banished for a whole year.

The cases of witchcraft are an unwelcome reminder of the superstition of an age that had surrendered long before to the enlightened tenets of the Reformed faith—a superstition, be it remembered, that was not confined to the unintelligent and illiterate but haunted the understandings of knowledgeable people. The case of James VI is notorious. In 1649 the Estates granted a commission to the magistrates, ministers, and elders of Haddington for the trial of three women charged with witchcraft. If found guilty, the judges were to "strangle them and burn their bodies to death." Unfortunately, the result of the trial has not been ascertained. Again, in 1677, the provost and bailies were directed by the Privy Council to try Elizabeth Moodie, whose case has been already referred to. The widow of John Moore, she was apprehended on a charge of having entered "into paction with the devil" and done other mysterious things. Lord Fountainhall pungently remarks on "that miserable bodie, Lisie Mudie" who, besides confessing to being a witch, "did also delate 5 other weemen in the toune of Hadington (two of them midwives) and a man as guilty of the same willanie; and, being confronted with them, I saw hir constantly . . . abide at hir delation, and bind them with particular tokens and circumstances, but they denied all." Fountainhall adds: "I did see the man's bodie searcht and prick't in 2 sundrie places . . . he seem'd to find pain, but no blood followed, tho the pins were the lenth of one's finger, and one of them was thrust in to the head." [1]

This old Scots judge laments that Haddington should give "harbor to such unhappie creatures," and goes on to cite the case of "Margaret Kirkwood in Hadington that hangs hir selfe; some say shee was so strangled by the devill and witches." Margaret Kirkwood "being wealthie, their ware severalls who put in for the gift of hir escheat; amongs others the Toune of Hadington, not only upon the account that they ware shireffs within them selfes . . . but because the toune of Hadington hes a particular clause in their charter of erection exeiming [exempting] them from the shireff's jurisdiction, by which they are in the present use and possession of repledging their burgesses from the shireff." [2] While narrating gruesome details regarding the punishment of witches, Fountainhall himself was not wholly emancipated from the superstition. He believed in the machinations of Satan in visible form, notwithstanding that he styles the evil one a "grand impostor." "The most part of the creatures that are thus deluded," he writes, "by this grand impostor and ennemy of mankind . . . are ather seduced by malice, poverty, ignorance, or covetousnes; and it's the unspeakable mercy and providence of our good God that that poor devill hes not the command of money (tho we say he is master of all the mines and hid treasures in the earth), else he would debauch the greatest part of the world." [3]

One of the women mentioned by Fountainhall as delated against was Margaret Phin, another "indweller in Hadington." She petitioned the Privy Council for her release from the tolbooth where, she declared, she was illegally detained. There is pathos in her circumstances. "A persone near eightie years of age," she was "most calumniouslie accused by ane unhappie woman who suffered at Hadington for witchcraft [i.e. Elizabeth Moodie], saying the petitioner was also guilty as she, whereupon the magistrates . . . without any further tryall or probation, put the petitioner in the tolbuith, where she hath remayned these three moneths bygaine in a most deplorable conditione both in respect of her great aige and sorrow for the losse of her good name, she being a person allevayes living under a very good report." All that can be learned further of Margaret Phin's case is that the Privy Council appointed a commission for examining this venerable person and others similarly charged. Her statement that Elizabeth Moodie tried to incriminate her along with other women is borne out by Fountainhall. But apart altogether from the trustworthiness of her evidence, the magistrates exceeded their powers by imprisoning her without investigating the details of her case.

And if witches were given short shrift, so were conventiclers who, in the Covenanting period, were a formidable body in East Lothian. In 1678 a proclamation was read at the Cross of Haddington warning the inhabitants to refrain from attending field meetings and listening to the fiery utterances of "vagrant, intercommuned, or rebellious preachers." Those acting contrary to the proclamation were to be punished "with all severity," such gatherings being held by the Government "in just horrour and detestation."

In the eighteenth century witchcraft was supplanted by smuggling—a more practical and profitable form of delinquency and marking significantly the change-over from ecclesiastical to secular interests. Smuggling was rife along the Lothian coast, much of the contraband being conveyed from Fife ports. Determined efforts were made

---

[1] *Historical Notices of Scotish Affairs*, i, 145-146. [2] *Ibid.*, i, 144-145. [3] *Ibid.*, i, 146-147.

for its suppression, not so much because it was illicit, as because it interfered detrimentally with the sale of liquors manufactured locally. This was really the basis of the town council's action when, in August 1744, it resolved to discourage smuggling as "fatal to the true interests of the community in so far as it lessened the consumption of spirits produced within its own borders." In accordance with the spirit of this resolution, certain people in the county made public their intention to favour alcoholic beverages of local manufacture instead of French brandy which hitherto had been sold in considerable quantities. The fact was deplored that "an expensive and luxurious way of living had shamefully crept in upon all ranks of people who, neglecting the good and wholesome produce of their own country, had got into the habit of an immoderate use of French wines and spirits in public houses and private families, which liquors were in a great part clandestinely imported and smuggled through the country." Tea-drinking was also discouraged. Among "the people of lower rank" the custom, we are told, was indulged in to an "extravagant excess." Tea then sold at ten shillings per pound. Though this sum represented more than it would do now, the price must surely have been beyond the means of the class of people desiderated. Was this attempt to curb the tea-drinking habit an astute bid for the consumption of local spirits?

But to return to the catalogue of minor offences. These show rather curious anomalies. In 1730 barbers were forbidden to dress the wigs of their customers on Sundays, or even to shave those who frequented their establishments on that day. This transgression, obviously a concession to religious susceptibilities, meant a penalty of £10 Scots, one half of which was given to the informer and the other half to the poor. In 1769 riding horses at a gallop through the streets was regarded as an offence, and rightly so. Nor can there be much sympathy for those persons who were fined sixpence for each of their pigs found wandering.

In 1738 six burgesses were appointed constables within the royalty. Very miscellaneous were their duties. One was "to challenge any person within the burgh or liberties thereof that shall be found wearing pistols or daggers," another to apprehend "all vagabonds, sturdy beggars, and Egyptians (gypsies)," a third to search public houses for "drunkards, Sabbath-breakers, and blasphemers." Personal attendance, and we may well suppose unpleasant duties, became seriously inconvenient if not repugnant, and gradually the view obtained that the town would be more effectually protected by a paid police. But this idea was not realised till much later. The "jougs" as a mode of punishment existed to near the end of the eighteenth century. In 1781 the town officers were dismissed for refusing to tie the hands of a woman convicted of theft, who had been ordered to stand in the "jougs." And so late as 1785 a thief was placed in the pillory with a board across his breast indicating the nature of his offence. The almost unbelievable treatment meted out to petty offenders contrasts with the lenient interpretation of confinement in the tolbooth. A prisoner might entertain his friends, who came and went as they pleased. Occasionally the jail door was left unlocked and incarcerated persons escaped. Another of the vagaries of the tolbooth was the employment of a piper to lessen the boredom of the captives.

The clamant need for burgh reform was first agitated in 1784. The obsolete, cumbersome, and inequitable method of electing town councils had long been apparent, but if the movement was to be crowned with success it was necessary that an influential municipality should take the initiative. This came about appositely in the above-mentioned year when the Lord Provost of Edinburgh, who was also preses of the Convention of Royal Burghs, issued a circular letter urging the need for reforming the constitution of burghs, as well as the encouragement of linen manufacture, extension of the fisheries, and coastal improvement. Haddington duly received a copy of the Lord Provost's letter, but its attitude was obscurantist. Its Parliamentary repre-sentative was instructed to support the increase of linen manufacture but to take no action in the case of burgh reform and fishery extension. The workings of local government sometimes are past finding out, and the policy as regards burgh reform is a case in point. As it was, the civic authorities of Haddington had no reason to fear that such a measure would be placed on the statute book, for the French Revolution and the reign of terror that ensued retarded its passing for more than a generation, the general feeling being that similar excesses would result if burgh reform were accomplished.

Not till 1818 was the movement given a fresh impetus. Lord Archibald Hamilton, M.P. for Lanarkshire, became chairman of a non-official committee of inquiry regarding the condition of the Scottish burghs. In this capacity he requested various towns to fill up a questionnaire. Haddington, however, persisted in its non-committal attitude, pleading that the communication was unnecessary in view of the fact that burgh reform was being considered by a committee of the House of Commons. The report of Lord Archibald Hamilton's committee, which was published in 1822, demonstrated the existence of deep-rooted abuses, the chief being the self-election of town councils. In the House of Commons Lord Archibald moved the abolition of this antiquated and unjust procedure, but the forces of reaction, particularly vested interests, were too strong for him. How far-reaching were the anomalies was plainly exhibited in Haddington so late as 1820 when, in response to a petition signed by all the Dissenting ministers and many inhabitants, the old Burgess Oath of "allegiance, assurance, and abjuration" was rescinded for a more up-to-date formula. As matter of fact the Burgess Oath had long been disused in many towns in respect that it required declarations offensive to a substantial section of the community as well as being inconsistent with the spirit of the times.

Not until the repeal of the Corporation and Test Acts in 1828 did Haddington cease its retrograde policy. On 25th November 1830 the town council petitioned in favour of burgh reform, but the measure was rejected by the House of Lords. Two years later the community petitioned for the re-introduction of the bill. This was brought about in 1833 when Jeffrey, the Lord Advocate, introduced two measures, one applicable to the ancient royal burghs, and therefore to Haddington: the other to the burghs that had recently been granted representation at Westminster. Both were passed, and henceforth town councils had a democratic basis.

On 5th November 1833 the ratepayers of Haddington enjoyed for the first time the privilege of choosing their representatives on the town council. In the reformed body, consisting of twenty-five members, the distinction between trade bailies and councillors was abolished. But, as already indicated, the council continued to elect a baron-bailie of Nungate and another for Gladsmuir, also two burlaw-bailies, whose duty was to settle disputes connected mostly with farming. Samuel Brown, son of the famous John Brown of Haddington, was the last to hold the provostship under the old dispensation and the first under the new.

CHAPTER X

Crafts—Trade—Industry

THERE is perhaps no better way of studying the old burghal life of Haddington, more especially its reactions to trade and industry, than by investigating the affairs of the various incorporations which, arising naturally out of the economic conditions of the Middle Ages, did not actually outlive their usefulness till the nineteenth century. Merchants and craftsmen were to a large extent a reflex of the life of the community, being closely bound up with civic administration. In remote times the laws of the burghs split every township into two communities, the division being regulated by the incorporations. A townsman either was a freeman or an unfreeman. If he was of the former he was a merchant or a member of one of the trading organisations and enjoyed all the rights and privileges—and they were substantial—inherent in such a position. If, on the other hand, he was unfortunate enough to belong to the unfree, his facilities for earning a livelihood were seriously curtailed.

The material about the merchants who flourished in Haddington in the sixteenth and seventeenth centuries is scanty, but the broad lines are fairly clear. Not only were the merchants less efficiently organised than the craftsmen, but they did not possess a gild till 1659—a somewhat late date. In spite of this, however, their influence was stronger, which was in part attributable to their having a monopoly of foreign trade. The distinction between the merchant and the tradesman was sharply drawn. The merchant bought and sold manufactured goods, likewise the raw material from which they were made, whereas the craftsman was exclusively an artificer, skilful with his hands. During the first half of the sixteenth century three Continental towns competed for a monopoly of Scottish trade—Antwerp, Middleburg, and Campvere. Haddington favoured the last-mentioned, which from 1444 till 1795 was the only staple port between Scotland and the Netherlands. In 1533 we hear of Philip Gibson, a merchant in the burgh, receiving a quantity of cloth. In 1552 a deputation from Haddington was sent to Flanders, its expenses being defrayed by the burgesses. Again, on 4th February 1642-43 there was signed in Haddington a declaration made by merchant burgesses of the royal burghs "trafficking from this realme (Scotland) to the Low countreys, anent the expediency of the supplying of the Conservator's place there in favours of Thomas Cuningham, factor in Campveir." Cuningham wrote an interesting journal covering the period 1640-54. The manuscript, now in possession of Edinburgh University, was printed and issued in 1928 as one of the publications of the Scottish History Society. The staple exports from Haddington were wool, hides, and sheepskins. In 1378-79 the burgh was fifth in the list of Scottish towns exporting wool, and in 1480-87 it was fourth.

In 1565 it was ordained that unfreemen were to buy wool, hides, or skins only from burgesses, and that before eleven o'clock in the forenoon on market days; and by an Act of 1579 no person could buy skins or hides except at booths. As regards the government of the town, the respective rights of merchants and craftsmen were clearly defined in Acts passed in 1658-59. While the merchants conducted their business in booths, they were entitled on market days, with a view to greater publicity of their wares, to erect a stall in the street, known as a "crame." Only staple goods could be sold in booths. In terms of an Act of 1557, "na collaris, stumpis . . . nor hose of any coloured cloth nor silks" were allowed to be disposed of at the crames. In 1554 these stalls, which were uncovered except in wet weather, were debarred "on the hiegate or in kirk doors or in common passages" except on Saturdays. Certain varieties of goods could not be sold at the crames, such commodities being reserved for booths. During the plague of 1569 "na kind of merchandise nor chapman's wares" were allowed to be sold, nor "cramery wares, fruits, towis, dishes, dublaris (wooden plates) nor secklike traffery."

Craftsmen were regarded as socially inferior to the merchants. In 1574 Haddington sent as its representative to the Convention of Royal Burghs one John Douglas, a cordiner (shoemaker). He was, however, ordered to remove himself on the ground that "na craftisman hes evir had, nolder aucht or suld haif, voit or commissioun amangis thame." As early as the fifteenth century the craftsmen were forming incorporations with legislative authority, and before the close of the sixteenth their primary objects were achieved—management of their internal affairs, a monopoly for each particular trade, and representation on the town council. In 1552 the deacons of the crafts together with the old and new council chose the provost, though, judging by a minute of June 1582, the deacons, it would seem, were not members, the phrase used being "provost, bailies, council, *and deacons.*" But much ambiguity lurks in the uncouth phraseology of that far-distant time. In 1576 the deacons desired to vote for the election "of ye provostry, baillery, and theasurey (treasurer)" but the council opposed in respect of an Act of the Convention of Burghs of 1561. So in regard to "the appearance of tumult and controversies . . . and for the stayment thereof, the haill deacons were content for the present year to sit w^t clois mouth . . . quhill tryell be had of ye said act." In October 1584, when a member of the Bothwell family was made provost, no deacons were to vote "but sic as are maist honest of ye craft, maist substantious, sic as feir God, tretaris of paix, keparis of ye lawes and statutes of ye burgh."

There were, of course, constant bickerings between freemen and unfreemen—those who were in possession of trading privileges and those who had none. The latter, however, sometimes contrived to circumvent their opponents by taking advantage of favourable opportunities. "Everywhere," writes Hume Brown, "in spite of the indignant protests of the freemen, enforced by the interested magistracy, unprivileged persons pushed their way into trade and commerce through the mere pressure of circumstances against which legislation was impotent." [1] Various instances will be recalled in this chapter.

Haddington had no fewer than nine trading incorporations—Baxters, Hammermen, Masons, Wrights, Fleshers, Cordiners, Skinners, Tailors, and Weavers. For the better protection of their common interests, these formed themselves into a body known as the Convener Court of Haddington. Its meetings were presided over by the convener, who wore official robes while from his neck hung a gold medal. These badges of office were supplemented so late as 1817 when Adam Jack, a member of the Wrights and Masons, presented a large horn, silver mounted and finely polished, on which were engraved the insignia of each of the nine trades as well as a representation of the convener holding nine arrows—a symbol of the unity of the crafts. The Convener Court owned two palls or mortcloths from which considerable revenue was derived. In 1724, the larger one having become dilapidated, a new one was ordered. When, in the middle of the eighteenth century, the hearse came into general use, it was proposed to secure one for the united incorporations, but there was doubt about meeting the

[1] *History of Scotland*, iii, 49.

expense and no further action was taken. In pre-Reformation times the incorporations were closely allied with the Church, taking part in the various festivals and maintaining altars in St Mary's. In 1537 it was decreed that no craft set up a workshop within the burgh unless it contributed eleven shillings "to uphald ye altar." The craftsmen also bore a part in the miracle plays which, as has already been noted, were a feature of the religious life.

It is impossible to review the history of all the nine incorporated trades of Haddington. But this need not hinder the elucidation of the economic life of the town, for in describing the working of one craft we are describing conditions and procedure that were substantially characteristic of all. Accordingly, it is proposed to confine attention to the Baxters and the Hammermen, the records of both crafts being still to the fore and fairly complete. In addition to being typical of the others, these incorporations furnish abundant material which sheds a strong and interesting light on the social life of Haddington during three centuries. The destruction of the old town records prevents any attempt to fix the chronological order of the nine crafts. There is evidence, however, to show that before the middle of the sixteenth century the town council had granted charters, Seals of Cause as they are called, to several trades whereby they were formally constituted and invested with rights and privileges.

In a printed paper of "Information" lodged in the Court of Session in 1807, it is stated that the Baxters (*i.e.* Bakers) craft was the most ancient. The Seal of Cause indicates that it existed before 1550. A charter was usually granted to a trade on application of its members, but in the case of the Baxters it was bestowed as a decreet after deliberation. What led to the Baxters' petition was the encroachments of unfreemen. The Seal of Cause ensured that bread baked by members was distinguished from that baked by outsiders, a mark being placed on the output of the former. The existing minute book of the Baxters' Incorporation covers only the period from 1677 to 1743 but stray references to its activities before that time can be gleaned from other sources. In the pre-Reformation period the Baxters had their altar in the parish church, and, later on, sat in their own loft, the front of which displayed a painting of the symbols of their trade—a sheaf and scales for weighing dough, the whole being set off with the motto: "Bread is the staff of life."

A large portion of the minute book is occupied with routine business—the election of office-bearers, the setting of the boxpenny for the year, the booking of apprentices and journeymen, regulations as to the baking and selling of bread, and punishments inflicted for breaking the laws of the craft. At intervals, however, we come upon illuminating information. The deacon had to answer to the magistrates that members furnished sufficient bread and of just weight. This entailed periodic visits to bakehouses as well as the inspection of bread exposed for sale on the street on market days. One deacon got into trouble through being too zealous. He was James Hislop against whom Alexander Thomson, baxter in Nungate, obtained decreet "for searching of mercat on Nungate Bridge" and seizing the bread "exposed to sale on the brig." Hislop was refused expenses by the incorporation on the ground that Nungate was beyond his jurisdiction. In 1703 the Baxters made war on the "hugsters" who bought bread from the craft and sold it at a lower price—rather an unprofitable transaction one would imagine. Another grievance centred in the "Penny Wedding." It was customary for those providing the viands for such functions to take their flour to the baker, a practice of which the craft disapproved on 2nd November 1715. That craftsmen should "bake loaves, shortbread, and pyes to public weddings, which was not of their flour but belonging to the makers of the said weddings" was deemed "prejudicial and detrimental to the said baxter craft." Therefore to prevent abuses, the craftsmen were in future to refuse to bake for such persons except with flour supplied by the incorporation.

The Baxters also chafed under the law whereby they were compulsorily thirled to the town's mills, and for some years there were organised attempts at evasion. In 1743 the town council were concerned that there were "no established rules as to the dues at the mills of the burgh" and appointed a committee to submit a table of such, which was approved. But this brought only temporary relief. In 1783 the craft's attitude towards thirlage was clearly revealed, George Allan, tacksman of the Haddington mills, bringing an action for abstracted multures (*i.e.* dues payable to the mill master) before the magistrates. Allan accused the Baxters of refusing to grind at the town's mills and of importing large quantities of flour without paying dry multures. Having won his case, Allan raised an action in the Court of Session of declarator of thirlage against the incorporation. The latter denied thirlage, and argued that the only title produced by the town was one conveying the mills simply *cum multuris*, which, in their view, was no grant of thirlage at all. It was also stated that the Baxters imported flour without any multure being asked. Unfortunately, there is no record of the decision of the Lords of Session.

Till 1796 the price of bread was proved before the magistrates by witnesses on oath, and from the evidence adduced the price was regulated and announced by tuck of drum on Monday mornings. Of equal importance to the craft was the price of grain, and in the year mentioned the Baxters engaged in wordy warfare with James Wilkie, who complained of connivance to raise the price of corn. Wilkie had James Kirk, the burgh schoolmaster, appointed to attend the weekly market and to report on the prices obtained for grain, likewise the quality supplied. Wilkie's action was resented by the craft who inserted the following announcement in the *Edinburgh Evening Courant*: "To the Public. Whereas the Bakers of Haddington have been falsely accused by James Wilkie, Esq., of Gilkerston, of using unwarrantable means to heighten the price of wheat in the public market, in order to raise the assize of bread, they do hereby positively deny the charge and challenge him, or any other person, to prove it." Whether Wilkie accepted the challenge is not known, but the incorporation some time after complained of the magistrates setting the assize by the return sent in by his official, which return "always comprehends a quantity of wheat not fit or proper to be made into bread, and in consequence of which the assize is always considerably below the wheat used by the Bakers." This the craft followed up with a memorial to Robert Dundas, the Lord Advocate, who gave his opinion that the magistrates were not entitled to include in their average the damaged wheat. The thirlage question came up again in 1798 when the incorporation were allowed a commutation of one shilling and sixpence per boll for grinding their wheat, in place of the multures fixed in 1743, conditionally that they ground all their wheat at the town's mills and ceased importing flour.

In 1805 steps were taken to deal with the growing encroachments of country bakers. James Smith, in Nungate, was complained against for bringing bread into Haddington and selling it not only to householders but to retailers. The defence was that the bakers of Nungate had for many years sold bread in the burgh without interference. The sheriff's finding, however, was that the privileges of the incorporation had been invaded—a decision which appears to have been upheld by the Court of Session.

It is interesting to recall that the Napoleonic menace made the Haddington bakers exceptionally busy. Among the craft's papers is a little account book containing a record of the bread supplied between 1805 and 1809 to the regiments stationed in the town for the purpose of thwarting a French invasion that seemed imminent. Some two hundred thousand loaves were baked by six craftsmen, the transaction being supervised by the incorporation.

In 1808 the craft had to meet an accusation of badly baked bread. The sheriff attributed the cause to the yeast being soured in transit. But this explanation did not satisfy the craftsmen, who took legal advice of Francis Jeffrey (afterwards Lord Jeffrey) who advised the incorporation to be content with the decision, adding that if good bread were baked, the sheriff's interlocutor would not be put into execution. On the other hand, fraud or gross negligence would make the craft liable to punishment whether the interlocutor was altered or not.

In the thirties of last century the abolition of thirlage was seriously canvassed. While of opinion that it had outlived its usefulness, the craft were evidently feeling that to be consistent they must renounce their monopoly. In 1832 they considered the disposal of their rights, though no practical step appears to have been taken. Their doom, however, was sealed in 1846 by an Act of Parliament which deprived the members of the right to carry on their trade to the exclusion of outsiders, though they were still at liberty to retain their corporate character. Obviously this was but an empty concession when the monopoly had gone, and the Bakers were not slow to appreciate the new situation. Matters were brought to a head by three craftsmen withdrawing from membership, which was followed by the others resigning in a body. Thus ended, within four years of the tercentenary of receiving their charter, the Incorporation of Baxters of Haddington.

Turning now to the Incorporation of Hammermen, which included allied trades, the first thing to be noted is that they probably were the strongest numerically of the nine crafts. As in the case of the Baxters, the earliest records of this body are missing; but the men of this craft had some form of organisation in the first half of the sixteenth century. Their altar in the parish church was dedicated to St Eloi. In 1553 the provost and bailies requested the craft to produce its Seal of Cause within five days. Such action would seem to indicate that whatever document of privileges the craft had, it had not been seen for many years, and was therefore a matter for investigation. Although not explicitly stated, the Hammermen probably produced their charter. At any rate it is a fact that their Seal of Cause existed in 1598. Accidentally burned in that year, it was felt that something should be done to remedy an anomalous position whereby the craft was exercising privileges in trade and obtaining representation on the town council on the strength of a document that no longer existed. Ultimately, in 1633, the Hammermen prepared a statement in which they set forth that "past memorie of man" they had been an incorporation, that they were "of auld erected and appoyntit in ane free craft" by the burgh, and that they had long been possessed of "ane ample gift of the freedom." But their Seal of Cause being non-existent, through no fault of their own, they supplicated the magistrates not only to ratify their former gifts but to grant new ones. Accordingly a new Seal of Cause was conferred which lacked nothing in comprehensiveness, embracing, as it did, goldsmiths, lorimers, clock-makers, pewterers, buckle-makers, potters, and swordslippers. Evidently the incorporation expected marked developments in industry, since the charter specifically states that none of these trades was then represented in Haddington. In 1633 only blacksmiths, locksmiths, saddlers, and cutlers were carrying on trade in the town. There were no goldsmiths, buckle-makers, or potters before 1806. Like other crafts the Hammermen suffered from infringements of their rights and were diligent in prosecuting unfreemen. But the irregularity continued, so much so that in 1688 efforts were made to secure additional protection.

The papers of this incorporation reveal interesting particulars regarding internal organisation, though it cannot be pleaded that there were important differences between this craft and others. It was almost the universal practice that one or more sons should adopt their father's trade. If the parent died prematurely, the son, if of sufficient age, was made a freeman in right of his father. Again, if the head of the household had no son, his son-in-law, even if only a journeyman, was admitted a freeman, provided he performed the usual essay satisfactorily. Occasionally a widow was allowed to carry on her late husband's trade. The chief source of revenue was the fees paid by freemen and apprentices. The latter, when "entered," paid £6 Scots as dues to the craft's box and an equal sum for a dinner. Fees were also payable to the clerk and officer. After a youth had served five years as an apprentice and two as a journeyman he presented himself for admission, and was given a piece of work to try his skill (*i.e.* the essay). If approved, he then took the oath of fidelity and secrecy, and having paid more fees could regard himself as a member of the craft.

On fair and market days goods might be exposed for sale on the street by unfreemen as well as freemen. If, however, articles were made by a member of a craft, the seller tendered a small payment to the craft concerned. The method of collecting these sums was peculiar. Every November the "boxpenny," as it was called, was rouped and awarded to the highest bidder, who was obliged to belong to one or other of the crafts. This person was empowered to visit the various stalls and collect the fee from every vendor whose goods fell within the liberty of one of the nine crafts. On the following Hallowmass the lessee of the "boxpenny" paid over the amount agreed on. It was an anxious day for him, for he might be either gainer or loser, the money collected depending on the number of vendors from whom dues were exigible.

The "boxpenny" was frequently the subject of dispute. For example, the chapmen, who were unfreemen, sold buckles on fair and market days. These goods were regarded as falling within the Hammermen craft, and for upwards of a century the chapmen paid the weekly "boxpenny" of fourpence without demur. But in 1755 John Bower, one of their number, refused payment on the ground that buckles were not a commodity belonging exclusively to the Hammermen. The dispute eventually found its way into the law courts and was decided in favour of the craft. The Hammermen also joined the Baxters and Cordiners in a protest against the tacksmen of the stalls in the High Street who demanded six shillings Scots yearly from every freeman who did business there on market days. This incident occurred in 1732, previous to which, it was alleged, there never had been any charge.

The Hammermen were never long without grievances. In 1691 they raised a hue and cry against the smiths and saddlers in Nungate and other places beyond the burgh on the score that they were underselling the craft. The materials used by these tradesmen were, it was pointed out, frequently obtained in Haddington. If such practices continued, the Hammermen "would neither be able to live nor pay the public burdens." After investigation the town council decided that inhabitants requiring a smith or saddler must employ a member of the incorporation. The Hammermen also obtained authority to seize any smithwork or saddlery taken out of the town. This was done in 1763 when John Smart, who set up a blacksmith's sign near West Port and refused to cease work, had his anvil and hammers seized. Sometimes the Hammermen themselves figured as interlopers, engaging in work that had nothing to do with their craft. In 1759 Andrew Cockburn, one of their number, was made town jailor, but instead of being expelled from the incorporation his fellow-craftsmen became security for him to the extent of £100, he in turn granting a bond over his heritable property. George Young, one of the deacons, acted more consistently. Becoming farrier to a cavalry regiment quartered in Haddington, and finding it impossible to attend to the affairs of the craft, he resigned office.

Although there is no mention in the Seal of Cause of copper- and brass-smiths, there was a tacit understanding that workers in these metals belonged to the Hammermen· At the same time the craft looked with a lenient eye on tinkers, who did a good deal of mending of copper and brass kettles, and even pursued their calling in the burgh. For half a century all the coppersmiths in Haddington learned their trade from John Hislop, who in 1778 was admitted to the freedom, though at first working "by tolerance of the Craft." Similar conditions prevailed in the pewterer trade. On the death in 1688 of John Hay, pewterer, his widow employed Simon Sawers as a journeyman, and for a century thereafter this trade was mainly in the hands successively of Simon Sawers, his son Robert, and his grandson Simon.

The pewter business had a strong competitor in the tinsmith, tin being cheaper than pewter. Eventually the tinsmith ousted the pewterer. Despite the fact that the lorimer belonged to the Hammermen craft, the making of the metalwork for harnesses was not engaged in locally till the eighteenth century was far advanced. The saddler, on the other hand, was associated with the craft from the beginning. The making and repairing of saddles, pads, and pillions was a prosperous business. From 1627 to 1640 the deacon was always a saddler. In 1655 the saddlers were complained against because in making cushions they did not procure the skins for covering them from Haddington skinners. The town council sided with the skinners, who in turn were found fault with by the saddlers for encroaching on their privileges. In 1634 certain merchants were reprimanded for importing saddles, and in 1652 the saddlers obtained a decision that merchants were not at liberty to sell horse-shoes, stirrup-bearers, stirrup-irons, bridles, or girths, this right being reserved to the Hammermen. The saddlery business declined in the opening decades of the eighteenth century with the result that in 1736 one saddler was sufficient for all the work in the town. Later on, however, there was a temporary revival. Many of the apprentices were sons of burgesses and farmers. Among the latter was John Laurie, who was tenant of Sandersdean. His son did not serve his apprenticeship in Haddington, but had important links with the craft. Peter Laurie ultimately made his mark, becoming Sir Peter Laurie, Lord Mayor of London.

Till the eighteenth century clockmaking was the province of the blacksmiths. Not till 1722 did it become a distinct business in the town. In that year Patrick Young was restricted to the making of clocks, watches, guns, jacks, and cutlery. From 1758 to 1769 William Veitch was the only clockmaker in the craft, but by 1776 the trade had made such headway that steps were taken to conserve the rights of those so engaged, as Alexander Hogg knew to his cost. A wheelwright, he was found repairing clocks and watches, which led to his tools being seized by the Hammermen's deacon, who declared that "a more flagrant and inexcusable encroachment of their privileges had seldom or never occurred."

Here and there in the minute books, which extend continuously from 1627 to 1806, are indications of the attitude of the Hammermen to national affairs—political, social, religious, humanitarian. The craft opposed Catholic emancipation but favoured the abolition of the African slave trade. As for the Reform Act of 1832, its passing was

Banner of Incorporation of Weavers, 1761.

hailed as a tremendous step in political progress. Much jubilation took place, and the banner (still to the fore) carried by the craft in a procession in honour of the event is inscribed: "By hammer in hand all arts do stand." Beneath is a representation of an anvil, thistles, and roses, together with the words: "The iron fetters which were riveted by oppression are now knocked off on the anvil of liberty by the hammer of reform."

The roll of Hammermen steadily declined in the nineteenth century till only five members were left, namely, George Young and George Spears, blacksmiths; Robert Porteous, saddler; William Aitken, watchmaker; and John Ferme, solicitor, who was clerk of the incorporation. The record of yearly payments ceased in 1868, and at or about that date the Hammermen as an organised body ceased to exist.

Only brief reference can be made to the other crafts. The Wrights and Masons seemed to have been conjoined, though they appear as distinct organisations in the list of the nine incorporations. The original charters probably dated from the fifteenth century, but a second Seal of Cause applicable to both crafts was granted in 1647. The claim of the Wrights and Masons to be patrons of the altar of St John the Evangelist in the parish church was disputed, but, on being referred to arbiters in 1530, was upheld. In the eighteenth century the Wrights and Masons built a tenement on the north side of High Street, adjoining the George Hotel, and there, in the upper flat, they had their convening room. The united incorporation included coopers, wheelwrights, plasterers, slaters, and glaziers. Regular meetings ceased with dwindling numbers, the last being held in 1863. In 1881 Andrew Dickson, joiner, was the sole member left. Up to that year the accumulated funds amounted to about £120 exclusive of the Wrights' and Masons' tenement in High Street, which was valued at about £400. Dickson applied to the Court of Session for power to make a more extensive use of the funds than was sanctioned by the original constitution. The judgment of the court was that the income might be spent on indigent dependants of members, assuming these increased. If, however, they did not amount to twelve, the income was to be applied by such members along with the magistrates, and by the latter if there were no members. The money was to be spent in defraying taxes, rates, repairs, in charitable objects authorised by the Seal of Cause, in paying school fees of descendants of members, and in promoting secondary education in Haddington.

The Seal of Cause of the Weavers is dated 1635, but it is doubtful if this was the original charter. This craft was divided into three classes. The strongest numerically was employed on woollen goods, the second on linen, while the third was composed of those who prepared the rough flax for the spinning wheel. In the eighteenth century, and earlier part of the nineteenth, the Weavers were a body to be reckoned with. They owned property in Poldrate which was sold in 1798 to George Jack, mason. Gradually, spinning in private houses was superseded by mechanical contrivances, and when the power-loom was introduced the collapse of the incorporation was inevitable. The minute book of the craft for the period 1786–1852 still exists. For long the Weavers owned a loft in the parish church on which was emblazoned the motto: "Improve your time, it is but little; 'tis swifter than a weaver's shuttle." Barclay, in his eighteenth-century account of Haddington, mentions that numerous weavers in Nungate engaged in the manufacture of coarse woollens. The last member of the craft was George Fairbairn, who lived at Athelstaneford. He died in 1873.

Considering that tanning was an early industry in Haddington, it is surprising to learn that the Skinners were a small body. In 1667 the magistrates recorded that "their predecessors erected the Skinners . . . in ane free craft . . . past memory of man." The craft probably existed in 1545, for in that year it was enacted that "na maner of man buy skynes, woll, nor hydes within ye burgh but freemen . . . under ye pain of escheiting of ye samyn." The records of the Skinners are continuous from 1682 to 1801, when they end with the signatures of William Pringle, deacon, and Henry Davidson, clerk.

Judging from the membership lists for the period 1682–1801 it would appear that the Skinners reached high-water mark in the late seventeenth and the opening decades of the eighteenth century when the numbers on the roll ranged from a dozen to twenty. Later on they became fewer. According to Martine, George McCullagh, who was entered in 1832, was the last member. Throughout the eighteenth century the predominant family in the incorporation were the Pringles, though the Wilsons ran them closely. It is a curious fact that from 1768 until the beginning of the nineteenth century the only members were either Pringles or Wilsons. In 1772 there were six Pringles and two Wilsons; in 1775, six Pringles; in 1776 five Pringles and two Wilsons; and in 1780 six Pringles and two Wilsons. In 1800 the incorporation was exclusively in the hands of the Pringles, the list of members being William Pringle, senior, William Pringle, junior, and William Pringle, *tertius*, together with Thomas, Andrew, and James Pringle. As the Pringles and Wilsons were not sufficient to occupy entirely the Skinners' seat in the parish church, the incorporation, being thriftily inclined, let the unoccupied portion. In 1781 the craft agreed to pay the church officer five shillings per annum for preventing unauthorised persons from entering the Skinners' pew.

A portion of the riverside behind the Episcopal Church is known to this day as the Skinners' Knowe. This ground, which seems to have been the exclusive property of the incorporation, was used by members for washing and dressing their skins and working their leather. Writing last century, Martine remarks that the Skinners' Knowe was "much altered, the Tyne having at one time run close to the [Episcopal] chapel garden wall." In March 1745 the Skinners complained to the town council that George Anderson, a tanner, had encroached on their portion of the riverside by erecting a shed and constructing a pond. Adjoining the latter the Skinners had a pond of their own. Anderson consequently was regarded as an interloper. The town council sided with the Skinners whose prescriptive right to the Knowe was a matter of ancient history. Another entry in the minutes, dated 1st June 1765, informs us that the Episcopalians were about to build a chapel on ground occupied by some old houses belonging formerly to Charles Lauder, a step which would "oblige the Craft to pull down the west wall of the Skinners' Knowe."

Alongside the Skinners may be conveniently placed the Cordiners or Shoemakers, who on 12th August 1635 were granted a renewal of their privileges. Although entrusted, in the days before the Reformation, with the upkeep of the altars of St Crispin and St Michael, the Cordiners, says Martine, were "the most unruly and ill-agreeing set of all the nine incorporated trades." The election of office-bearers was usually the occasion for wrangling, and in 1806 was so keenly contested that matters had to be settled in the Court of Session. The Cordiners attended for many years the fairs of Dunbar and Gifford.

There is some dubiety regarding the Seal of Cause of the Fleshers. In 1579 the town council requested the craft to produce their charter, but they responded by saying that it could not be found. Whereupon the magistrates, then concerned about the shortage of butcher meat, ordained that henceforth it should be lawful for all fleshers outside the burgh to sell to the community. The Fleshers claimed that their privileges were derived from a charter of James V. In the burgh records we read: "The Counsall having considered that they did indulge the Flesher Craft in their freedom in the year 1680, notwithstanding they had not a sufficient number, and finding that they are now [1683] in as few a number, have discharged them of their freedom till they make up their number to the satisfaction of the Counsall." In the hope of remedying matters, it was decided that in future two weekly Flesh markets should be held instead of one. Members of the incorporation were enjoined to apportion their beef for sale before nine o'clock in the morning, otherwise landward fleshers would be allowed to "break their beef." In 1690 the Fleshers were still unable to regulate supply and demand, and therefore were subjected to the competition of the landward tradesmen. In November 1757 an Act was passed decreeing that the slaughtering of animals for human consumption was to be done in a building set apart for the purpose and at the public expense. Hitherto the Fleshers had slaughtered cattle and sheep not only in the streets but at their own houses. Down to 1757 the Flesh market was held in High Street. It was then removed to Newton Port and in 1804 to Hardgate.

An illuminating account of the state of the nine incorporations at the passing of the Burgh Reform Act is to be found in the reports of the Commissioners on the Municipal Corporations of Scotland, published in 1835. This general survey shows that the Haddington crafts were then moribund. Indeed the retention of their exclusive privileges had almost become a matter of indifference. Very few persons had entered the crafts during the previous thirty years, and the day was approaching when the whole system on which craft organisation was based would receive its quietus. In 1835 the Wrights and Masons owned some heritable property, a hearse and harness, and funds amounting to £50, the annual income being about £40 yearly. The Hammermen had about £180 in money, the Cordiners £20, the Fleshers only £5. In addition to a sixpence paid quarterly by each member, the Fleshers levied a penny on every ox, a halfpenny on every calf, and twopence halfpenny on every score of sheep and lambs killed by members. As for the Baxters and Weavers, they had no funds, while the Tailors were a few pounds in debt.

From persons well acquainted with the affairs of Haddington the Commissioners obtained the opinion that the exclusive privileges of the incorporated trades were prejudicial to the community, and that the crafts themselves would not sustain serious injury by their being abolished. But the trades opposed abolition (somewhat half-heartedly) on the ground that such a step would bear inequitably on those lately admitted to membership unless they were compensated for the entry money. The Tailors considered that the extinction of their privileges would make it difficult for members to pay the existing debt. The Cordiners, again, regarded abolition as inflicting "positive injury." The Hammermen, while viewing their privileges as valuable, were not apprehensive of "serious injury" being sustained if they were taken away. The Baxters attached little importance to their favoured position, but complained much of being thirled to the town's mills, to which they paid sixpence more for each boll of wheat ground than outsiders. Since any one might now sell bread within the royalty, and a considerable quantity was imported daily by persons living beyond the town, the Baxters felt that baking was the only privilege that remained.

Sufficient has already been said to show that Haddington was a trading community from an early date. Robert II granted 250 merks to the Earl of March from its customs, and facts have been given indicative of the important position the town occupied in the fifteenth century in the matter of dues levied on wool and hides.

Situated at the heart of a great agricultural district, the staple industry of Haddington consists in all kinds of farm produce, a vast amount of which changes hands in the weekly markets. The grain market existed in the thirteenth century and formerly was the largest in Scotland. When Martine wrote in the nineteenth century Haddington was still occupying the premier position. The quantity of grain sold in the town from 1st October 1858 to 30th September 1859 amounted to 83,114 quarters, valued at £158,061.

But while agriculture has been always pre-eminent, manufactures on a moderate scale have been carried on in Haddington since the seventeenth century. After the collapse of the New Mills Cloth Manufactory (see p. 49) various attempts at industrial expansion were made, but with limited success. In 1709 William Stead intimated through the Press that there was being "made at Haddington . . . all sorts of fine and coarse cards, such as fine scribbling and Spanish cards . : . Likewise all sorts of coarse wool." Twenty years later there was a lint manufactory at the East Haugh, and in 1730 a woollen establishment was started in Nungate, while a spinning school was opened within the royalty.

Haddington seems to have been late in the day in acquiring a reputation for cloth manufacture. There may have been spasmodic attempts in early centuries, but it was not till the New Mills Cloth Manufactory was launched, towards the end of the seventeenth century, that a venture of some magnitude was in progress. After its failure no industry deserving notice appeared in the town until the establishment in 1750 of the Tarred Wool Company. The real promoters of this concern were Andrew Fletcher (Lord Milton) and Lord Deskford. Premises measuring 123 feet by 45 were erected at the East Haugh, and Andrew Meikle, the inventor of the drum-thrashing machine, supplied the mechanical apparatus. Being a waulk or fulling mill, a large volume of water was needed. Unfortunately this was not available, and the Company had to be content with the mill lade which was already harnessed for the town's malt industry. The water supply was a serious problem, especially during dry seasons, and there was litigation between the Company and the town. In the end the undertaking was not a success, and a new Company was formed which, after conducting operations on a smaller scale, was in turn dissolved in 1775.

The business was then acquired by one Sawers, who had been clerk to the former Company. Sawers carried on for a number of years, manufacturing blankets of excellent quality. In 1789 the mill and machinery of the old Tarred Wool Company was acquired by William Wilkie, merchant in Haddington, who, after conducting the business for half a dozen years under difficulties, granted a thirty-eight years' lease of the property to Hay Smith. The latter was enterprising, installing machines for grinding indigo and other dye-stuffs. Mustard was also a speciality, for which an additional force of water was obtained. But Hay Smith's experiments led to a financial crisis, and in 1803 a fifteen years' lease of the mill was taken by James Dawson, who resumed the cloth industry.

The Tarred Wool Company had competitors in the town which doubtless accounts to some extent for its ill-luck. In 1771 there was a bleachfield controlled by Andrew Dickson and Thomas Croumbie, whose plain linen cloth was wrought at twopence, damasks and cambrics at fourpence, and lawn at threepence per yard. Dickson also manufactured several varieties of white thread, the bleaching of which was done "at reasonable prices." In 1815 the site of Dickson's bleachfield was utilised by Alexander Dunlop for the erection of a distillery. In 1788 a steelyard was opened, but particulars are not forthcoming. Again, in 1842–43, the West Flour Mill was erected at a cost of £1377, 16s. 4d., and a few years later the East Flour Mill in Poldrate was renovated and brought up to date.

The opening of the nineteenth century witnessed the starting of printing and publishing concerns that were remarkable in a country town. In 1804 there was set up the East Lothian Press, first in premises in Hardgate and then in High Street. The founder was George Miller, who in 1789 had opened a bookshop in Dunbar which, after twenty-five years, had a stock valued at over £10,000. Miller also organised and managed a circulating library which in 1809 contained 3500 works. Later, he entered the printing business. Dunbar, however, did not prove advantageous for this concern, and the East Lothian Press was removed to Haddington, from which town, between 1812 and 1833, he issued a series of useful and instructive publications. The history of the East Lothian Press has been described, not inaptly, as "an epitome of the civic, commercial, and literary activities" of Haddington.

From the East Lothian Press, in the management of which Miller was assisted by his son James, there issued *The Cheap Magazine*, which catered for the farm labourer and the remote villager. According to Robert Chambers, the periodical was "in some respects in advance of its age" and provided "a considerable mass of paper and print once a month for fourpence . . . calculated to instruct as well as amuse the two classes who mostly require instruction, the young and the poor." The periodical lasted barely two years, which is rather strange, considering that its circulation averaged from 12,000 to 20,000 copies a month. It was followed in January 1815 by *The Monthly Monitor and Philanthropical Museum*, of which twelve numbers appeared. This journal was on the same lines as its predecessor, but more literary. Apart from these publications and the *Haddington Register*, an almanac compiled by James Miller and containing the kind of information found in county directories, the East Lothian Press issued reprints of popular works like Burns's poems, Allan Ramsay's *Gentle Shepherd*, Thomas Boston's *Crook in the Lot*, and the *Shorter Catechism*, the last-mentioned, rather surprisingly, embellished with a woodcut of Dunbar Castle. Nor must we omit Miller's edition of *Robinson Crusoe*, of which there was a "prodigious impression." Paisley, of all places, took 2500 copies, Edinburgh and Glasgow 500 each, and the United States 500.

In 1819 Miller got into financial difficulties, and from then till 1833 the East Lothian Press was managed by his son James, who printed for the father of Samuel Smiles, author of *Self-Help*, and Hew Scott, the future compiler of *Fasti Ecclesiæ Scoticana*. James Miller, besides bringing out an edition of John Brown of Haddington's *Dictionary of the Bible* and the effusions of local bards and pamphleteers, himself entered the field of authorship with the *Lamp of Lothian*, the types used being set up by the author. Unfortunately, the younger Miller was unsteady in his habits, which accounts for the East Lothian Press ending its existence in 1833.

The Millers were not the only publishers in Haddington at this time. The Neills conducted a bookselling and publishing business there for about one hundred and twenty years. In 1771 the business was superintended by Archibald Neill, who also had a printing concern in Edinburgh. An edition of the Psalms by John Brown of Haddington was printed and sold "by Archibald Neill, the Publisher, at the Stationery Warehouse, back of the City Guard, and at his shop in Haddington." Neill's son George extended the business. In 1833 he took over James Miller's *Annual Register*, and some years later began publishing *The Monthly Advertiser*. In 1840 he printed a catalogue of Haddington Subscription Library. George Neill was succeeded in 1848 by his son Adam, who introduced as a feature of the *Annual Register* a series of illustrations of quaint buildings in Haddington and vicinity. Adam Neill and his son George continued the family business till the latter's death in 1888. Adam died in the following year when the concern passed into other hands.

Another publishing firm was that of George Tait. Possessing literary ambition, Tait founded in 1822 the *East Lothian Magazine, or Literary and Statistical Journal*, which aimed at describing the antiquities, agriculture, and natural history of the county. Only one volume, covering from April to December, appeared. Yet Tait was venturesome enough to launch, in July 1830, another periodical, edited by himself. Known as the *East Lothian Literary and Statistical Journal*, it bore a marked resemblance to its predecessor and was as short-lived.

The newspaper industry dates from 1859, the first number of the *Haddingtonshire Courier* being issued on 28th October of that year. This, the earliest weekly newspaper published in East Lothian, was founded by David and James Croal. Six hundred copies of the first issue were printed on a hand-press formerly used for the *Caledonian Mercury*. The circulation rapidly increased, and the paper has now been published for more than eighty years. A nephew, John Pettigrew Croal, who began his journalistic training in the *Courier* office, was editor of the *Scotsman* from 1905 to 1924. Another weekly newspaper was started in 1881—the *Haddingtonshire Advertiser*, the proprietor and editor of which latterly was William Sinclair. After his death in 1914 the journal passed into the hands of A. W. Jolly, Aberdeen. It ceased publication in 1923.

CHAPTER XI

Social Life

IT might be plausibly urged that social amenities in Scottish towns in bygone centuries did not differ essentially, that the manners and customs of one community were not in any important sense distinguishable from those of another. This, however, is a superficial view, the validity of which is shaken by a close acquaintance with local circumstances. The peculiarities of character and temperament met with in a community in Aberdeenshire, for example, were not always the same as those encountered in a Lowland burgh. Haddington, like any other small town in a rural district, had its idiosyncrasies. Interesting sidelights on these have been exhibited in previous chapters, but nowhere perhaps is so vivid a picture of domestic relationships, so penetrating an insight into the nature of the social bond, as in the records of the town council and the old court books of the burgh. James Robb was probably the first to appreciate the value of those sources, to which in a booklet dealing with the town he has devoted a section. Moreover, Robb did excellent work in making transcriptions from the burgh records of much that is quaint and picturesque, and occasionally of incidents that are very far from being such. The transcriptions are comprehended in seven volumes, and as they never got beyond manuscript form they have been drawn upon in this work. From them, as well as from other sources, it has been possible roughly to set forth the dominant features of the old life of Haddington.

At an early period, owing to its being on the line of march between the Borders and Edinburgh, the town felt the full force of the sporadic visits of the English. The inhabitants were in constant peril of being attacked, and penalised, if not with their lives, at any rate with a pretty thorough appropriation of their property. Their houses, most of which were of timber, were constantly being burnt. Consequently the life of the community was hard and distracting, and sometimes of abject misery. Thus a constantly recurring problem was how the burghers could be protected from the incursions of the "auld enemy," how they were to ward off assaults which brought so much devastation in its train.

Haddington, as has been pointed out, never was a walled town in the usual acceptation of the term, certainly not in the mediæval period. It is true that after the memorable siege of 1548–49 a rude system of defence was introduced, but its aim was principally against the entry of plague-stricken persons and other unwelcome "foreigners": it was not a serious attempt at fortification. The idea of security from the enemy in whatever guise he approached the town underlay the injunction of 1534 that all burgesses dwelling outside the royalty must come within, otherwise they would lose the freedom of the burgh. But many, finding it convenient to live outside, ignored this decree of the town council. At all events the practice was persisted in, and defaulters were warned that the penalty would be strictly enforced if they did not "set up their beds in the town."

This emphasis on the corporate idea had, as a matter of course, an important bearing on the social life of the community. When inter-communication with other parts of the country was rare such isolation inevitably gave rise to angularities of character and temperament, and developed manners and customs that differentiated the burghers from those of other municipalities. In the sixteenth and seventeenth centuries the social life of the town had little of the sweetening influences associated with later times. Life was drab and full of grinding toil, while happy intervals were few and far between. Most men lived dangerously, the doctrine that might is right being alarmingly prevalent. Lawlessness in its most ugly forms was constantly encountered. Human life and property were held cheap, and crimes of every kind were committed· with impunity. While the penalities imposed in the majority of cases were drastic enough, it is evident that the defenders of law and order had their hands full. Street brawls were common. These would occur with startling suddenness and occasionally set the whole town in an uproar. Fortunately they were usually of short duration, but while they lasted were menacing and not easily quelled. A few excerpts from the records will make clear social conditions at this time.

In 1583 it was decreed that any person causing a tulzie and thereby drawing blood was to be imprisoned for nine days. "Backbiters and speakers to the hurt and slander of neighbours and all other perturbaris of the quiet estate of this burgh" were to be confined for twenty-four hours or more, while "all drunk in time of preaching," or disobedient to the magistrates, or found out of their houses after ten o'clock at night without cause were to receive a similar punishment. More serious crime is foreshadowed in the case of Cuthbert Symson and his wife who in 1580 were attacked by four men with "swordis . . . batteris and utheris wappynis." Armed men prowling about the town was not uncommon, and sometimes the result was not merely assault to the effusion of blood but "cruell slauchter." In 1571 a poor watchman was badly mauled by two men who laid about them with "quhingeris [whingers], dagers and stanes": they would have killed him, had he not defended himself with great agility. One feels sympathy, too, for John Vallance who in 1614 was assaulted "under cloud of night," his only offence being that, at the instigation of the magistrates, he had removed the seat of the Baxters' incorporation in the parish church, which had been placed there without authority. His action was resented by two members of the craft, who struck him from behind with heavy sticks. They were warded and put in irons, which seems lenient punishment for a cowardly assault on a man who had merely done his duty.

The parish minister then was George Grier, who appears to have suffered much at the hands of William Stoddart, swordslipper, who shouted from a window numerous blasphemies concerning the minister as well as slandered his wife. The cause of offence was that the Hammermen's seat in church had been removed. Stoddart was placed in the stocks at the Cross, and, after publicly repenting in the kirk, was warded. In 1615 the town was much perturbed by young men patrolling the streets at night carrying swords and other weapons which they used somewhat freely on harmless folk. So the decree went forth that no person was to walk the streets at night armed with "sword, stalfe or the like." If any did so, they would be classed as vagabonds bent on unlawful errands, and would be punished accordingly. We also find the magistrates deploring the increasing prevalence of "drinkein, playing at cartis [cards] and dyce, and sic uyer games in ye nycht," especially among "prophane, young and insolent personis," who were responsible for most of the disreputable conduct. Those who sold wine, ale, beer also were blamed, and it was enacted that no one was to frequent a tavern or be supplied with "miet, drink, candill, tabill, cairts or dyce" after nine o'clock at night in winter and ten in summer. Evidently much of the riotous behaviour was traceable to the tavern, and this was a courageous attempt to mitigate the evil.

Now and then there was a touch of comedy in the nature of an offence, as in the

Remains of supposed Palace in which Alexander II was born.
Site now covered by County Buildings.

[*Drawn by Adam Neill, bookseller.*

High Street a Century Ago.

[*To face p.* 120.

case of John Wilkie, who was warded for abusing the magistrates. Finding incarceration rather boring, he managed to enlist the services of Richard Scougall, the town piper, who relieved the captive's weary hours by "playing all ye nyt in ye tolbuith and upoun ye wall heid" thereof. And there was the unfortunate bellringer who got into trouble for being remiss in his duties when "the preaching was about to begin." For this paltry offence he had to remain in irons during the pleasure of the minister whose intention to preach had not been duly announced. Nor was this all. The negligent bellringer had to remain in ward till he atoned for his fault publicly in the kirk or at the market cross.

A very curious case illustrating the insecurity of life and property is reported in the *Privy Council Register* under date 1st August 1662. The complaint was at the instance of John Brown, merchant burgess of Haddington, who was "in peaceable possession of three acres of arable land on the east side of Nungate." One October day in 1661 he was working on his farm when George Brown, indweller in Nunraw, and Margaret Alinstoun, his wife, assaulted him and his servants with swords and other weapons. They also forcibly "loused his plough and did break the same, took the brankis and halters off the horses' heads and therewith did most cruelly stryk at the said complainer's face" and "beat and abused him most unchristianly." George Brown and his spouse, the *Register* entry adds, were "the more encouraged" to commit this "great wrong and oppression" as "there is now no sheriff court kept at Haddington for want of a sheriff depute." What the end of this case was is not disclosed, but assuming the complaint of the merchant burgess was justified, it was high time that the services of a sheriff depute were available and persons engaged in their lawful calling should be protected from such ruffianly conduct.

In the eighteenth century important changes were being wrought in the social structure of Haddington. There was now a travelling public, not by any means large, but still causing an infiltration of sufficient strength to modify to some extent those peculiar excrescences, quaint symbols of insularity some of them, to which reference has been already made. The presence of numerous inns and hostelries was an indication that people were moving about more than they used to do. Most of these were relatively small concerns catering for the physical wants—food, drink, and, it might be, a night's lodging—of farmers who had arrived in the town to attend the markets, or of carriers who brought some of the goods to be sold there. These inns or taverns were usually primitive and the amount of comfort to be obtained was negligible, but they suited the needs of the local farmers and their servants, and were much frequented.

Dr Alexander Carlyle in his *Autobiography* affords an interesting glimpse of what frequenters of some of these establishments had to put up with. He writes: "By this time (1742) even the second tavern in Haddington (where the presbytery dined, having quarrelled with the first) had knives and forks for their table. But ten or twelve years before that time, my father used to carry a shagreen case, with a knife and fork and spoon. . . . When I attended in 1742 and 1743 they [the tavern] had still but one glass on the table, which went round with the bottle." [1] But be their deficiencies what they may, the hostelries were the rendezvous for the convivial life of the town. Here the Dandie Dinmonts would foregather on market days and, amid much din and bustle, implement a bargain and ratify it with strong drink. Apart from the taverns, there were several reputable inns which found their *clientele* in the

[1] New ed., 1910, pp. 71–72.

well-to-do who, arriving from remote parts of East Lothian, had to make a short stay in the town and required passable accommodation. These inns did not make their appearance till the eighteenth century had run most of its course. They served, however, a useful purpose in the period immediately preceding the coming of the railways.

Apart from these establishments, all of them commercial, were the Blue Bell and the George. Both were of the better class, made some pretension to luxury, and were popular with travellers from England. At both commodious stabling could be had, and they were recognised as halting places for stage coaches. Although the Blue Bell is no longer to the fore, the building in which this inn was housed still exists. Occupying part of the south side of High Street, its façade is distinguished by a tower-shaped structure of rather picturesque design, while in a spacious courtyard behind are premises which once provided excellent stabling. The Blue Bell dated back to the middle of the eighteenth century but may have existed before that. In 1764 it bore the name of the White Hart, and in that year George Gall sold the business to James Fairbairn, owner of the George and Dragon. He it was who changed the name to "Blue Bell and Post House." From this inn the Haddington "Fly" departed daily for Edinburgh. The coach ran as far as Birsley Brae, where passengers were transferred to another vehicle which completed the journey. The Blue Bell also was the place of departure for Richard Blackwell's two-horse coach "The Good Intent" and Walter Peacock's "Lord Nelson." These were local coaches carrying few passengers. In the latter part of the eighteenth century two four-in-hand coaches, on their way to and from London, changed horses at the Blue Bell. These were the "High-flyer" and the "Telegraph." For a whole year they were in opposition, but as this was unremunerative they amalgamated under the name of the "Union" and as such ran for many years. The Blue Bell ceased business in 1855.

When the George was established is not known. But in 1764 it was owned by James Fairbairn, who, as mentioned, was also associated with the White Hart, renamed the Blue Bell. Unlike the latter, the George still flourishes. It was originally known as the "Old Post House," then as the "George and Dragon," and in later times simply as the "George." This establishment was also famous in coaching days. For many years during last century the Yellow and Blue Mail, which ran between Edinburgh and London, changed horses at the George. Because of its spacious and even handsome rooms the George has all along been popular for social functions. In 1778 the members of the Caledonian Hunt met there, and in the post-Reform period, when political electioneering was afoot, the rival candidates made the George and the Blue Bell their headquarters. It also was the meeting-place of various farming societies and of a body known as the Orinoco Whist Club.

The George in its long history has had numerous proprietors. In an advertisement, dated 22nd January 1772, some interesting particulars may be gleaned as to its size and general appearance. "The house consists of four flats or stories besides garrets. . . . In the second flat there is a large dining-room, a parlour, four bedrooms . . . a bar with shelves, and a small room fit for a dairy or such like use. In the third flat there are three elegant bedrooms . . . and in the fourth flat there are three good rooms for servants." The kitchen had all cooking appliances, and there was a wine cellar. Stabling for twenty-three horses and a coach-house for four carriages also formed part of the establishment, likewise a byre, a place for feeding pigs, and two high lofts. In 1772 the premises were for sale, and, as an inducement to prospective buyers, it was intimated that a pipe conveyed water from a pump well to the kitchen. In 1822 there was built a large room adjacent to the site of the Knight Templars Preceptory. The George has interesting literary associations. It was patronised by Jane Welsh Carlyle, wife of the Sage of Chelsea, when she revisited her native town—the "hateful Haddington" of earlier years. Carlyle himself more than once stayed at the George.

Among other inns that flourished in the town a century ago were the Britannia (now the Commercial); the Star, which stood at the west end of High Street and faced down that thoroughfare; and the Heather, also in High Street, a rather tumble-down building reached by an outside stair. Market Street had three inns—the Black Bull, the Gardeners' Arms, and the Crown. The first two still carry on and can look back on a history extending over the greater part of two centuries. The Crown was much frequented by East Lothian carriers. In Kilpair Street was the Lamb, to which the town council usually resorted after the Riding of the Marches. There was also the Fox and Bay Horse, situated at the top of High Street, and tenanted at one time by George Dawson, father of the famous racehorse trainer who had his stables at Gullane. The ceiling of this inn was covered with square Norwegian logs, while the elaborately carved oak door is said to have once adorned the old Collegiate Church of Haddington. In Brown Street, next to the George, was the Bee Hive, while in Hardgate was the King's Arms, a plain, three-storeyed building with a little courtyard in front. The old building, which survived till a few years ago, had a panelled dining-room. At the beginning of last century a coach ran to Edinburgh from the King's Arms. Another Hardgate inn was the White Swan, which at one time was kept by David Philip, a Crimean veteran, who on each anniversary of the battle of the Alma hoisted a flag above his establishment. When the Volunteer movement began, the name of this hostelry was changed from the White Swan to the Rifle Arms. Above the entrance was a painting of two soldiers with rifles, together with the motto: "Defence not Defiance."

In coaching days Haddington had close on a dozen inns, a number, it would seem, disproportionately large. But it must be remembered that, with the exception of the Blue Bell and the George, none catered to any extent for the long-distance traveller. So far as the latter was concerned, the accommodation provided was probably ample, having regard to the fact that the number of persons passing along the king's highway on foot, or on horseback, or in the stage-coach, was limited. Besides, Haddington was too near the Scottish capital to make it a halting-place unless for special reasons. Still, it were wrong to suppose that the smaller inns did not share in the patronage of the travelling public. They relied mostly, however, not on people coming from a distance, but on local farmers and grain merchants from Edinburgh. On market days these would come in dozens, attended in many cases by wives and daughters. A large amount of catering had therefore to be done, the amount being greatly increased on the occasion of the two annual fairs, also on Hiring Friday, when Market Street would be crowded with farm servants of every description. The latter, for the most part, supplied their physical wants at the stalls that lined the streets.

In the eighteenth century and earlier part of the nineteenth there was little time, and perhaps little inclination and less opportunity to cultivate the fine arts. But a section of the townsfolk reinforced by a sprinkling of the county gentry interested themselves in the drama. The performances were usually held in an apartment above the old Episcopal meeting-house in Poldrate, which disappeared about 1850. That vocal and instrumental music was performed here, likewise one or two plays, there can be little doubt. Unfortunately, particulars have not been ascertained, but looking to the fact that accommodation was strictly limited, it may be reasonably assumed that these entertainments were private affairs, in which performers and a few friends constituted the entire audience. According to Martine, "the gentry and respectable folk of town and county" patronised theatricals in a barn in Sidegate, where Stephen Kemble and his company formed a special attraction. Plays, including John Home's *Douglas*, were also occasionally performed in another barn at West Port.

It was sports and pastimes, however, more than music and the drama, that fostered closer fellowship among the community. From a remote period the inhabitants engaged in various recreations. Archery, bowling, quoits, horse-racing, and, in later times, golf were all vigorously championed. So far back as 1539 there is mention of a game of "cuittes" (quoits). In 1598 the Privy Council ordered that Monday, instead of Sunday, should be observed as a holiday for pastimes. Towards the close of the seventeenth century football had its followers.

Archery vies with quoits as the earliest form of recreation to be practised in the town. In 1563 "bow buttis" were erected on the Sands near Nungate Bridge, but archery had been practised before this. We read: "The Council thought it necessary for the exercise of our Sovereign Lady's (*i.e.* Mary Queen of Scots) lieges in archery that there be ane payre of bow buttis biggit on the Sands in the place where bow buttis used before to stand." Ten merks were paid for the erection of the butts. In 1574 reference is again made to the "pair of buittes" at the Sands. Archery seemingly became popular. In 1606 there were two pairs of butts—one for adults and another for the youths of the town. The Sands also was the place where pupils of the grammar school engaged in a ball game: hence the familiar local name of Ball Alley.

Haddington all along has been specially identified with bowling. Indeed it is credited with being one of the first places in Scotland where the game was played. It may well be so, for the project for a bowling green on the Sands to the south of Nungate Bridge was first mooted in 1657 when the town council approved of a scheme and instructed the burgh treasurer to purchase bowls and to engage a greenkeeper. But despite these practical measures the scheme remained in abeyance till 1662 when certain sums of money that had been collected for the "pretendit building of ane bridge at Saltoun" were somehow appropriated and spent in the erection of "ane house at and wall about and laying out the ground of ane boulling greir in the Sands." This project, unlike the earlier, materialised. The ground, now part of Lady Kitty's Garden, was ready in November 1669 and was rouped in the patrimony of the town. In June 1670 a nineteen years' lease was granted to Robert Miller, apothecary, who, by arrangement with the town, built a three-storey house adjoining. Miller was at great "pains, charges, and expenses" but the upkeep of the green was found to be expensive and was abandoned. After many years a scheme for the construction of a bowling green to the north of Nungate Bridge was launched. In 1749 Robert Thomson and George McCall were granted a long lease of the "waste ground at the bridge." This ground, which became the "old bowling green," has been in continuous use for nearly two centuries, and is still used. The palmy days of the old green by the side of the Tyne may be said to have ended in 1890, when it was found that there were more bowlers than could be accommodated comfortably. This led to a new green being laid out on a site fronting Wemyss Place. A bowling club is said to have been formed in 1709.

Wapinschaws, which were a regular feature of the sixteenth century, may in a sense be regarded as pastimes. Strictly speaking, their primary purpose was serious. They were periodic gatherings for the purpose of seeing that every man was armed in accordance with his station in life, and ready to take the field in defence of his country. None the less, wapinschaws were often transformed into spectacles in which various feats of martial valour were performed, thus providing entertainment for onlookers as well as for those taking part. These military displays were held on the town's lands at Gladsmuir.

In the seventeenth century horse-racing had many devotees in Haddington. In 1660 (the year of the restoration of the Stuarts and the revival of all forms of sport and entertainment, these having been repressed under Puritan rule) a number of horses were entered for a prize—a silver cup bearing the arms of Haddington. The race was run on 29th May, the birthday of Charles II, the course being "from Wintoun gray stone to the West Port." Another race was "from Nisbet loanhead to the West Port." In 1661 the *Caledonian Mercury* announced that "the race of Haddington is to be run on 22nd May next," the prize being "a most magnificent cup." To the announcement is appended this very curious note: "This same ancient town, famous for its hospitality, has many times smarted by the arms of enemies. Yet this glorious revolution [*i.e.* the restoration of the Stuarts] hath salved up all their miseries, as very well was made apparent by the noble entertainment given to the Lord Commissioner at the Lord Provost Seaton his lodging, when his Grace made his entry to this Kingdom." Horse-racing under the auspices of the town council continued into the nineteenth century. In 1862 the East Lothian Steeplechase was run along the ridge of the Garleton Hills.

A sharp check to various forms of recreation was administered in 1798 when it was enacted in Haddington that these should be discontinued while Britain was at war with France. It was permissible, however, to drink "a few glasses of wine" at the Cross on the King's Birthday. But with the return of normal times a strong impetus was given towards wholesome and health-giving recreation, one result of which was the institution in 1833 of the Tyneside Games in Amisfield Park. These became an annual affair and attracted the community in large numbers. At the first anniversary of the Games, on 8th October 1834, a stand holding six hundred people was "crowded with ladies of the first rank and fashion, with a great display of East Lothian beauty." In 1867, by which time the Tyneside Games had come to an end, another opportunity for sport and pastime was afforded by the establishment of the Haddington Games. Two years earlier, Haddington Golf Club had been instituted, the course being at Amisfield Park.

Dancing was largely engaged in during the winter months. The county gentry forgathered at the Assembly Room, while humbler devotees found their pleasure in inns and taverns. On 7th March 1772 the *Edinburgh Evening Courant* announced a Subscription Assembly in the Town Hall. Dancing was to begin at five o'clock. Strangers might be introduced by a subscriber. No doubt the early hour was intended to suit the convenience of those who came from remote parts of the county and had to get home at a reasonable time by means of slow-moving vehicles on rough and, it might be, snowbound roads.

The social life of Haddington early in the nineteenth century was enlivened by various organisations. Most of these served a practical purpose, though a few were run on purely social lines. The following are mentioned in the *East Lothian Register* for 1820: Caledonian Society, Nungate and Haddington Brotherly Society, Haddington Friendly Society, Haddington Benevolent Society, Constitutional Society of Weavers of East Lothian, United Society of Smiths of East Lothian, Dyers and Others Society, Haddington Widows' Society, Haddington Savings Bank, Haddington Dispensary, and Female Penny Society for the Relief of the Poor. There was also a Carters' Society whose chief function seems to have been to race their horses on the Monday following the summer Fair (15th July). The leading personage at the Carters' fête bore the esoteric title of "My Lord." He headed a procession of men accompanied by horses gaily decked with flowers. The town's drummer and piper also took part. When passing the burgh school "My Lord" would dismount from his horse and request the rector to give the scholars a holiday in order that they might witness the horse races, which were run from Smail's Pond, just outside the West Port, to St Laurence House.

From time to time processions were organised under the auspices of the town. A time-honoured personage who attended these was "Jock o' the Green," who usually went in front attired in what Martine calls "a bower-shaped erection covered with flowers and shrubs," this headgear being supposed to represent "a bower in the Garden of Eden."

An important organisation that has ripened into old age, though without its natural force becoming abated, is the East Lothian Agricultural Society. Founded in 1819 by several of the leading farmers, it really incorporates an earlier organisation established by General John Fletcher of Saltoun in 1804 which possessed funds amounting to £1700. In 1810 was instituted the Haddington New Club. It was mainly recruited from the nobility and gentry, though in later times it became more democratic. In 1842 the membership numbered 55 together with seven honorary members. The New Club, which existed for upwards of half a century, met quarterly in the George Hotel, and appears to have been mainly social.

Freemasonry locally dates from 1599 when the Haddington St John's Kilwinning Lodge (No. 57) received its charter from Grand Lodge of Scotland. Another hoary organisation is the Ancient Fraternity of Gardeners in East Lothian which has had a lodge in Haddington since 1676. Early in the nineteenth century numerous friendly societies were founded which, besides promoting social intercourse, have worked for the betterment of those connected with them. The East Lothian Mutual Assurance or Friendly Society, established at Haddington in 1830, included among its benefits a sick fund, a deferred annuity fund for affording allowances to members for life who had attained the age of sixty, and a life assurance fund which provided a sum on the death of a member. The Haddington Lodge of the Order of Oddfellows, known as the Tyneside Lodge, dates from 1843. There were also local lodges of the Ancient Order of Foresters, and the Independent Order of Good Templars, both of many years' standing. Long ago the various friendly societies, either singly or together, marched in procession through the streets.

The poor of Haddington have never been without generous friends. Charities or mortifications of one kind or another have existed for at least two centuries. Bequests to the poor, as distinct from money bestowed out of public funds, appears to have been inaugurated in 1735 when a certain William Wood remembered the indigent to the extent of £50. Not a large sum, it is true, but it must be borne in mind that the purchasing power of money was greater then than it is now. Wood's donation was followed by Captain Seton's, amounting to £160. In 1774 John Hume, a native and a carrier by occupation, bequeathed to the town council a tenement at the junction of High Street and Sidegate (now replaced by another building). Part of the proceeds of Hume's tenement was to be expended annually in binding one of the inhabitants as an apprentice, while the residue was to be devoted to religious and charitable purposes. The industrious poor were also benefited by David Gourlay, distiller, Haddington, who in 1801 set apart the interest of £1290, likewise the rent of a piece of ground known as Gourlay Bank, north of the town. The distribution of the Gourlay bequest was entrusted to the ministers of the parish. Later still, James More did not forget the stock from which he had sprung. More succeeded to the estate of Monkrigg after a lawsuit in regard to the will of George More of Monkrigg, his cousin. James More was the founder of the Monkrigg Benevolent Fund for aged and poor persons belonging to the parish, which has benefited hundreds of people during sixty years and more. Each beneficiary receives £5 a year. More also bequeathed £300 to the town council in aid of a new school that was to be dedicated to the memory of John Knox, but the money went to founding a bursary bearing the donor's name. Finally, in 1812, the town council, who all along had succoured the poor, resolved to distribute twelve guineas annually among necessitous burgesses, and gave an undertaking to augment this sum to fifteen guineas when there was no more property tax.

There used to be two red-letter days in Haddington, both connected with the farming interest, when rustic life poured into the town, mainly on business intent, though after bargains had been struck there was much jollification, usually orderly and good-natured. What for many generations was known as Hiring Friday was held early in February. From ten o'clock in the morning till five o'clock in the afternoon, Market Street was filled with a bustling crowd of farmers and farm servants, all anxious to drive advantageous bargains. On Hiring Friday the tavern keepers looked with eager expectancy for plenty of custom, and seldom, if ever, were disappointed. The conditions of agricultural labour were then more stringent, and the lively scenes of Hiring Friday were in a sense the manifestation of a reaction. Every hind had to provide an outworker or "bondager" for labour on the farm, though when the hind had a "halflin" son or a grown-up daughter the custom did not press with undue severity. For the right to live in a cottage, the farm servant had, in lieu of rent, to give twenty-one days' labour in the harvest field, but when a "bondager" had to be engaged, lodged, and fed, the custom became expensive. In 1845 or 1846 feeling against the necessity of providing an outworker was particularly strong, and on Hiring Friday the hinds met on the East Haugh to organise opposition to a system which had become almost unbearable. After the meeting the protestants marched in a body to the market, and before the hiring ended the result of the East Haugh protest was apparent; fully half the hinds had broken their pledges. The "bondager" system was terminated in 1866, and it is pleasant to record that it was the farmers themselves who abolished it. Hiring Friday came to an end in 1925. The employment of farm servants is now gone about in other ways.

The other great day in Haddington, when the rural life of the place was much in evidence, was the annual show of the East Lothian Agricultural Society. It was held in Amisfield Park, lasted two days, and was attended by huge crowds.

CHAPTER XII

Schools and Schoolmasters

In his *Burgh Schools of Scotland* James Grant has brought together a group of striking facts regarding primary education under the ancient Catholic Church of Scotland. The schools then were of two classes—church and burgh schools. The whole scholastic system, however, was so entirely a part of the religious organisation of the country that, even when the burgh bore all expense, the school notwithstanding was mainly under the control of some ecclesiastical body. Thus we find the Abbot of Holyrood patron of the grammar school of Haddington, though it is plain from the burgh records that the town was responsible for its maintenance. Moreover the teachers were almost invariably of the clerical order and with their pedagogic duties frequently combined service of some sort in the parish church. Equally significant is the fact that anterior to the Reformation, and, perhaps later, the pupils were largely destined for a sacred vocation. Considering that John Knox was in priest's orders in his early days, it is a fairly safe deduction that the career of ecclesiastic was marked out for him when he entered the grammar school of Haddington.

Of educational beginnings in the burgh we know very little. That a school existed as early as the fourteenth century is proved by documentary evidence. In the *Exchequer Rolls* (No. 35) occurs an entry under date 1378 of payment of £3, 15s. 2d. to the master of the school of Haddington by command of Robert II. Again, the *Chamberlain's Accounts* for 1383–84 show that £4 was paid, also by royal warrant, for the board *pro mensa* of a poor scholar in the town.

With the coming of the Reformation the educational system, like so much else, underwent a drastic change. It was denuded of its priestly character, while the doctrine and government of the new religion were given free scope in the instruction of youth. Schools were set up in various parishes in East Lothian after the manner prescribed in the first Book of Discipline, which, it may be noted in passing, was chiefly the work of a Haddington man—John Knox. On 6th October 1559 the burgh obtained its first Protestant schoolmaster—Robert Dormont. The town council deemed it expedient to fee Mr Robert Dormont to be schoolmaster of the burgh with twenty-four merks per year and to allow 12d. yearly of schoolhouse fee for "ilk toun bairn," while the assistant teacher, always termed "the doctor," was to receive fourpence per term from each parent or guardian whose children attended the school. The council also undertook to find Dormont "ane chalmer" (schoolhouse), for which no rent was to be paid. Altogether an interesting glimpse of school management at the time of the Reformation.

Dormont was not dominie for long, being succeeded in 1563 by Thomas Cumming. The latter's duties were of wider scope, and he was admonished by the town council to be an exemplar to those who waited on him for instruction. Cumming was to teach diligently in "gramatik, lres [letters], in laytne toung and moralie vertu." His remuneration was to be seventy merks yearly. In addition, each scholar was to pay him "xij^d of skoilaigs silver alanerlie" every term. An increase of income came in 1571 when the town council ordained that all annuals of the chaplainries and altars connected with the parish church should be given to the master of the school, or to a reader, for teaching the children in the kirk what presumably was religious knowledge. In

1572 the offices of parish minister and schoolmaster were combined in James Carmichael, details of whose career are given in Chapter III. Carmichael, who was one of those scholars who made Scotland famous for classical learning, encouraged his pupils to take part in dramatic representations. Of this we are reminded in 1574 when the town subscribed £10 from the Common Good to be expended by the schoolmaster on costumes "and other necessaries for the play."

But the arrangement whereby the offices of parish minister and schoolmaster were held by one person was found impracticable. Even with the assistance of Walter Balcanquall, reader in the parish church (who had been appointed in 1573), Carmichael found he had more pastoral work than he could accomplish. Consequently, after the joint appointment had been given a fair trial, he was set apart exclusively for ministerial duty. In 1577 James Panton became schoolmaster. He too had an assistant who was styled "doctor." This personage, who was to have "ten libs mony of fye quarterlie" with "ane chalmer" (house) free, had his physical wants supplied by "all the bairnis yair day about." In other words, the doctor's "meat" was a responsibility with which the parents of the scholars were charged. How it fared with Panton history does not record, but there is some ground for believing that the opening of the new school in 1579 led to a desire for a master of higher attainments. Anyhow Panton relinquished his post after two years, and John Ker, previously a regent in St Andrews University, reigned in his stead.

Ker is reported to have come under an obligation not to absent himself from the school for three days without permission. It is also stated that he was empowered to collect what fees he could from pupils residing beyond the burgh, an indefinite arrangement and, it may be supposed, most unpleasant for Ker, since it is not difficult to imagine cases of haggling between schoolmaster and parents. But such remuneration was of course supplemental to the salary paid by the town, namely "thre skoir of pundis money" annually. In Ker's time the "auld schule" was repaired and transformed into a lodging not only for the dominie but for the parish minister "and others the town has need of." The "auld schule" lasted throughout the Catholic period and was attended by Knox. It occupied ground opposite the old bowling green and extended from the East Port to the dovecot facing Nungate Bridge. The building therefore overlooked the Tyne, while behind ran the old road to St Mary's. Knox, we are told, talked and wrote Latin with the facility of an educated churchman, which possibly is to be attributed to the fact that in the "auld schule" pupils were punished if they spoke their mother tongue. As school hours lasted, with brief intervals, from early morning till nightfall, an intelligent boy could hardly pass through such discipline without acquiring more than a smattering of Latin. Yet the banning of the vernacular in school hours must have been but temporary, for Knox could write his mother tongue not only with ease but trenchantly, as any one may discover who peruses his *History of the Reformation.*

While the grammar school attended by Knox came to an end in 1578, the building remained and, as we have seen, was used for extra-scholastic purposes. And this could be done the more readily since the new school was built alongside the old. What may be described as the second grammar school of Haddington was in continual use from 1579 till 1755 when the third school was erected on the south side of Church Street.

The strong partiality for Latin was in 1583 extended to the teaching of music. In that year there was formed a song school. John Buchan, the first teacher, was provided with a house and "ane chalmer" in which to teach. Robert Gray, who was appointed head of the song school in 1607, appears to have been precentor in the parish church as well. Three years later he had a successor in Patrick Dunbar, who not only taught vocal music but how to "play upon virginallis, lute, gutharie, and sic (other) instruments." Dunbar led the psalm-singing in the kirk, and in summer "in the grammar school at even." In this way the scholars were made familiar with the psalter. Dunbar seems to have died in office, for in 1614 the town council, "at the request and desire of my Lord Chancellor," appointed James Dunbar, "son to umquhile Patrick Dunbar to be master of ye Sang Schole."

Greek is first mentioned as being taught in Haddington in 1591. John Callender, who was then appointed master of the grammar school, obliged himself to "instruct the said school and haile bairnis . . . sufficiently in the Latyne and Greek grammar . . . and in all classic authors necessary." In 1594 the Presbytery tested Callender's capacity to teach the ancient classics, and investigated, more naturally perhaps, the state of religious education. In 1596 it was decreed that in future all schoolmasters within the bounds must undergo a test, but as to its nature we are not enlightened.

In 1606 there was heartburning over a rival and unauthorised school in Nungate. The matter came before the magistrates in the form of a petition by William Bowie, the burgh schoolmaster, who complained that parents were withdrawing their children from his school and sending them to one in Nungate kept by a Mr Burnside. As the position then stood, this was irregular, and it was enacted that no parent put a child to school within a mile of the burgh seminary. The magistrates also ordered the Nungate establishment to be closed. It would be interesting to know the motive that induced parents to desert the town school. Was it due to Bowie's inefficiency or unpopularity, or was it merely a matter of convenience? A similar complaint was lodged in 1617 against John Mercer, and again the magistrates righted matters by ordaining that no one was to teach in Haddington save Thomas Paterson, master of the grammar school.

In 1623, when Alexander Seton held the post, the salary was substantially increased. It was in future to be two hundred merks yearly, while the "doctor" was to receive £20. Seton was also paid two shillings by parents for each of their children attending the school, a source of revenue which must have been considerable. As for the land-ward children, Seton could be as extortionate as he pleased, the parents having to pay what he demanded. His position was also safeguarded by the prohibition of a rival school. In return, Seton was to give unremitting attention to his duties. For place of abode he was assigned "the haill houses above the said school with ane laich cellar"; also "the haill laich houses above . . . ye auld schule." School discipline at this time was difficult to preserve, and the town council agreed "to assist, maintain, and defend ye said Mr Alexander in correcting and repressing ye insolence of ye scholars."

Seton, who was the father of William Seton, provost of the burgh, sued in 1642 Robert Ker of Whitehill and William Edgar, burgess, as cautioner, for £100 for Robert Ker's (presumably a son) board and lodging for a year. There was also an unsettled bill of four rex-dollars for teaching him Latin, and another for twenty shillings expended on a pair of shoes for this pupil. The curious may read Seton's somewhat fulsome epitaph (he died in 1645) in Haddington Churchyard. There, on an imposing tombstone, is a Latin inscription which Monteith, in his *Theater of Mortality*, translates thus:

> Here lies a man, who tamèd wayward youth,
> Instructing them with letters and with truth.
> The easy minds he greatly did improve,
> Inform'd the ignorant, by special love;

SCHOOLS AND SCHOOLMASTERS

He did disclose all myst'ries, and reveal
What most abstruse, as hidden under seal.
Consider him aright, for truly he,
Priest of the Muses, well may naméd be.

Female education, though it was extremely meagre, existed in the sixteenth century. Isabel Spence, who is mentioned in 1586 as having been succeeded by Marion Lindsay, spouse to James Cockburn, appears to have been the earliest female teacher. Jane Halyburton was teaching the girls in 1600, and in 1609 the "maiden bairns" were taught reading and sewing by Marion Redpath. The post had been offered to Elizabeth Donaldson, who not only "disdainfully refused it," but opened a rival school which, despite its being attended by "ane great number of maiden bairns," was closed by the magistrates. At this time the girls were put to weaving on attaining the age of fourteen.

In 1672 the schoolmaster was Edward Jamieson who, refusing to take the oath of allegiance, was deprived. The Bishop of Edinburgh used his influence to secure Jamieson's reinstatement, but the town council would not agree. Early in the eighteenth century the fortunes of the school were in the hands of Thomas Watt, who published a Latin grammar at Edinburgh in 1714. One of his noted predecessors, James Carmichael, also won fame in a similar manner. Carmichael's Latin grammar was published in 1587 and was dedicated to James VI.

Towards the close of the seventeenth century the day's work at the grammar school began at six o'clock in the morning, but in 1699 it was resolved, in the interest of the pupils' health, that from Hallowmas to Candlemas the assembling hour be nine o'clock. If school hours were long and arduous, some relaxation was afforded in the form of play-acting. In 1682 the entrance door of the bowling green was removed for the convenience of scholars taking part in a dramatic performance, which seems to imply that it took place in the open air. This novel feature of school life became prominent after 1724 when John Leslie was headmaster. Leslie was a friend of Allan Ramsay, author of the *Gentle Shepherd*, who describes the Haddington dominie as "a gentleman of true learning." A play having been acted by the scholars on 8th March 1724, Leslie claimed expenses for the erection of the stage. In doing so, he informed the magistrates that the performance had been received "with a general applause."

The scholars again exhibited dramatic talent on 26th August 1725, acting a tragedy, the *Siege of Damascus*, by John Hughes, a dramatist of the Queen Anne period. From a paragraph in the *Edinburgh Courant* we learn that the performance was held in the forenoon, that those who took part were "Noblemen and Gentlemen's children, scholars of the Grammar School," and that everything passed off to the "great satisfaction and surprise of many ladies of Quality, Nobility, Gentry, and crowds of other spectators, who, notwithstanding the storminess of the day, resorted thither to have the pleasure of that diversion." The reference to "crowds of other spectators" makes it almost certain that the tragedy of the *Siege of Damascus* was performed in the open air.

Miller in his *Lamp of Lothian* tells us that Allan Ramsay on one occasion "introduced his young Thespian heroes to their auditors." And from other sources we learn that the Scots pastoral poet composed a prologue for a performance of Dryden's *Aurengzebe*, given by the Haddington schoolboys in 1727. The prologue is printed in Chalmers's edition of Allan Ramsay's works. It ends:

"Get seven score verse of Ovid's Trist by heart,
To rattle o'er, else I shall make ye smart!"
Cry snarling dominies that little ken:—
Such may teach parrots, *but our Lesly men.*

131

SCHOOLS AND SCHOOLMASTERS

From the town council the boys of the grammar school received every encouragement to develop their histrionic talents. On 5th August 1729 the magistrates communed "with Mr John Lesley anent a stage for the schoolboys to act a comedy upon." Later, the town treasurer was instructed "to provide trees and dales (deals), and other materials for the stage." These preparations probably were connected with a performance of *Julius Cæsar* followed by one of the *Gentle Shepherd*. At any rate both works were acted on 27th August. Allan Ramsay was present and supervised his own production and possibly *Julius Cæsar* as well. The poet also composed prologues for both works. In the one preceding the Shakespearean play Ramsay is conscious that some may question the propriety of callow youth attempting a representation of *Julius Cæsar*, but repels the idea triumphantly (as he thinks). He asks:

> Is it for Boys to act the fatal doom
> Of Julius Cæsar and the fall of Rome?

and bids those retire who can derive "no Pleasure from this Play."

> Our Souls, tho' young, are of a British growth,
> They warmly breathe for Liberty and Scowth.

In the prologue to the *Gentle Shepherd* Ramsay states that his pastoral was preceded by *Julius Cæsar*. Evidently the juxtaposition of the Shakespearean play and the *Gentle Shepherd* made him a little uneasy. The pastoral poet suspects that the diction of his own work may offend but is resolved to treat any objection with disdain.

> Though they're but Shepherds that we're now to act,
> Yet, gentle Audience, we'd not ha' ye mistake
> And think your entertainment will be rude.

A reference to the leading characters in the *Gentle Shepherd*, with which the prologue concludes, gives Allan another opportunity of introducing the name of the Haddington schoolmaster.

> Thus give us leave to pass our None-age time on,
> We'll all be Pates and Lesly 'll be our Symon.

"Honest Allan" again was to the fore when Leslie's pupils gave a performance of Addison's *Drummer*, supplying an epilogue in which he compliments the Haddington scholars.

> Hey boys! The day's our ain! The ladies smile;
> Which over-recompenses all our toil.
> Delights of mankind! tho' in some small parts
> We are deficient, yet our wills and hearts
> Are yours; and, when more perfect, shall endeavour,
> By acting better, to secure your favour.

Ramsay's epilogue, it is interesting to add, was spoken by Charles and Maurice, sons of Colonel Cockburn of Clerkington. But enough perhaps has been said of the histrionic accomplishments of the grammar school of Haddington and of Allan Ramsay's association with their efforts.

In spite of these rather engrossing diversions, the school maintained its reputation for proficiency in classics. But while Greek and Latin occupied chief place in the curriculum a feeling gradually arose that the requirements of a liberal education were not being fully met unless the ancient tongues were supplemented with English. Tradi-

132

tional study was first modified in 1731 when English was made more prominent, one Donaldson, who had been assistant to Leslie, being appointed to teach the subject, together with writing and arithmetic. But, according to Miller, it was not till 1750 that "a proper teacher of English was appointed" in the person of Alexander Smart, which rather suggests that Donaldson's qualifications had not been up to standard. Smart had upwards of sixty scholars. By his time a large number of pupils was coming forward who had little use for Greek and Latin but much for English, writing, arithmetic, geography, and other essentially vocational subjects. The mediæval grammar school had outgrown its usefulness, and the English school was its modern counterpart. The trend of education now was in the direction of instructing pupils how to speak and write their mother tongue with accuracy and, it might be, with some pretensions to grace.

This significant departure in educational standards synchronised with the erection of a new grammar school which, including a house for the master, cost £5906 Scots. The building was erected in 1755 and still exists—a massive, plain, red sandstone structure on the south side of Church Street. As regards the schoolhouse, Barclay, writing in 1785, states that it contained "the best accommodation for boarders of any he knew." Alongside the grammar school was erected in 1761 a building for the teaching of English and allied subjects, which was under the supervision of John Abernethy, who had formerly been schoolmaster of Gifford.

Under James Watson, who was appointed rector in 1763, and his successor, James Johnston, who came to the office twenty years later, the school was given a fresh lease of life, many of the future representatives of well-known Haddington families receiving their education there. When Watson resigned in 1783, the magistrates advertised the vacancy in the *Edinburgh Advertiser*, and, with a view of attracting candidates, gave a circumstantial account of the state of the grammar school.

Haddington is known to be a place remarkably well situated for a grammar school and the accommodation of Boarders, being in a pleasant, healthful, and fruitful country, abounding with provisions of all kinds, at a moderate distance from the Metropolis, to and from which there is access by Stage Coaches two or three times every day.

The School-rooms are large and airy, the Dwelling-house [schoolhouse] is large, roomy, convenient, well-finished (being built within these thirty years), in every respect fit to accommodate a large family and a number of boarders; independent of which, and a good garden, the School fees and Candlemas gifts alone, payable to the Rector and his Assistant or Doctor, have been known to yield over £100 Sterling yearly, and they will also between them be entitled to a yearly salary of 400 merks Scots.

The Languages to be taught at this School are Latin, French, and Greek; and as the salary, school fees, profits of Boarders, and other encouragements are reckoned handsome, and may be increased by proper care, good behaviour, and ability of the Teachers, so the Magistrates flatter themselves that persons of this description only will apply, personally, or by letter, without loss of time. N.B. Preachers, or those having a view to Church settlements, need not apply for this.

After a "comparative trial," James Johnston was found "best qualified," and, as already mentioned, was duly appointed to succeed James Watson. By this time not only were educational ideals heightened and broadened, but the social aspect received more attention. Close friendships were formed which were kept in repair in after years. In 1765 we hear for the first time of former pupils dining together at the Blue Bell Inn, where youthful associations were recalled. Another forgathering took place in the following year—this time in the Star and Garter Inn, Edinburgh. Again, in 1772, the former Haddington pupils held a reunion at the premises of George Bain, in Old Assembly Close, Edinburgh. Nor was the physical welfare of the scholars neglected. In 1779 the thin end of the wedge of athleticism in the modern sense was introduced, in the shape of ball games at the Sands. Previously there had been no more exalted vision of recreation than cock-fighting, and, unfortunately, such disgusting and degrading exhibitions continued to be witnessed in the town till the end of the eighteenth century. On Fastern's E'en there was usually a football match in which both masters and scholars took part.

In the *Statistical Account of Scotland* (1791) the salary of the rector is stated to be 400 merks Scots, while that of the English master is set down at £15 sterling. The latter also was expected to give tuition in the rudiments of music. James Johnston, the rector, accepted boarders at £20 per annum, who were lodged in apartments above the school. About this time, too, the magistrates, along with the ministers of the town, began to visit the grammar school on Examination Day, when prizes were awarded to the dux and a quantity of sweets to each scholar.

Till 1731 the grammar school was the sole educational establishment, but after that date there were furtive attempts to open private schools in which modern subjects were a speciality. Towards the close of the century Richard Hay was English master, though he seems to have devoted much time to arithmetic, as he was the author of a work bearing the somewhat fatuous title of *Beauties of Arithmetic*. In 1814 Hay was induced to resign on receiving an annuity of £30 per annum. He, however, apparently reserved the right to open a private establishment in which the curriculum was comprehensive, for it included English, writing, arithmetic, geography, as well as ultramodern and commercial subjects like book-keeping, mensuration, and land surveying.

The nineteenth century opened with William Graham in the seat of authority at the grammar school. Graham, who had previously been schoolmaster at Dirleton, was rector for thirty-eight years. Martine bears contemporary witness that he was "a very successful teacher, and, although a little pedantic, was much esteemed in society." During his time the school was largely attended by sons of the landed gentry and well-to-do farmers, some of whom had careers of distinction at Edinburgh University. In 1801 Graham had twenty-seven boarders under his care, and as late as 1817 he advertised in the *Edinburgh Courant* that boarding accommodation was a feature. Every Sunday the scholars in residence were marched to the parish church, where they occupied a large, square pew.

Another chapter in the history of the grammar school was begun in 1809. As has been noted, arithmetic had been taught in the English school for many years, but it was now deemed essential to instruct pupils in the higher mathematics. This led to the erection of a new building adjoining the English school, which became known as the Mathematical school. For its first teacher it had no less a person than Edward Irving, who was recommended in response to a request made to Professor Leslie of Edinburgh University. Irving, who was described by Leslie as "a lad of good character and of superior abilities," presented the Professor's testimonial to the magistrates, who duly appointed him. In 1812 Irving was offered a scholastic post in Kirkcaldy at a higher salary. He wished, however, to remain in Haddington conditionally that his remuneration was increased to what he was being offered by Kirkcaldy. "The kind treatment and good encouragement which I have uniformly received from the Magistrates and the people in and about Haddington," Irving wrote, "have attached me strongly to my present situation and render me unwilling to leave it." A proposal to increase his remuneration by £15 was, however, defeated, and on 29th September Irving intimated his acceptance of the Kirkcaldy appointment.

While master of the Mathematical school Irving was "a tall, ruddy, robust, handsome

From painting by John G. Spence Smith, R.S.A.

Group of Old Buildings in Mitchell's Close.

[*To face p.* 134.

youth." He "won the confidence of his advanced pupils," says Mrs Oliphant, his biographer, as well as made his way "into the homes and society of many of the worthy inhabitants of Haddington." Among these was Dr John Welsh, whose daughter Jane had lessons from Irving. A friendship grew up between teacher and pupil which, as every one knows, was a central episode of Irving's career. In due course Jane Welsh became the wife of Thomas Carlyle. Although teaching mathematics in Haddington, Irving's ultimate intention was to enter the ministry of the Church of Scotland. It is reported of him that round the supper table he would ventilate the peculiar religious opinions that afterwards made him famous, a habit which sometimes brought him into conflict with the parish minister—Dr Robert Lorimer. During his stay in the town Irving devoted much time to astronomy and, accompanied by some of his pupils, would sally forth on dark nights to study the stars.

Irving's successor was James Brown. Soon after he had taken up his duties it became clear that the Mathematical school could not support a master unless he taught other subjects as well. This led, in 1814, to the Mathematical department being affiliated with the English school under Brown's supervision. He resigned in the following year, on being appointed minister of the Scots Church at Calcutta, and Thomas Cumming, his assistant, was promoted to his place. The new assistant was Patrick Hardie, who in 1822 succeeded Cumming. Hardie, who formerly had a seminary of his own in St Ann's Place, turned out some first-class pupils, the most noted being Samuel Smiles, author of *Self-Help*. Hardie was a favourite with his scholars, who, in 1837, erected a handsome stone over his grave in Haddington Churchyard.

In 1822 the heritors approved of the establishment of a parish school, but the scheme was discouraged by the town council on grounds of economy. Two years later the project was again mooted, but not till 1826 was it realised. A parish school supported by the landward heritors was erected in Lodge Street, though, when sites were considered, it was actually suggested that the ruins of St Martin's Chapel be pulled down and the parish school erected there. Fortunately what would have been an act of vandalism was prevented. James Johnstone, the friend of Thomas Carlyle, was the first parochial schoolmaster. He had several highly efficient successors. Indeed, when (as will be shown presently) the burgh school entered upon decadent days, the parish school came to its own, and was in fact responsible for the education of the great majority of the youth of the town. In 1872 it came under the direction of the newly appointed School Board, when the name was changed to Landward Public School, and continued as such till the late eighties of last century. The old parish school with the master's house adjoining still exists, though it has long served other purposes.

But to return to the grammar school. In 1838, the rectorship being once more vacant, the town council appointed a committee to consider improvements in the management. The result was the adoption of a recommendation to the effect that "the most extensively beneficial plan" would be to appoint one rector and two assistants, who would be responsible for the curriculum of the three burgh schools. Robert Burns Nichol was made English and French teacher, and John Davidson mathematical and writing master. Greek and Latin were assigned, as heretofore, to the rector.

From 1838 to 1843 the last-mentioned office was held by William Maxwell Gunn. His academic career had been unusually distinguished and was crowned with the honorary degree of Doctor of Laws from Edinburgh University. Educated at the High School of Edinburgh, where he won the gold medal in the rector's class, Gunn began his teaching career by becoming the first rector of the Edinburgh Southern

Academy, which he opened in 1829. When he relinquished the Haddington rectorship it was to become one of the classical masters of the High School of Edinburgh.[1] Gunn was the author of several textbooks dealing with the ancient classics. Much interested in religion and theology, he also wrote *Biblical Criticism in Scotland* and *Religion and National Education,* as well as edited for the Wodrow Society the *Select Works* of Robert Rollock, the first Principal of Edinburgh University.

Gunn's scholastic reputation notwithstanding, the English and French classes of Nichol were the largest, partly because of the vocational importance of the subjects and partly owing to the teacher's popularity. A strict disciplinarian, Nichol introduced a novelty in the shape of a weekly court at which all cases of alleged misbehaviour were investigated and the offenders punished. Nichol himself acted as judge, and selected from his pupils a prosecutor and a jury. One of the cases tried had reference to Anthony Carrick, who was accused of throwing the keys of the school into the Tyne.

With Maxwell Gunn's removal to Edinburgh in 1843 the glory of the old grammar school may be said to have departed. His successor was the Rev. William Whyte, who, although in orders, appears to have been wholly associated with pedagogic pursuits. Before coming to Haddington he was classical master in George Watson's Hospital, Edinburgh, where, it may be presumed, he had some reputation, otherwise he would not have been given the Haddington rectorship. But however that may be, Whyte became a thorn in the flesh of the magistrates and council, and under his supervision the grammar school seriously declined. Remiss and inefficient, Whyte was constantly squabbling regarding his salary. On the other hand, many parents had so little confidence in the rector's character and ability that they withdrew their children. Frequently during Whyte's rectorship the town's schools were in a lamentable state. At one time there were only eleven pupils in a school capable of accommodating from two to three hundred, and with an assistant the attendance did not increase beyond fourteen. Only two dozen scholars attended the school examination in 1866, which caused the *Haddingtonshire Courier* to allude to "the melancholy spectacle now annually presented at what is still called the Examination of the Burgh School." Even fewer pupils presented themselves in the following year, and the local newspaper was constrained to refer to "the once famous and flourishing Burgh Schools of Haddington." It was suggested to Whyte that he should resign, and this he was willing to do, provided the magistrates made him "a handsome offer worthy the acceptance of a preacher of the Gospel and a veteran classic." A retiring allowance of £60 was proposed on the understanding that Whyte severed his connection with the school and vacated the rector's house. But there was no response to this overture, and the moribund condition of education in the town continued. In 1864, and again in 1868, Whyte's dismissal was considered, but no action was taken. He remained master of the situation for other six years.

After Whyte's departure strenuous efforts were made to raise the burgh school to its former status. In the hope of attracting pupils of all ages, a primary department was inaugurated under the charge of William Goodfellow, who came from Wales. This

---

[1] It is noteworthy that at least two headmasters and one "doctor" of the grammar school of Haddington gained the subsequent distinction of being Rectors of the High School of Edinburgh—Hew Wallace, William Skene, and Alexander Matheson. Wallace was appointed in 1650, and held office till his death six years later. Skene, again, was Rector of the High School from 1680 to 1717. Matheson received the post in 1759. Previously he had been "doctor" in the Haddington seminary as well as tutor to Sir David Kinloch of Gilmerton, Bt. Because of his successful rectorship, Matheson was admitted a burgess and guild-brother of Edinburgh. One of his pupils was the celebrated Dugald Stewart. Alexander Adam, who was to become the most famous of all the Rectors of the High School, was an assistant to Matheson. See Steven, *History of the High School,* pp. 106–108.

step was taken on the recommendation of the recently constituted School Board. The primary children met in the English school, which was also used for the teaching of the classics and mathematics. But the decadent state of the burgh school throughout most of Whyte's rectorship was not easily ended. Indeed many parents transferred their children to the parish school, which had a competent headmaster in Thomas Henderson, who had previously taught at Morham. Further complications arose with the presence of educational rivals. Private schools for both sexes now existed, one or two of which displayed a tolerably high standard of teaching and produced a few scholars who made their mark in the world. Chief among these institutions was Paterson Place Academy, which the Rev. John Paterson, a former United Presbyterian minister, carried on till 1854, when it was taken over by Walter Haig, another worthy pedagogue. Then there was Flora Bank private school under the superintendence of Charles Macnab. Several schools for young ladies also existed, notably that for which Mrs Croley and Miss Finlay were responsible.

The town's schools having to contend with these private establishments, various steps were taken for putting the former on a stronger basis. In 1876 there was talk of uniting the burgh and parish schools, but the Education Department were unfavourable. The truth is, the historic school of Haddington was nearing its end. In April 1879 the old grammar school building was advertised for sale, also the English school and the premises in which Edward Irving taught mathematics. The grammar and English schools were sold in the following May and June, the former for £600. Both buildings were converted into small dwellings. Thus terminated the old grammar school of Haddington which had existed continuously from the fourteenth century and probably earlier—a period of five hundred years. Truly, it was "ane end of ane auld sang," to use the saying of Chancellor Seafield at the passing of the Scottish Parliament.

A comparatively recent big-scale achievement was the rearing of the Knox Institute. As far back as 1870 it had been proposed to erect a memorial to Haddington's greatest townsman—John Knox, and that it should take the form of an educational institution was right and proper in the case of one who laboured so zealously for the establishment of parish schools throughout Scotland. But seven years elapsed before plans were finally approved for the erection at the west end of the town of a large, imposing, and up-to-date higher grade school. The Knox Institute was opened for teaching on 1st October 1879 under the rectorship of J. C. Graham, M.A., previously a classical master in Merchiston Castle School, Edinburgh. The formal opening, however, did not take place till the following January, the ceremony being performed by Mr Arthur J. Balfour of Whittingehame, afterwards first Earl Balfour. In front of the building was placed a life-size statue of the Scottish Reformer, the gift of the Misses Traill, Aberlady. The statue, which is carved in freestone, was the work of D. W. Stevenson, A.R.S.A. Knox is represented in Geneva gown, and his left hand rests on an open Bible.

The inauguration of the Knox Institute reacted precariously on Walter Haig's Academy in Paterson Place. This school had all along attracted a good class of pupil, the fees being much higher than those obtaining in the public schools. Haig's Academy, as a kind of secondary school, found a powerful rival in the Knox Institute. By this time Walter Haig had grown elderly, and not long after, the seminary, of which he had been for many years the respected head, was closed. Haig, who took up residence in Edinburgh and died there in 1904, was presented by former pupils with a purse containing one hundred sovereigns, together with a silver salver.

137

SCHOOLS AND SCHOOLMASTERS

The advance in educational methods affected prejudicially the town's schools as well, and when, in the rear of the Knox Institute, there was erected an elementary school affording the same teaching as was given in the burgh and parish schools but with superior equipment and greater efficiency, it was seen that the days of the latter were numbered.

A chapter that has education for its theme may fitly close with a brief description of several cultural institutions that arose in Haddington when the means of mental improvement were not so evenly distributed as they are now. Most of them came into existence early in the nineteenth century and betokened an active interest in the things of the mind.

First of all, there were the efforts to stimulate intelligence and promote general education among adults through the medium of books. The Gray Library, being a superb collection of recondite works, may be reckoned in a category by itself: the generality of townsfolk could derive little benefit from it. Still, the town council, at least for a time, regarded this benefaction as a nucleus round which a modern library might be built up. Ratepayers could borrow from the Gray Library, a catalogue of which was compiled and printed in 1828 by James Miller, author of the *Lamp of Lothian*; but this concession was rarely taken advantage of. The persons who profited were persons from a distance, scholars like Dr Thomas M'Crie who, when writing his famous biography of John Knox, applied for some books in the Gray Collection which he wished to consult. His request was granted, and, be it said to his credit, the volumes were returned in due course. All outside borrowers were not so punctilious. When in 1833 the state of the Gray Library was investigated, as it appears to have been periodically, it was found that no fewer than sixty volumes were missing. Some were traced to a minister's library in Glasgow, others were discovered in Duns, while a number were in the custody of Dr Hew Scott, who used them in the compilation of *Fasti Ecclesiæ Scoticana*. One volume, a Hebrew grammar, found its way back to the Gray Library after an absence of more than fifteen years.

The town council's effort to augment the Gray Collection with modern literature was only partially successful, probably the chief reason being that fiction was excluded. Early last century, however, an impetus to reading for general instruction and entertainment was given by the founding of the Haddington Subscription Library. It was designed to meet the popular demand, the main contents consisting of light literature in which novels were conspicuous. What may be described as the instructional type of book, especially on the scientific side, was supplied by the "itinerating libraries" of Samuel Brown. Instituted in 1817, these operated throughout the county, though knowledgeable persons within the burgh were catered for as well. But Samuel Brown's scheme did not enter into serious competition with Haddington Subscription Library.

In addition, a circulating library was opened in 1814 by George Miller, the founder of the East Lothian Press, but it only lasted a few years. A small library was also conducted under the auspices of the Haddington School of Arts. It comprised chiefly scientific works, "an unalterable rule" being "that no novels, plays, or books of an immoral or irreligious tendency" were to find a place on the shelves. When the Haddington School of Arts came to an end in 1853, its library, numbering more than a hundred volumes, was handed over to the Town and County Library then being formed.

CHAPTER XIII

Buildings Old and New

HADDINGTON, in spite of its being one of the ancient royal burghs, has few antiquities. The statement may savour of paradox, but it has reluctantly to be admitted as actual fact. The reason is not far to seek. Throughout its long chequered history, and because of its strategical position, the town was repeatedly subjected to devastating incursions by the English. With fire and sword the enemy did terrible havoc. More than once, as we have seen, Haddington was almost razed to the ground, which was not difficult where buildings were mostly thatched. Again and again the town had to be rebuilt, though always on the old site and in general conformity with the original lay-out.

Consequently the periodic upheavals prior to the sixteenth century went far to preclude the survival of buildings dating back to early times. Indeed, with the exception of the parish church of St Mary and St Martin's Chapel (the latter for long a hopeless ruin), no existing structure is older than the sixteenth century. Numbering not more than half a dozen, these for the most part consist of portions of masonry incorporated with more recent buildings, and are to be seen at the far end of certain closes off the main streets. The late Dr Wallace-James discovered one excellent example in the form of a "secret" stair built into the thickness of the wall of a tenement on the south side of the High Street, which had once belonged to James Oliphant, an early provost of the burgh, and Thomas Punton, a bailie. Be that as it may, it is true none the less that most of the buildings that we see to-day have no history: they belong to the eighteenth century or, as can be discerned from their pseudo-classical design, to the earlier part of the nineteenth.

What is now Court Street was at one time designated King Street, thus doing obeisance to a well-founded tradition that in this quarter, when Haddington was a regal town, stood the royal palace which had associations with William the Lyon and Alexander II. That a palace was situated here is vouched for by Fordun, the chronicler, who, while not always to be relied on, was at any rate living sufficiently near the time covered by his narrative. From Fordun we derive the information that a "palace" stood "at the west end of the High Street," and that in it, as recorded in the opening chapter, Patrick, sixth Earl of Athol, was murdered in 1242. In 1833 the site chosen for the County Buildings necessitated the removal of several blocks of dwellings and one or two nondescript structures. Among the latter was a fragment of arched Norman masonry, which, it has been suggested, was all that remained of the palace of the early Scottish kings. Miller, who was residing in the town at the time of the demolition, says the fragment consisted of a vault and part of an arched passage leading thereto. A drawing of this ruin, made by Adam Neill, bookseller, and reproduced in the *East Lothian Register* for 1834, shows masonry which in design and texture might have been contemporaneous with William the Lyon and Alexander II.

The older portion of the County Buildings (extensive additions have been made of recent years) was erected from a design by William Burn, a noted though rather uninspired Edinburgh architect. Fortunately, Burn was more successful with the Haddington structure than he was with most of his buildings. It is in the Tudor style and cost £5500. Most of the stone was obtained from the Jerusalem quarry in the vicinity,

139

but part of the façade is constructed of polished stone from Fife. Immediately to the east of the County Buildings is the Corn Exchange, which was erected in 1854 after a plan by Robert William Billings, author of *Baronial and Ecclesiastical Antiquities of Scotland*.

At the junction of High Street and Market Street, and particularly arresting as one enters the town from the Edinburgh road, are the municipal buildings. The earliest portion of this composite structure was designed by William Adam of Maryburgh, hardly less celebrated as an architect than his son Robert. Hopetoun House, one of the noblest mansions in the kingdom, the old Royal Infirmary of Edinburgh, and the old Town House of Dundee (the last-mentioned ruthlessly demolished a few years ago) were all creations of William Adam.

The Town House of Haddington was contracted for on 10th June 1742 by Robert Reid, mason, and George Pirie, wright. But there were delays, and actual building operations did not take place till 1748. Sixty feet long and thirty-six wide, the original structure conformed strictly to Adam's design. It was adorned with a steeple which was a landmark for more than eighty years. Accommodation was provided for the town council and the sheriff court, while on the ground flat, facing south, was the local jail consisting of three cells. When these were full, prisoners were relegated to the third storey. Below was the apartment in which the town council transacted business —a rather surprising and, one would suppose, a very awkward arrangement. Moreover, the jail was insecure, and the escape of prisoners was not unusual. Joseph John Gurney, the Quaker philanthropist, inspected the building in 1819, and was severe in his criticism. Gurney's strictures, however, were more than confirmed in 1835 by the commissioners appointed to report on the municipal corporations of Scotland. We read: "The jail was not upon a good construction. It was not supplied with water, the cells were badly ventilated, and there was no proper provision for cleanliness."

To the west of the Town House there was added in 1788 what may be termed the Assembly block, which led to a considerable modification of the Adam building. Above the existing arch on the ground floor was erected what came to be known as the Assembly Room. It was reached by the broad staircase that is still to the fore. Below accommodation was provided for carriages and sedan chairs. The project for an Assembly Room was first mooted in 1774 by a group of gentlemen of East Lothian headed by Mr Charteris of Amisfield. The original idea was to build on Little Sands, but as a site there could not be obtained, the waste ground west of the Town House was fixed upon. The town council favoured the idea "provided the said room was built on pillars," so that the markets for bear and oats might still be held below, a stipulation which was agreed to. Owing to various causes the Assembly Room was not completed till fourteen years later. Towards the project the town council subscribed twenty-five guineas on condition that that body had the use of the building on "necessary public occasions." On the other hand, the county gentlemen came under an obligation to furnish "a new prison room," an arrangement not so puzzling when it is remembered that the civic authority had provided the site. The holding of the markets below the Assembly Room was ultimately abandoned, and on the ground was built the sheriff-court room (which was in use till 1833 when it was removed to the new County Buildings), also offices for the sheriff clerk and town clerk, as well as accommodation for the burgh and county records. The present finely proportioned steeple dates from 1830–31. Planned by Gillespie-Graham, the architect of the spire of the old Assembly Hall on the Castle Hill of Edinburgh, it is 170 feet high, and was built by James M'Watt, mason.

From Macgibbon and Ross' "Castellated and Domestic Architecture of Scotland."

Bothwell Castle (so-called), Hardgate, as it was Fifty Years Ago.

[*To face p.* 140.

Proceeding down High Street, we come to the Cross of Haddington situated in the centre of the causeway. Gifted in 1881 by Daniel and John Bernard of Holme House, it replaces an earlier structure. Indeed it is the third Cross, if not the fourth, to be erected in the ancient Croce Gait. The probability is that a Cross was set up as far back as the reign of David I. Most likely it would be cruciform, as most crosses of that period were. But however this may be, a pre-Reformation Cross existed till 1693. Regarding this antiquity there is an illuminating entry in the burgh records under date 11th September 1693. "The same day the Counsell after report made by the committee who were appoynted to relieve the bill given out by John Jack, mason, and his accompt of charges and expenses in buying and working a long stone and some small stones *for building ane new crosse*, allows him fourtie pund Scots in full of his accompt." The Cross erected by John Jack was situated near Fishmarket Wynd (now Cross Lane). For many years the exact site was unknown, but in 1926, in course of causeway operations in High Street, the foundation stone, sixteen inches square, was accidentally uncovered. From this basement, says Martine, rose four steps surmounted by a rounded stone pillar "as thick as a man's waist, with the figure of an animal of some doubtful species, not unlike a monkey, on the top of it." [1] This Cross was about twelve feet high from the causeway. After serving for one hundred and eighteen years, the Cross of 1693 perished about 1811 as the result of a freak. A person, evidently anxious to show physical prowess, climbed to the top of the shaft, and in doing so brought the whole structure to the ground. By a singular coincidence a similar mishap overtook the Cross erected by Messrs Bernard, the goat being again smashed as the result of a youthful frolic. In 1936 a new goat was set up.

When the Cross of 1693 was destroyed, the town council, not being in a position to erect another of stone, reared a wooden pillar some yards farther east, which did service until, like its predecessor, it met with an untoward fate, being set on fire. After its destruction, which happened within living memory, there was no Cross till 1881, when, as already stated, the present one was erected through the munificence of Messrs D. & J. Bernard. It rests on a basement of three broad steps. Out of this massive square pedestal rises a slender shaft fully twelve feet high, the whole being crowned at a height of twenty-five feet by the Haddington goat in rampant posture, and bearing between the forepaws a gilded pennant on which the letter H is emblazoned. On one side of the pedestal are the words: "The + of Haddington," the inscription being taken from the old town seal. On the west angle the figure of the goat is repeated, with the traditional tree. The north shield, again, has within it the figure of a muzzled bear and the crest of the donors of the Cross, which was placed there by request of the town council. Facing the east is the lion rampant of Scotland, while the southern shield is filled with a monogram of the date of erection.

It is perhaps unnecessary to state that the Cross figured in most of the important events in the history of Haddington. Many proclamations, royal or otherwise, were (and still are) made there, and in olden times the Cross was the rallying place of the burghers when summoned to fight the English. The Cross also was associated with public rejoicings. Until well into the nineteenth century, it was customary on the King's Birthday for the leading burgesses to assemble round it and, with libations of wine, celebrate the auspicious occasion. But in progressive times the boisterous proceedings and crude entertainment associated with the King's Birthday came to be regarded as in questionable taste and the practice fell into desuetude. The "jougs," which were last used in 1785, were beside the Cross. In front of the George Hotel

---

[1] The animal was a unicorn. A portion of this relic is preserved at the Public Library.

141

stood the Tron, an ungainly wooden erection for weighing wool, hides, tallow, cheese, and other commodities. The dues of the Tron were paid both in kind and in money. Every pack of wool paid a fleece and twelve shillings Scots; a stone of cheese, one shilling Scots; and an ox or cowhide, six pennies. Paving stones mark the site of the Tron.

In Market Street formerly were two buildings that might well be numbered among the antiquities of Haddington. One was the mediæval Tolbooth, which occupied ground facing Newton Port. It was removed in the middle of the eighteenth century when a new place of detention for lawbreakers was erected at the Town House. The demolition of the old Tolbooth was by no means premature, though regrettable on historical grounds, being insecure as well as dilapidated. In 1732 its ruinous state was so obvious that the town council, who had hitherto held their meetings there, were compelled to remove to the town's library, then housed in the pre-Reformation schoolhouse. At the same time the steeple with its clock and bell was pulled down as dangerous. We have no detailed description of the Tolbooth, but as it had a draw-bridge, the repair of which was ordered in 1658, it is presumed that the building was castellated. On the roof was a bartizan, probably battlemented, and reached by a turnpike stair. Here in troublous times a sentinel was posted. In 1532 it was decreed that Matthew Hunter should "walk on the tolbooth head nightly." The building was a three-storey one. The town council met in an apartment on the first floor, while at the street level accommodation for prisoners appears to have been provided.

Of the antiquity of the Tolbooth there can be no doubt, for it existed previous to the earliest burgh records, which begin in the fifteenth century. It is also known that in 1539 repairs were carried out and the roof covered with slates. Some old-time customs were associated with the Tolbooth. Here, when accused persons did not appear after being summoned, their names were thrice called, after which, if they were burgesses, they were declared unfreemen. The jailor, for the better performance of his office, had an "able-bodied and qualified servant." Both jailor and assistant wore a sword. They took turns of duty, mainly to see that no prisoner escaped, a circumstance that tells its own tale. And there was lax discipline as well. Those confined in the cells could be visited by relatives or friends, who might bring "ale, beir, wyne, or other drink" to revive the drooping spirits of those in durance vile, though the jailor had orders not to allow any one "to drink excessivelie or be debaucht," a duty which at times must have been attended with difficulty. But even more curious is the fact that all prisoners had to pay a fee to the jailor, who was empowered to deny them their freedom until it was paid.

In 1741 subscriptions were collected for the erection of a new Tolbooth. The magistrates applied for financial aid to county gentlemen who, at Quarter Sessions, passed a resolution to the effect that the building having "become almost intirely ruinous," "noblemen, gentlemen, and other inhabitants of the shire" should, "out of their benevolence and for the publick good," contribute "towards the said necessary building." A committee, including Lords Tweeddale, Belhaven, and Drummore, Sir Robert Sinclair, Sir Hew Dalrymple, was appointed to confer with the magistrates as to the building of a new jail, which in the end, as has been noted, took the form of apportioning part of the new Town House, then in course of erection.

The other antiquity in Market Street was a building that went by the pretensious name of Blair's Castle. How it received this designation, it is impossible to say, for, save the fact that it was demolished about a century ago, almost nothing is known about the building. It stood east of the office of the *Haddingtonshire Courier*, projected into the street, and was approached by a flight of steps, underneath which were large vaulted cellars. A story was long current that a subterranean passage led from Blair's Castle to Lethington (Lennoxlove).

One of three roundels (the others were in Hardgate and Sidegate) was situated in Market Street, close to the town steeple. Roundels (which were not peculiar to Haddington) contained wheel stairs and projected beyond the line of neighbouring buildings, the one in Market Street even reaching beyond the pavement.

In Hardgate are the ruins of a mansion which, fifty years ago, was in such good preservation that Macgibbon and Ross, in *Castellated and Domestic Architecture of Scotland*, described it as "one of the best specimens of old Scottish domestic architecture left in Haddington"—a mansion that "would still make an interesting residence for any one over whom historic associations had any sway, and, if kept in proper order, would preserve a most picturesque feature of the town." But the fair vision conjured up by these learned authorities on Scottish architecture has been doomed, for the building is now an utter ruin.

Popularly but erroneously known as Bothwell Castle, it was really the town residence of the family of Cockburn of Sandybed, now represented through the Haldanes of Gleneagles by the Earl of Camperdown. The titles of the property make clear that the Cockburn family owned the mansion before and after Bothwell's time. Further confirmation is afforded by the burgh records. In August 1770 the widening of Hardgate was being considered, and in a minute of the council occur these words: "Mr Buchan [of Letham] has cheerfully agreed to remove the dyke of his garden opposite to his house *known by the name of Sandybed house.*"

"A rare example of a nobleman's house in his county town," the so-called Bothwell Castle is elaborately described and illustrated by Macgibbon and Ross, who inspected the building while still intact. The main block fronted Hardgate. It was formed by two wings extending to the river and enclosing a small courtyard. At the south-west angle may still be seen the lower portion of a circular tower, in which was the chief entrance, though at one time there was another in the centre of the main block. Above the doorway is a weather-worn panel with a moulded border, the receptacle of a coat of arms. Within the tower was a staircase which probably gave access to the two upper floors and attic before the erection of the stair built out on the courtyard between the wings, which are three storeys high. A remarkable feature of the mansion was a rectangular dovecot, forming part of the main structure and situated at the east end of the south wing. Usually dovecots were erected some distance from the house, but the Hardgate building was singular in having this appurtenance joined to the mansion itself. The interior of the latter, as it was fifty years ago, showed that it had been finished with care and taste. A drawing, dated 1897, and preserved in the National Art Survey of Scotland, displays wood panelling (with which most of the rooms were lined) and iron door fittings—excellent examples, it is believed, of local craftsmanship. The windows in the main block had seventeenth-century details but had been enlarged, while those in the wings belonged to a still earlier date. The kitchen in the north-east wing was vaulted and had a large arched fireplace. There were at least a dozen apartments besides kitchen and cellar accommodation.

At the intersection of High Street with Hardgate there existed till about a century ago what Martine describes as a "curious old building" at the east end of which was a carved stone inscribed *Gloria Dei*. This is believed to have been the Preceptory of the Knights Templar in Haddington. John Richardson, well known in his day as lawyer and antiquary, was born in this tenement in 1793. He describes the staircase leading to the upper flats as handsome, its railings being of massive oak. On the roof was fixed the cross of the Knights Templar and in the basement were vaulted chambers. Opposite this building was the Custom Stone, so called from the fact that the tacksmen of the customs used to transact business there. A massive block of dark whinstone, the Custom Stone was removed many years ago to the East Haugh, where it may still be seen.

Proceeding southwards from Hardgate and entering Sidegate, there stood till comparatively recent times, on the east side, an L-shaped house with roundel pierced by two small windows. Built about the beginning of the seventeenth century, it was the mansion of Provost George M'Call and subsequently of the Hay Donaldson family. M'Call was Postmaster of Haddington, and in 1723 and again in 1728 was chief magistrate. His daughter Janet married Hay Donaldson, who was town clerk of Haddington for some years previous to his death. His son, who bore the same name, was a Writer to the Signet and law agent for the town council of Haddington. He also was the confidential legal adviser as well as intimate friend of Sir Walter Scott, who describes him as "a sound and true Pittite [in politics], and, though a very gentlemanlike and indeed an accomplished man, goes little into society, is extremely temperate, and dedicates his time almost entirely to his business." And when Hay Donaldson died in 1822 Sir Walter spoke of him as "an excellent man, who long managed my family affairs with the greatest accuracy and kindness." When Martine wrote his *Reminiscences of the Royal Burgh of Haddington* the mansion of Provost M'Call (who owned the park in which the Knox Institute is built) and the Hay Donaldsons was still to the fore. He characterises it as "one of the few specimens of the old style left in the burgh." In front was a little courtyard in which grew some fine trees.

But while this "grand old house" is gone, there still exists on the east side of Sidegate a building which may well be regarded as the finest specimen of domestic architecture in Haddington still remaining. Haddington House, as it is called, may, it is hoped, be renovated and revert some day to its original form. But while it is not likely that it will ever again be the town house of a notable county family, everything should be done to preserve the mansion which, architecturally and historically, is of outstanding interest.

The front of Haddington House is extremely quaint, and has arrested the attention of architects and antiquaries. Especially noteworthy are the porch and entrance door, reached by a stair with a stone balustrade and square pedestals on which rest stone bails. The porch is supported on pillars and has a circular timber roof, while the doorway has a broad moulded architrave. On the lintel are carved the initials A.M. and K.C., with the date 1680. The seventeenth-century style is also displayed in the glass door with its small panes and moulded astragals, the latter arched at the top. The interior consists of small panelled rooms with good fireplaces and pilaster decorations. There is also an oriel window, but this is a late insertion. Probably the best view of Haddington House is to be obtained from the churchyard. From this viewpoint the whole aspect is particularly pleasing. In the spacious garden behind is a horizontal sundial bearing the same initials as those displayed above the main entrance together with the date 1688. The initials are those of the original owners, Alexander Maitland and his wife Katherine Cunningham. In 1673 Maitland was made a burgess in token of "many favours done to the town." He served for a period in the town council, and it was he who submitted to his civic brethren a message from the Duke of Hamilton to the effect that it was the pleasure of James VII that no magistrates be elected in the meantime. In 1689 Maitland, as acting Provost, was one of the commissioners of the royal burghs at the Convention which met in Edinburgh.

Ancient House in St Martin's Gate, Nungate.

[*To face p.* 144.

BUILDINGS OLD AND NEW

With the exception of the Church of St Mary there is no antiquity of Haddington that calls forth more admiration by reason of the charm of its setting and the beauty of its outline than Nungate Bridge. This structure not only delights the eye but quickens the historic imagination, for the changes it has witnessed are manifold and extend far along the vista of the centuries. While the precise date of erection is uncertain, it is quite unhistoric to assert that the bridge belongs to the seventeenth century. In a communication to the *Scotsman* for 2nd January 1912 the late Dr Wallace-James mentioned a thirteenth-century deed (*Carta Prioratus S. Andrea*), in which the structure across the Tyne at Nungate was even then (*c.* 1282) referred to as "the old bridge." It is also known from a printed document that in 1293 Sir William Lindsay left money for the repair of the bridge. Other sums devoted to a like purpose are mentioned in charters dated 1311 and 1356. Again, in 1350, Hugh Giffard, Lord of Yester, "for the weal of his soul and those of his predecessors and successors," gave, granted, and confirmed to the foundation, site, and construction of the east end of Nungate Bridge, two pieces of land in the village of Giffordgate for "the benefit and upkeep of the said bridge, with free ish and entry to all wishing to use the said bridge."

Clearly, then, a bridge existed at Nungate in the thirteenth century, and, on the face of the evidence, a long time before that. It is generally believed that the structure was built by private enterprise. Yet the notion that the burgh of Haddington had nothing to do with its erection is inconsistent with an entry in the minutes of the town council for 27th August 1672 where it is explicitly stated that the east end was "built be thame." The council on this occasion ordered the removal of the "jougs" fixed thereon and that a stone panel inscribed with the town's name and arms be placed there instead. A possible explanation is that while at first the town had no claim on the bridge, it afterwards obtained possession of the east end and rebuilt it.

Nungate Bridge spans the Tyne at a point where the river is about 100 feet wide. Built of warm red sandstone, it consists of three arches, while two additional semi-circular ones (on land) were constructed in the eighteenth century to lessen the gradient from Nungate. Slezer's *Theatrum Scotiæ* shows the bridge as it was in 1693. Rounded arches carry a roadway at a high level, the approaches being steep. But though Slezer figures the arches as rounded, they are dissimilar. The western one is three-centred and the other two are slightly pointed. The bridge measures almost fifteen feet across the parapet and is sufficiently wide for two-way vehicular traffic, though not of a heavy order. In the retaining wall at the east end, facing southwards, are several carved stones which possibly may have been removed from the parish church. One has a weather-worn inscription but all that is decipherable is the date 1565. On the south face of the western arch is an iron hook from which delinquents sentenced in the burgh and sheriff courts were hanged.

Much havoc was caused to Nungate Bridge during the Siege of Haddington in 1548–49. Soon after, it was repaired, and to this day the extent of the renovation is discoverable, the stone then used being different in colour and texture from the rest of the fabric. Further repairs were carried out in 1608 and again in 1639. By 1758 the bridge had again become dilapidated. Justices of the Peace and Commissioners of Supply undertook the work of renovation. The town council, when asked to contribute towards the expense as well as undertake the management, pointed out that the bridge was "no part of the royalty," yet in respect that it was of convenience to the townsfolk, they agreed to contribute £50 sterling. So that as late as the eighteenth century, and indeed till 1849, it was a moot point as to who owned Nungate Bridge.

It were wrong to suppose that from early times Nungate Bridge existed merely to afford the inhabitants of Haddington access to the burgh of barony on the far side of the river. Past the bridge ran a road which probably traversed a portion of ground now incorporated in the churchyard, and was intended for traffic when the town ports were closed. Indeed there is something to be said for Martine's view that the road leading to the west end of the bridge "seems originally to have turned to the south and up to the church, and not towards the town as at present." In this connection the situation of the burgh of barony and the adjoining hamlet of Giffordgate in relation to Haddington is important. Giffordgate was on the Yester estate, while Nungate arose on the lands of the Abbey of Haddington. Giffordgate could be reached from the town by riding or driving across the ancient ford, but the townsfolk for the most part made use of the bridge. While Nungate and Giffordgate were outside the royalty and formed no part of the burgh's possessions, the daily life of those who lived there was so closely associated with the burgh that there was little exaggeration in stating their abode as simply "Haddington."

Until the nineteenth century the Nungate Bridge was the only means by which vehicular traffic could cross the Tyne at Haddington unless by the ford at the Sands, though two timber foot-bridges existed in the eighteenth century. In 1817 was opened Waterloo Bridge, linking up Haddington with Gifford and the Lammermoors, but the best part of a century elapsed before another bridge carrying vehicular traffic was constructed. In 1901 the Victoria Bridge, which crosses the Tyne a short distance from Hardgate and joins Whittingehame Drive, was opened. It is spacious and ought to serve the community for many years.

Until a few years ago Nungate could boast of quite a number of ancient houses. Macgibbon and Ross in *Castellated and Domestic Architecture* have a drawing illustrating a "plan and style of building" which found favour in this suburb during the seventeenth century and early part of the eighteenth, and was adopted no doubt as a means of defence. The Nungate houses were entered from a courtyard shut off from the roadway by a high wall through which was a wide gateway, which, when closed, gave effective security from all intrusion. These houses, so characteristic of the period, have wholly disappeared. One remained till comparatively recent times near the bridge. It bore the date 1658 over the entrance doorway, which was formed in a small angular porch. This building was the last good example in Nungate of a seventeenth-century house, though until the end of last century it had a formidable competitor in the dwelling of James Farmer, with its wainscotted rooms and decorated ceilings, the latter with emblematic mouldings of scriptural scenes.

INDEX

ABBEY, 9, 22, 41, 146; Parliament at, 2; burnt by Edward III, 6; Tyne floods and, 6; Henry IV at, 7; Margaret Tudor and, 8; treaty with French at, Mary of Lorraine at, 14, 15; French camp, 17; St Martin's Chapel and, 26; buildings, lands, 29, 30; seals of, revenues, English invasions and, 29; prioress' duties, educational facilities, 30; Queen Mary and, 31; New Mills owned by, 47; Defoe sees remains of, 55; Nungate lands owned by, 83

Abbey Bridge, 29

Abbot of Unreason, 22

Abercromby, Patrick, author of *Martial Achievements*, 11

Aberlady, 6, 30, 56, 65, 66, 67, 97, 137; French at, 13, 14; English troops at, 17, 18; de Termes fortifies, 20; John Gray, minister of, 37, 54; burgesses and, 42; Jacobite army lands, 53; Riding of Marches, town's harbour, 86; shipping, highway to, anchorage sold, 87

Abernethy, John, teacher in English school, 133

Academy, Paterson Place, 137

Ada, Princess, and burgh, 3; grants lands to Alex. de Martin, 26; founds Abbey of Haddington, 29

Adair, John, his plan of Haddington, 82 *n.*

Addison's *Drummer* acted by schoolboys, 132

Agnew, Sir Andrew, 70, 71

Agriculture, 116

Aitchison, Misses, of Alderston, gifts to St Mary's, 25

Aitken, Wm., watchmaker, 113

Alderston, 87

Alexander II, 3, 4, 139; born in Haddington, 2

Alinstoun, Margt., 121

Allan, Geo., tacksman of town mills, 109

Altars in St Mary's, 25

Amisfield, formerly New Mills, 47, 57, 67, 78, 125, 127; Lothians and Border Horse at, 78, 79

Amisfield Mains, 66

Ancient Monuments Commn. and St Mary's, 25

Anderson, Geo., merchant, 52 *n.*

Anderson, Geo., tanner, 114

Anderson, Geo., jun., tanner and Jacobite, 59

Anderson, John, saddler and Jacobite, 59

Annand, Sir David de, of Tranent, 28

Annual Register, 117

Archæologia Scotica, 82

Archery at the Sands, 83, 124

Archibald, Robt., Anti-burgher congregation, 35–36

Argyle, heads Scots army, 14, 16; attempts to oust English, 17

Arran, Governor of Scotland, 8, 15, 18, 32; and siege, 11; opposes Treaty of Haddington, 14; and French prowess, 16; and French defeat, 19; complains of d'Essé, 20; daughter educated at Abbey, 30; tries to capture Bothwell, 39

Artillery Park, 66

Arts, Haddington School of, 138

Assembly Room, Haddington, 69, 73, 76, 78, 92, 125; origin of, 140

Assize, 101

Athelstaneford, 26, 32, 56, 113; Jas. Carmichael, minister of, 33

Athol, Patrick, sixth Earl of, murdered, 4, 27, 139

Auld Register of Haddington, 81

"Auld Schule," 129

Aytoun, John, provost, 32

BAILIARY of Haddington, 27

Bailies. *See* Magistrates

Baird, Sir David, of Newbyth, Bt., 69; Cobden's controversy with, 74

Baird, Sir John, of Newbyth, 52 *n.*

Baird, Robt., of Newbyth, M.P., 69

Baird, Sir Wm., younger, of Newbyth, 52 *n.*

Bakers (Baxters), 111, 115; supply bread to James VI's retinue, 42; and Parliamentary reform, 68; ancient craft, encroachments by unfreemen, minute book, and St Mary's, 108, 120; war on "hugsters," and "Penny Wedding," 108–109; thirled to town mills, price and quality of corn, complaint against country, supply bread to military, 109; badly baked bread, monopoly ended, 110

Balcanquhall, Robt., and Laud's Service Book, 34

Balcanquhall, Walter, 33, 129

Bald, Sir Hugh, obtains land in Nungate, 30

Balfour, A. J. (Earl of Balfour), banqueted, 78; bids God-speed to local troops in War of 1914–18, 79; opens Knox Institute, 137

Balfour, Jas. Maitland, of Whittinghame, M.P., 69

Baliol, John, 4

Ball Abbey, 124; bonfire at, 78

Bara, barracks at, 56

Barberfield, 85

Barbers, forbidden to work on Sundays, 104

Barclay, Dr Geo., of Middleton, account of Tyne flood (1775), 63; description of town and parish, 82; and fairs, 91; and grammar school, 133

Barker, Alex. le, 5, 94

Baron-bailie, 95, 105

Barracks, 66; at Lennoxlove and Bara, 56; offer to erect additional, 62

Barthol, Bower, precentor and Jacobite, 59

Bass, uniforms of garrison supplied by New Mills Cloth Manufactory, 49

Baxters. *See* Bakers

Beanston-moor, 50

Bearford (Beirfoord), Lady, 44

Beaugué, Jean de, his account of siege of Haddington, 10; other references, 11, 12, 13, 14, 15, 16, 17, 18

Bee Hive Inn, 123

Begbie, lands of, 29

Beggars, 99, 104; invade town, 88, 89; licensed, 90

Behaviour, disorderly, among young, 120

Belhaven, Lord, 142

Bellenden, Sir John, acquires lands of St Laurence hospital, 26

Bellenden, Sir Lewis, 26

Bellevue, 85

Bellman, town, 98–99; put in irons, 121

Bells of parish church carried away by English, 24

Bernard, D. & J., donors of present Cross, described, 141

Bertram, Walter, Provost of Edinburgh, endows altar, 28

Billeting problems, 55, 62, 95

INDEX

Billings, R. W., architect, 140

Binning, Lord, Lieut.-Col. of Haddington Militia, 67

Birlie's (or Burley's) Walls, 82

Birsley Brae, 122

Bisset, Wm. de, and Athol murder, 4

Black Bull Inn, 123

"Black-paling footpath," 66, 84

Blacksmiths, 110, 111, 112

Blackwell, Richd., his stagecoach, 122

Blackwood, Robt., shareholder in New Mills Cloth Manufactory, 48

Blair's Castle, 142–43

Blue Bell Inn, 55, 73; officers of Cope's army at, 57; popular with travellers, commodious stabling, described, formerly White Hart, owners of, 122; former pupils dine at, 133

"Blue Bell and Post House," 122

Boer War, Haddington and, 78

Bolton, Jas. Carmichael, minister of, 33

"Bondager" system, 127

Books published in Haddington, 117

Booths, 102, 106, 107; tacksman's demands, 111

Bothwell, Francis, fifth Earl, made provost, hunted by James VI, 40

Bothwell, Jas., fourth Earl of, assigned Abbey endowments, 30; apprehends Cockburn of Ormiston, escapes from enemies, 39

Bothwell, Patrick, third Earl, requests money from town, summoned for treason, 39

Bothwell Castle, Haddington. See Cockburn of Sandybed

Bothwell family, 107; and Haddington, 39

Bouglass, Alex., millwright and Jacobite, 59

Bourke, Hon. R., of Colstoun (Lord Connemara), 77

Bower, mediæval chronicler, 6, 7; and Franciscan friary, 27

Bower, John, refuses payment to Hammermen, 111

Bowes, Sir Robt., 15

Bowie, Wm., schoolmaster, complains of rival school, 130

Bowling, 83, 124, 129, 131

"Boxpenny," 111

Bread, price of, proved before magistrates, 109; badly baked, 110

Bridges, timber foot-, 146

Bright, John, addresses meeting in Haddington, 73–74

Britannia Inn, 123

Britannia Wynd, 82

Broad Wynd, 82

Brodie, Wm., of Dunbar, 76

Brook, Col. Alex., commands 8th Royal Scots, killed in action, 79, 98

Brook, John, Victorian provost, 98

Broun, Patrick, of Colstoun, 1, 41

Broun, Wm., of Stottencleugh, provost, 94, 95

Brown, Geo., provost, 44

Brown, Geo., indweller in Nunraw, 121

Brown, Jas., teacher of mathematics, 135

Brown, John, of Haddington, 70, 105; his career, 35–36; friend and correspondent of Countess of Huntingdon, 37; Dictionary of the Bible, his edition of Psalms, 117

Brown, John, merchant burgess, 121

Brown, Samuel, provost, 105; presents address to Earl Grey, 69; "itinerating libraries," 97, 138

Brown St., 123

Bryce, Dr Moir, 29; and Franciscan friary, 27

Buchan, John (Lord Tweedsmuir), commends 8th Royal Scots, 79

Buchan, John, of Letham, 143; acquires Gladsmuir, 86

Buchan, John, music teacher, 129

Buchan Hepburn, Sir Archd., Bt., Convener of East Lothian, 80

Buckles, within Hammermen craft, 111

Buke of Auld Register of Haddington, 24

Burgess-ship, obligations, privileges, 99; enrolment of nobility and their retainers, the "Assurance," 100. See also Burgesses

Burgess Oath, 105

Burgesses oppose ecclesiastical policy of James VI and Charles I, 33; as constables, 104; wool, hides, and skins to be bought only from, 106; necessitous, 127

Burgh administration, 101

Burgh of barony, 146

Burgh Court, 1, 2, 24, 29, 101

Burgh reform, non-committal attitude, 104; ultimately in favour, 105

Burgh School. See Grammar School

Burghal lands, 85

Burgher congregation, 36

Burn, Wm., architect, 139

Burnet, Gilbert, minister of Saltoun, in later years Bishop of Salisbury, 54

Burns, Robt., and Brown of Haddington, 35

Burnside, —, school teacher, 130

"Burnt Candlemas," 6

Butts footpath, 85

Caesar, Rev. Dr, Tranent, 77

Caledonian Hunt meets in George Inn, 122

Caledonian Society, 125

Callender, John, teaches Greek and Latin, 130

Campvere, town's trade with, 106

Candlemakers, 87

Caponflat, 27

Carlyle, Alex., minister of Inveresk, 56; describes march of Cope's army, tumult in Haddington caused by false alarm, one of scouting party, 57; on Jacobite sentiment in East Lothian, 58; writes pamphlet on Militia Bill, 60; and taverns, 121

Carlyle, Jane Welsh, 75, 92; at George Inn, 123; and Edward Irving, 135

Carmichael, Jas., minister of Haddington, friend of Andrew Melville, revises Second Book of Discipline, abridges Acts of General Assembly, opposes prelatic policy, 33; aids sufferers in fire (1598), 90; schoolmaster and author of Latin grammar, 131

Carriers, East Lothian, 123

Carters, 68, 125–26

Castlewards of Bailiary of Haddington, 27

Catholicism in Haddington, 22, 23

Chalmers, Dr, and Provost Brown, 97

Chalmers, Robt., Auld Licht minister, 36

Chamberlain, royal, 2

Chantry chapels, 32; in St Mary's, 26

Chapels in town and vicinity, 26

Chapmen sell buckles on fair and market days, 111

Charities, 126

Charles I, ratifies charter of James VI, 42; and lands of Gladsmuir, 86; grants additional market, 92

Charles II, 125; birthday celebrated, 45

INDEX

Charles Edward, Prince, 59
Charteris, Lady Catherine, 83
Charteris, Col. Francis, purchases New Mills, 49
Charteris, Hon. Francis, younger, of Amisfield, 65, 69; marries Lady Frances Gordon, 57
Charteris of Amisfield (1774), and erection of Assembly Room, 140
"Charteris's Dykes," Cope's army marches by, 56, 57
Cheap Magazine, 117
Chesters, reservoir at, 91
Chevalier de St George, 53
Chinese bridge, 63
Cholera, in Haddington, 88
Church pageants, 22
Church of Scotland, 70, 71
Church St., Grammar School in, 129, 133
Churchyard, 83, 85
Clarges, Sir Thos., M.P. for Haddington Burghs, 45
Claverhouse's dragoons in Haddington, 50
Clay Barns, 85
Clerkington, 13, 16, 27, 29, 67; French troops at, 12; lands of, 24, 29; mansion swept away by floods, 63
Clockmakers, 112
Cloth industry, 116
"Coal and Candle" proclamation, 91
Coal mining, 6; at Gladsmuir, 86
Coalburn, 85
Cobden, Richd., addresses meeting in Haddington, 73–74; entertained at Archerfield, 74
Cockburn, Andrew, town jailor, 112
Cockburn, Col., of Clerkington, 132
Cockburn, Geo., bailie, 97
Cockburn, Geo., younger, merchant, 52 *n.*
Cockburn, Henry, obtains sasine of Aberlady, 86
Cockburn, Henry, "late Provost," receives poor relief, 89
Cockburn, Sir Jas., of Clerkington, gift to Franciscans, 27
Cockburn (Cokburne), Jas., of Wester Monkrig, provost, 41 *n.*
Cockburn, Capt. Jas., 45–46
Cockburn, Jas. (1586), 131
Cockburn, Janet, 60
Cockburn, Patrick, first minister of Haddington, 33
Cockburn, Sir Thos., of Clerkington, gift from Franciscan friary, 29
Cockburn, Sir Wm., chaplain at St John's altar, 25
Cockburn of Ormiston, apprehended by Bothwell, 39
Cockburns of Sandybed, town house in Hardgate, erroneously called "Bothwell Castle," 39; description of, 143
Commercial Hotel, 123
Common Good, 129; and Aberlady harbour, 86
Common Loan, 42
"Commone Douket," 27
"Company trading to Affrick and Indies," 51–52
Congilton, Sir John, and friary, 28
Congilton, Warden, 28
Constables appointed, 104
Convener Court of Haddington, 107
Convivial life, 121
Cook, John, minister of Haddington, 71
Cope, Sir John, writes to Lord Tweeddale, 56; encamps at Haddington, 56; a false alarm, 57; alters marching orders, 58
Copper- and brass-smiths, 112
Cordiners. *See* Shoemakers

Corn Exchange, 92, 140; troops quartered in, 78
Corpus Christi procession, 23, 101
"Corydon of Haddington," 33
County Buildings, 139–40
Court of Council, 101
Court St., 84, 139
Covenanters, 103; sympathies of burghers with, 34, 42
Crafts. *See* Incorporations
Craftsmen, and Church festivals, 23, 101; and Guild Court, 102; and town council, 95; rights of, 106; social standing, early organisation, 107; and miracle plays, 108
Craig, Sir Thos., acquires lands of St Laurence's hospital, 26
Crail Church, connection with Abbey of Haddington, 29
Crames, goods sold at, 106, 107
Crawford, John, Earl of, High Treasurer of Scotland, admitted burgess, 46
Croal, David and Jas., founders of *Courier* newspaper, 118
Croal, John P., editor of *Scotsman*, 118
Crocegait (High St.), 4, 82, 141
Croft, Sir Jas., governor of Haddington, 20
Crofts, town's, 84
Croley, Mrs, her school for young ladies, 137
Crombie, Dr, North Berwick, 75
Crombie, Patrick, Jacobite, 59
Cromwell, retreats to Haddington, skirmish with Covenanting army, 43; proclamation anent, at Cross, 44
Cromwellian union, acquiesced in by burghers, 44
Cross of Haddington, 39, 42, 64, 72, 76, 78, 121, 125; Charles II celebrations at, 46; Old Pretender proclaimed, 53; King's Birthday celebrations, 66; markets near, 92; proclamation anent Covenanters, 103; stocks at, 120; history of, 141
Cross Lane, 82
Croumbie, John, founds Militia Insurance Society, 66
Croumbie, Thos., owner of bleachfield, 116
Crown Inn, 123
Crummye, John, gift to St Mary's, 25
Cumberland, Duke of, presented with freedom of burgh, 58
Cumming, Thos., schoolmaster, 128, 135
Cuningham, Thos., factor in Campvere, Haddington favours his appt., 106
"Cunnars," ale and wine, 99
Cunningham, Katherine, 144
Cunningham, Robt., one of Cope's scouting party, 57
Cunningham, Capt. Wm., 66
Custom Stone, 63, 75, 144
Cutlers, 110

DALRYMPLE, Sir ADOLPHUS, M.P., 69
Dalrymple, Sir David, of Hailes, M.P., 69
Dalrymple, Sir Hew, 142; parliamentary representative, 56, 69
Dalton, Daniel, 45
Dalyell of Binns, 46
Dancing, 125
Darien Company, 47, 48; Haddington's contribution to, 50–51, 52 *n.*
Darnley, in Haddington, 40–41
David I, 1, 3, 23, 26, 81, 85, 141; and parish church, 24

David II, 5; grants trading rights, 6
Davidson, Col. Sir David, 75
Davidson, Henry, clerk to Skinners, 114
Davidson, John, mathematical and writing master, 135
Davie, —, merchant, 74
Dawson, Geo., innkeeper, 123
Dawson, Jas., and cloth industry, 116
Deacons of crafts, 107
Defence, against Napoleon, 66; town's system of, 119
Defoe's description of Haddington, 55
Denham, John, gardener and Jacobite, 59
Deskford, Lord, 116
D'Esse, commands French forces, 11; reconnoitres, 12; plans general assault, 15, 16; invested with Scottish regalia, 15; appeals to Arran for help, retires to Musselburgh, 18; attack that failed, 19
Dickson, Andrew, provost, and Wesley, 37; watches movements of Jacobite army, 56
Dickson, Andrew, owner of bleachfield, 116
Dirleton, 56, 134; charitable bequest to, 28; Cobden at, 74
Dissenting ministers and Burgess Oath, 105
"Doctor," assistant school teacher, 128, 129, 130, 133, 136 n.
Dods, Col. Chas. S., 75
Dods, Jas., bailie of Nungate, 83
Dods, Wm., provost, 75; favours Parliamentary reform, 68
Donaldson, Elizabeth, opens rival school, 131
Donaldson, Hay, town clerk, 144
Donaldson, Hay, W.S., son of above, law agent for town, friend of Sir Walter Scott, 144
Donaldson, Thos., schoolmaster and Jacobite, 59
Dormont, Robt., first Protestant schoolmaster, 128
Douglas, John, bailie, to escort first minister of burgh, 32
Douglas, John, session clerk, Bolton, 63
Douglas, John, shoemaker, 107
Dovecot at "Bothwell's Castle," 143
Drummer, town, 46, 98, 109, 126
Drummond, Geo., famous Lord Provost of Edinburgh, arrives in Cope's camp, 57
Drummore, Lord, 142
Dryden's Aurengzebe, acted by schoolboys, 131
Dunbar, Alex., vicar of Crail, 29
Dunbar, Jas., master of song school, 130
Dunbar, Patrick, Earl of, 5
Dunbar, Patrick, music teacher, 130
Dunbar, 20, 67, 90, 92, 114, 117; occupied by Scots army, 10; fortified, 18; skirmish at, 19; battle of, 43, 44; fugitives from, in Haddington, 44; Hanoverian troops land at, 56
Dunlop, Alex., erects distillery, 116
Dunpender Law (Traprain), 39
Durham, Bishop of, claims town, 4
Dyers and Others Society, 125

East Haugh, 116, 127; military drill on, 66; hustings set up, 68; Tarred Wool Co. at, 116; Custom Stone removed to, 144
East Linton, Scots and French forces at, 20
East Lothian, constituency formed, 77
East Lothian Agricultural Society, 126, 127; entertain Lord Tweeddale, 73
East Lothian Magazine, 68, 118

East Lothian Mutual Assurance or Friendly Society, 126
East Lothian Press, 117, 138
East Lothian Register, 125, 139
East Mill Haugh, 83
East Port, 15, 18, 85, 129; fortified, 13; Philip Stanfield's head exposed on, 49
East United Presbyterian Church, 36
Ecclesiastical importance of Haddington, 22
Edgar, Alex., provost, 51
Edgar, Wm., burgess, 130
Edmonston of Barnhouse, 40
Education, female, 131
Edward I, 5; attempts capture of town, 4
Edward III, 2, 5; makes war on town, 6; destroys original parish church, 24; burns friary, 27, 90
Edward VII, 72; marriage celebrations, 75–76
Elcho, Lord, 73, 77
Elliot, Wm., sheep stealer and town hangman, 99
Elm House, 85
Elvingston, 58
English garrison, assisted by burghers, 11; evacuates town, 20, 21
English School, Church St., 54, 85, 133, 137
"Ensign Maitland," 46
Episcopal Church, 37, 85, 123
d'Essé. See D'Esse
Eve, prioress of Haddington, 5
"Examiner of Goods," 99
Exports, staple, from Haddington, 106

Fairbairn, Geo., last of Weavers, 113
Fairbairn, Jas., innkeeper, 122
Fairholm, Geo., compiles list of East Lothian persons concerned in Forty-Five, 59
Fairs, 84, 88, 92, 111, 114, 123, 126; early popularity, 91
Fall, Capt., of Dunbar, M.P., 69
Farmer, Jas., his dwelling in Nungate, 146
Farquharson, Provost, 76
Female Penny Society for Relief of Poor, 125
Ferguson, Robt., of Raith, first county M.P., entertained in Haddington, statue erected to his memory, 69, 70
Fergusson, Robt., poet, interview with Brown of Haddington, 35
Ferme, John, clerk to Hammermen, 113
Ferme, Capt. W. T., 75, 77
Field, Wm., tacksman, indemnified for losses sustained by presence of Jacobites, 58
Finlay, Miss, her school for young ladies, 137
Fire, measures to cope with disastrous outbreak (1598), 90
Fish market, 92
Fishmarket Wynd, 82; Cross near, 141
Flanders, deputation to, 106
Fleming, John, wants supplied by town, 89
Flesh market, 92, 115
Fleshers, 42, 114; competition of landward tradesmen, 115
Fletcher, Andrew, of Saltoun, and Militia Bill, 60, 62, 64
Fletcher, Andrew (Lord Milton), promotes Tarred Wool Co., 116
Fletcher, Genl. John, of Saltoun, 126
Flora Bank private school, 137
Flour mills, 116, 117

Flower of Fame, 11
"Fly" coach, Haddington, 122
Football, 124, 134
Forbes, Joseph, wright, 59
Ford at Tyne, 146
Foresters, Ancient Order of, 126
Forrest, Alex., and Gimmersmills, 30
Forrest, David, of Gimmersmills, friend of Knox, 29, 32; granted charter by James VI, 41
Forrest, Geo., fiar of Gimmersmills, 41, 96
Forrest, John, provost, 29
Forrest, Marion, 44
Fortifications, Defoe and town, 55
Four Burghs, Court of, 2
Fox and Bay Horse Inn, 123
Franchise, town and extension of, 76, 77
Franciscan friary, 9, 32; Lord Athol buried in, 4; burnt by Edward III, 6; retinue of Margt. Tudor at, 8; skirmish near, 16, 18; the "Lamp of Lothian," 23, 27; and St Laurence Hospital, 26; site of, buildings, 27; Robert the Bruce and James IV benefactors of, 27; and Haliburton charity, Letter of Alienation, friary pulled down, 28; wardens and chapter, 29; town wall bounds, 85
Free Trade demonstration, 73–74
Freemasonry, 126
Freemen and unfreemen, 107
French, forces at siege, how composed, 11; night attack, 18; threat of Napoleonic invasion, 66
French Revolution, town council and, 65
Friar Gowl, 27
Friary. *See* Franciscan
Friendly societies, 126
"Frier Douket," 27
Froude, his account of siege, 18, 19
Fulwell, Ulpian, account of siege (1548–49), 10, 11, 12, 13, 19

GALL, GEO., Blue Bell Inn, 122
Gallow Green, 85, 99
Gallowgreen parks, 62
Games, Haddington, 125; ball, 134
Garden, Francis (Lord Gardenstone), one of Cope's scouting party, 57–58
Gardeners, Order of Free, 76, 126
Gardeners' Arms Inn, 123
Gardiner, Colonel, commands dragoons, 56; a false alarm, 57
Garleton Hills, 81; Wallace's army on, 5; French soldiers posted, 12; artillery at, 13; James VI's cavalcade on, 41; signal station, 66; bonfire, 78
Garvald, 97
Gaukroger, Geo., commands local Rifle Volunteers, 75
Gemmill, Lieut.-Col. Wm., D.S.O., 79
Gentle Shepherd, Ramsay's, performed by schoolboys, 132
George II, town sends address to, anent Jacobite rebellion, 56; proposed address after Culloden, 58
George III, town council congratulates, 60, 62, 65, 67
George IV, congratulated on escape from attempt on his life, 67; subscription for statue to, 68
George Inn, 55, 69, 76, 97, 113, 141; popular with travellers, early owners, coaching days, social functions, described, 122; literary associations, 123; New Club meets at, 126
George Inn Wynd, 82

George and Dragon Inn, 122
Gibson, Philip, buys cloth at Campvere, 106
Giffard, Hugh, Lord of Yester, bequeaths land in Giffordgate for upkeep of Nungate Bridge, 145
Gifford, 114, 133, 146
Giffordgate, 83, 145, 146
Gillespie-Graham, architect of town steeple, 140
Gimmersmills, and siege, 13; prioress of Abbey and, 29; leased by A. Forrest, 30; Forrest family and, 32; James VI and, 41 and note
Gladshot, 85
Gladsmuir, lands of, 42, 67, 77; Covenanting army at, 43; lands granted by David I, 85; industrial experiments, constituted a parish, acquired by Buchan of Letham, Riding of the Marches, 86; plague victims sent to, 88; baron-bailie, 95, 105; wapinschaws at, 125
Gladstanes, Archp., made burgess, 33
Gladstone, W. E., offered freedom of burgh, 77
Goatfield, 66
Golf Club, Haddington, 124, 125
"Good Intent" stagecoach, 122
Good Templars, 126
Goodfellow, Wm., schoolmaster, 136
Gourlay, David, distiller, his bequest, 126
Gourlay Bank, 66, 126
Gowl Close, Hardgate, 39
Graham, J. C., rector of Knox Institute, 137
Graham, Wm., rector of grammar school, 134
Grain market, 116
Grammar School, Abbot of Holyrood and, town council responsible for upkeep, in pre-Reformation times, early masters, 128; buildings repaired, Latin only to be spoken, 129; Greek taught, ill-behaviour, 130; long school hours, play-acting, 131–32; English taught, new school erected, description of, former pupils' reunions, athleticism, 124, 133–34; boarders, Edward Irving a master, 134–35; management improved, 135; decline of, troublesome rector, 136; the last phase, buildings sold, 137
Gray, Andrew, 53
Gray, Jas., and vicarage of St Mary's, 25
Gray, John, his famous library, 37; career, 53–54; early printed books described, 54; missing volumes, 138
Gray, John, builder, part of Friary site feued to, 29
Gray, Robt., bailie, 53
Gray, Robt., head of song school, 129
Greendykes, 79
Greengelt, 97
Grey, Earl, receives address from magistrates, 69
Grey de Wilton, Lord, commander of English forces, 10, 11, 16, 18, 30; request for preachers, 12; leads reinforcements, 15
Grey Friars. *See* Franciscan friary
Grier, Geo., minister of St Martin's Chapel, 33, 120
Guild Court, 101; jurisdiction of, 102
Gullane, 67, 90; Jacobite troops landed at, 53
Gunn, Wm. Maxwell, rector of grammar school, career, 135–36
Gunpowder Plot commemorated, 46
Gurney, J. J., philanthropist, and jail accommodation, 140
Guthrie, Richd, founder of St Laurence's hospital, 26
Gypsies (Egyptians), 104

INDEX

HADDEN, Capt. W., 75

Haddington, first Earl of, and Gladsmuir, 42

Haddington, Thos., second Earl of, killed at Dunglas, 42–43

Haddington, Thos., seventh Earl of, and John Wesley, 37; urges need for militia, 61

Haddington Benevolent Society, 125

Haddington Burghs, 68, 77, 95

Haddington Dispensary, 125

Haddington Friendly Society, 125

Haddington House, Aberlady, 87

Haddington House, Sidegate, finest specimen of domestic architecture locally, 144

Haddington New Club, 126

Haddington Register, 117

Haddington School of Arts, 97, 138

Haddington Stone, 85

Haddingtonshire Advertiser, 118

Haddingtonshire Courier, 118

Haig, Walter, Paterson Place Academy, 137

Haldane, Robt. and Jas., buys church for Independents, 37

Haldane, R. B. (Viscount Haldane of Cloan), 77

Haliburton, Sir John, charity for East Lothian poor, 28

Haliburton, Sir Wm., of Carlowry, 28

Halyburton, Jane, female teacher, 131

Hamilton, Jean, daughter of Regent Arran, 30

Hamilton, Nisbet, of Archerfield, entertains Cobden, 74

Hammermen, 23; and St Mary's, 25, 120; numerically strongest, early constitution, Seal of Cause, allied trades included, 110; unfreemen, internal organisation, "boxpenny," grievances, 111–12; attitude to national affairs, 112–13; decline of craft, 113; funds, 115

Hangman, 90, 99; scourges Edinburgh hangman, 50–51

Hangman's Acres, 42, 85

Hardgate, 81, 85, 91, 97, 115, 117, 123, 143, 144, 146; French cavalry in, 12; Independent chapel, 37; tanneries, 82; Provost Vass's house, 95

Hardie, Patrick, schoolmaster, 135

Hardyng, John, his *Chronicle*, 7

Haugh, 67, 76

Hay, Lord Arthur, killed in action, 79

Hay, Lady Elizabeth, becomes Duchess of Wellington, 73

Hay, Jas., Jacobite, 59

Hay, John, pewterer, 112

Hay, John, of Aberlady, complaint against Provost Seton (1667), 96

Hay, John, of Alderston, 52 *n.*

Hay, John, tenant in Duncanlaw, 67

Hay, Richd., English master, and author of *Beauties of Arithmetic*, 134

Head Burgh Court, 101

Heather Inn, 123

Heathery Hall, 85

"Heid roumes," 84

Henderson, Thos., headmaster of parish school, 137

Henry III, burns town, 4, 90

Henry IV, passes through town, 7

Henry, Prince, son of David I, 3

Hepburn, Alex., chirurgeon, 44

Hepburn, David, of Waughton, 86

Hepburn, Isabel, prioress of Abbey, 29, 31

Hepburn, Janet, "abbess of St Clare's monastery," 29

Hepburn, John, and town council, 39

Hepburn, Robt., of Beanston, 89

Hepburn, Wm., of Beanston, 89

Hepburns of Nunraw, right to appoint a bailie of Nungate, 83

Herd, town, 99

Heriot, Helen, wife of Sir Thos. Craig, 26

Hermanflat, 41 *n.*

Hertford invasion, 8, 9, 10

Hides, buying and selling of, 106

High School of Edinburgh, rectors of, formerly in Haddington, 136 *n.*

High St., 63, 90, 91, 92, 113, 115, 117, 122, 123, 126, 139, 140, 141; width of, 81; south frontage, 82. *See also* Crocegait

"Highflyer" stagecoach, 122

Hinds, oppose "bondager" system, 127

Hiring Friday, 123, 127

Hislop, Jas., baker, 108

Hislop, John, coppersmith, 112

Hodges, 85

Hogg, Alex., wheelwright, 112

Holy Blood altar, St Mary's, 25

Holy Rood altar, St Mary's, 25

Holyrood, Abbot of, patron of grammar school, 128

Home, John, describes march of Cope's army from Dunbar, 56–57; his *Douglas* acted, 124

Hope, Geo., of Fenton Barns, 74; entertains Cobden and Bright, 73; and franchise extension, 76

Hope, John Thos., younger of Luffness, 69

Hope Park, cavalry barracks at, 66

Horse-racing, 124, 125, 126

Hostelries, 121

Houston of Clerkington, 42

Howden, Dr Thos., 78

Hughes, John, his *Siege of Damascus* acted by schoolboys, 131

"Hugsters," 108

Hume, David, on preaching of Brown of Haddington, 35

Hume, Jas., 102

Hume, John, his tenement in Sidegate, 63, 126

Hunter, Matthew, 142

"INCORPORATION of the Woollen Manufactory at New Mills," 49

Incorporations, nine trading, their insignia, 107; closely allied with Church, 108; account of, 115; privileges prejudicial to community, 115

Independents, 37

Industrial enterprises, 92, 116

Inns, 121–22, 123

Irvine, Margt., 60

Irving, Edward, mathematical master, 134–35, 137

"Itinerating libraries," Samuel Brown's, 97, 138

JACK, ADAM, member of Wrights and Masons, 107

Jack, Geo., mason, 113

Jack, John, mason, and town Cross, 141

Jacobite army in Haddington, 53, 58; prisoners in town jail, 58; list of East Lothian persons involved in rebellion, 59

Jail, accommodation criticised, 140; Tolbooth, 142

Jail Wynd, 82

James II, assembles army in town, exempts burgesses from payments on salt and skins, 7

James III, holds council, 8; and Haliburton charity, 28

James IV, in Haddington, 8; gift to friary, 27

James V, holds councils at Haddington, 8, 23; endows hospital of St Laurence, 26; charter anent fairs, 91; sanctions weekly market, 92; charter (1542), 101; Fleshers' charter, 115

James VI, 131; narrowly escapes drowning in Tyne close to Haddington, 40; coronation approved by burghers, grants charter in favour of David Forrest of Gimmersmills, 41; charter to town, 42; and Gladsmuir, 85; and town fairs, 91; and provostship, 95

James VII, 49, 144; visit to Haddington, 47

James Francis Edward, Prince (Old Pretender), birth celebrated by burghers, 50; proclaimed as James VIII, 53

Jamieson, Edward, schoolmaster, deprived for refusing oath of allegiance, 131

"Jock o' the Green," 126

John, King, burns town, 3, 4, 90

John of Furde, gift to St Mary's, 25

John of Gaunt, visits town, 6

Johnston, Jas., rector of grammar school, 133; extends boarding system, 134

Johnston, Wm., postmaster, 52 n.

Johnstone, Jas., first parochial schoolmaster, 135

Jolly, A. W., 118

"Jougs," 104, 141

Julius Cæsar performed by schoolboys, 132

KER, JOHN, schoolmaster, 129

Ker, Robt., of Whitehill, sued by schoolmaster, 130

Kerr, Robt., minister of Haddington, 34

Kerrington, Sir Thos., chaplain, St Mary's, 25

Kilpair St. (Caleperys), 81, 82, 123

King St., 139

"Kingis Yaird," 27, 85; conveyed to burgh, 28

King's Arms Inn, 123

"King's Belcher in the Freris," 27

King's Birthday celebrations, 66, 67, 125, 141

"King's Kist," 86

King's Meadow, 6

Kings, early Scottish, and Haddington, 3

Kinloch, Capt., of Gilmerton, 75

Kinloch, Sir David, of Gilmerton, Bt., 136 n.

Kirk, Jas., burgh schoolmaster, reports on grain prices, 109

Kirkwood, Margt., accused of witchcraft, 103.

Knights Templars Preceptory, 123, 143–44

Knox, John, 23, 33, 127, 129; describes French attack on garrison of Haddington, 18; date of departure of English, 19; birthplace, 22; and St Mary's, 25–26; relations with Wishart, 31; Protestant influences, 32; attends grammar school, 128; a local memorial, 137

Knox Free Church, 36

Knox Institute, 13 n., 42, 144; Provost Brook and, 98; opened, 137

Kyle, David, 96

LADY KITTY's Garden, 83, 124; during siege (1548–49), 18

Lamb, Hon. Wm., M.P. for Haddington Burghs, 69

Lamb Inn, 123

Lammermoors, 81, 146; Scots army crosses, 8

"Lamp of Lothian," 23; Miller's, 117

Lauder, Chas., 114

Lauder, Chas., procurator fiscal and Jacobite, 59

Lauder, Jas., merchant, 86

Lauder, Jean, wife of Geo. Forrest of Gimmersmills, 41 n.

Lauderdale, Duke of, retainers made burgesses, 46, 100

Laurie, John, Sandersdean, 112

Laurie, Sir Peter, Lord Mayor of London, 112

Lawson, Geo., of Selkirk, John Brown's successor in Divinity professorship, 35

Lawson, Jas., Knox's successor in St Giles', 33

Lea, Thos., provost, presents address to Queen Victoria, 72

Legge, Capt. Roger, 44, 45

Lennoxlove, 67; supposed subterranean passage, 143. *See also* Lethington

Leper hospital at St Laurence, 26

Leslie, John, schoolmaster, friend of Allan Ramsay, interest in drama, 131–32, 133

Letham Mains, 85

Lethington, 30; Richard III and, 8; Scots army at, 12; burned, 20; James VII at, 47; barracks at, 56. *See also* Lennoxlove

Liberty Hall, 85, 86

Library, "itinerating," 97; Haddington Subscription, 117, 138; Town and County, 138; Public, 36, 37, 84

Lillie, Wm., Deacon Convener of Trades, 86

Lilly, Alex., wright and Jacobite, 59

Lindsay, Lady Margt., 28

Lindsay, Marion, female teacher, 131

Lindsay, Robt., weaver and Jacobite, 59

Lindsay, Sir Wm., of Luffness, gift to Franciscan friary, 27–28

Lindsay, Sir Wm., repairs Nungate Bridge, 145

Linen manufacture, 105

Lint manufactory, 116

Linton Bridge, 15

Livingstone, Jas., town piper, 98

Loanings, 85

Lockman, 99

Locksmiths, 110

Lodge St., 135

"Lord Nelson" stagecoach, 122

Lorimer, Robt., minister of parish and then of St John's Free Church, 36; and Edward Irving, 135

Lorimers, 112

Lothians and Border Horse, 78

Lucerna Loudoniæ, 6

Luffness, fort at, 20

Lundie, Dr Jas., provost, and national militia, 61

Lydgate, 66

Lyle, Paul, 90

M'CALL, GEO., provost, and bowling green, 124; mansion in Sidegate, 144

M'Call, Wm., merchant, 86

M'Call's Park, 42, 144

M'Cullagh, Geo., last of Skinners, 114

M'Cullagh, Jas., Methodist preacher, 38

Macdonald, Sir J. H. A. (Lord Kingsburgh), contests Haddington Burghs, 77

Macgregor, Donald, town piper, 98

Mackenzie, Sir Geo., of Rosehaugh ("Bluidy Mackenzie"), employed in town litigation, 35
Mackenzie of Newhall, Lieut.-Col. Hay, 66
Mackintosh of Borlum, proclaims Old Pretender at Cross, 53
Maclaren, Duncan, former Lord Provost of Edinburgh, 74
Macnab, Chas., teacher, 137
M'Watt, Jas., mason, 140
Magistrates, granted office of sheriff, 8; and Franciscans, 32; provide food and accommodation for retinue of James VI, 42; contribute to cause of Prince Charles Edward, 59; search for able-bodied seamen, 60; and repeal of Roman Catholic disabilities, 64; present address to Earl Grey, 69; and Nungate bailie, 83; and Gladsmuir lands, 86; measures to combat plague, 88; and poor relief, 89; gold medals for, 95; extensive powers, and sheriff court, 101; and price of bread, 109; grant new Seal of Cause to Hammermen, 110; close unauthorised school, 130, 131. *See also* Town Council
Main, A. Mathieson, provost, 97 ; plants tree commemorating Diamond Jubilee of Queen Victoria, 78
Mainshill, lands of, 39
Maitland, Alex., owner of Haddington House, 144
Maitland, Dame Alison, 30
Maitland, Chas., son of Robt., 46
Maitland, Robt., Deputy Governor of the Bass, 46–47
Maitland, Hon. Thos., M.P., 69
Maitland, Wm., of Lethington, obtains Abbey lands, 30
Maitlandfield, 85; proposed railway station at, 92
Major, John, and Franciscan friary, 22, 27
Malcolm IV, grants toft to Kelso monks, 3
Malloch, Andrew, procurator-fiscal, 89
Manufactures in town, 116
Margaret, Princess, daughter of James II, 30
Market Street, 81, 84, 85, 92, 123, 127, 140, 142, 143
Markets, 87, 93, 99, 106, 109, 111, 116, 121, 123, 140; more important than fairs, regulations, 92
Marriages, runaway, solemnised in Episcopal Church, 37
Martin, Alex. de, Sheriff of Haddington, 26; gift of lands to Abbey, 83
Mary of Guise (Lorraine), 14, 15, 31, 39; persuades army to return to Haddington, mounts tower of St Mary's, 16
Mary Queen of Scots, 2; and French marriage, 14; bestows Abbey endowments on Bothwell, 30; in Haddington, 40–41
Mason, Wm., 102
Masons. *See* Wrights and Masons
Mathematical school, 137; taught by Edward Irving, 134–35
Matheson, Alex., schoolmaster, 136 n.
Mauchline, Sir Patrick, 8
Mauchline, Sir Thos., chaplain, St Mary's, 25
Meadowaikers, 41 n.
Meal market, 92
Meikle, Andrew, and Tarred Wool Co., 116
Melville, Andrew, 33
Mercer, John, teacher, 130
Merchants, 101; representation on town council, 95; rights of, 106; and craftsmen, 107
Methodist chapel, 38
Michaelmas Fair, 42, 58, 60, 91

Middle Raw, 81, 82
Middleton, Earl of, banqueted, 46
Military, town responsible for upkeep of, collisions with civilian population, 55–56
Militia, Haddington, 50; local Rifle Volunteers embodied in, 67
Militia Bill, Haddington and, 60; farmers and manufacturers hostile, 61
Militia Insurance Society, 66
Mill Wynd, 85
Miller, Geo., printer and publisher, 117; his circulating library, 138
Miller, Jas., author of *Lamp of Lothian*, 117, 131, 133, 139; compiles catalogue of Gray Library, 138
Miller, Robt., bailie, 52 n.
Miller, Robt., apothecary, 124
Mills, burghers and ownership of, 42; Bakers thirled to town, 109
Minister and schoolmaster, offices combined, 129
Miracle plays, craftsmen and, 108
Mitchell, Major T. B., 79
Monck, in Haddington, 44, 45
Monkrigg, 127
Monkrigg Benevolent Fund, 127
"Mons Meg," drawn through Haddington, 8
Monthly Advertiser, 117
Monthly Monitor and Philanthropical Museum, 117
Moodie, Elizabeth, charged with witchcraft, 97, 102–103
Moore, John, 102
Moray, Regent, arrives with army in Haddington, 39; his Regency approved by burghers, 41
More, Geo., of Monkrigg, 127
More, Jas., of Monkrigg, his bequest, 126–27
Morham, 137; parish church, 49
Mortcloths, revenue from, 107
Morton, and Constabulary of Haddington, holds Privy Council meetings in town, 41
Morville, Richd. de, 3
"My Lord," 126
Myrton, Sir Wm., 29

NAESMITH, ROBT., 96
Napoleonic menace, local trade and, 67
National Covenant, burgesses and, 34
Navy, town council encourage recruiting, 65
Neill, Adam, his drawings of quaint buildings in Haddington, 117–18, 139
Neill, Archd., bookseller and publisher, 117
Neill, Geo., printer and publisher, 117
Neill, Geo., jun., 118
Neilson Park, 92
Neilson's Wynd, 82
New Licht congregation, 36
New Mills Cloth Manufactory, 116; notable industrial experiment promoted by Sir Jas. Stanfield, 47; site of, business details, twenty-five looms working, cloth for Dalzell's dragoons, English cloth imported, 48; uniforms for garrison on Bass, causes of decline, winding up, 49; Defoe on failure of, 55
"New Wark," 13 n.
Newton Port, 79, 85, 92, 115, 142; Anti-burghers in, 36; Public Library in, 54
Nichol, Robt. B., English and French teacher, 135, 136
Nicholas V, Pope, and St Mary's, 25
Nisbet, Wm., younger, of Dirleton, 64

INDEX

Nisbet loanhead, 125
North Berwick, 56; Jacobite troops landed at, 53
North Port, 15, 28, 84, 85 and note
Nungate, 13, 26, 30, 47, 108, 111, 121; and Tyne floods, 6, 63; abbatial lands, 29; antiquity of, a burgh of barony, 83, 95, 105; bakers on their defence, 109; weavers in, 113; woollen concern, 116; unauthorised school, 130; outside royalty, ancient houses in, 146
Nungate Bridge, 27, 83, 124, 129; during siege, 15, 18, 145; Defoe and, 55; hangings at, 99, 145; bread sold on, 108; town council and, architectural features, disputed ownership, 145
Nungate and Haddington Brotherly Society, 125
Nunraw, 29, 121; grange of Abbey, 30

ODDFELLOWS, 126
Office of Works renovates St Martin's Chapel, 26
Old Bank House, 85
"Old Post House," 122
Oliphant, Jas., provost, 94, 139
Orchards, fame of town's, 4
Original Seceders, 36
Orinoco Whist Club, 122
Our Lady, altar of, St Mary's, 25

PALACE, royal, at west end of town, 4, 139
Palmer, Sir Thos., 13, 15, 16; supervises defences of Haddington, 10, 12; taken prisoner, 16
Panton, Jas., schoolmaster, 129
Parish school, supported by landward heritors, 137; serious rival to grammar school, 135
Parliamentary Reform Assoc. formed, 76
Paterson, Rev. John, Paterson Place Academy, 137
Paterson, Thos., schoolmaster, 130
Paterson, Sir Wm., of Granton, made provost, 49–50
Paterson Place Academy, closed, 137
Patronage, Church, petition for abolition of, 70, 71
Peacock, Walter, his stagecoach, 122
"Penny Weddings," bakers and, 108–109
Pewterers, 112
Philip, David, innkeeper, 123
Phin, Margt., accused of witchcraft, 103
Pillory, 104
Piper, town, 98, 126
Pirie, Geo., wright, 140
Pirie's Wynd, 82
Pitt Ministry (1797), magistrates and, 65
Plague, 84, 85; outbreak of, during siege, 19, 20; measures to combat, 87; frequent visitations, 88; goods forbidden during, 107
Play-acting by school pupils, 131–32
Poldrate, 27, 28, 81, 123; Episcopal meeting-house in, 37, 54, 59; Weavers' tenement in, 113
Poor, problem of, 88–89, 125
Poorhouse, 89, 90
Porteous, Robt., saddler, 113
Ports, 84, 88; watching of, 85
Post-house, 55
Postmaster of Haddington, 144
Presbytery of Haddington, 53; petition against Service Book, 34; dines at tavern, 121; tests schoolmaster's qualifications, 130
Pretender, Old, 100
Pringle, Wm., deacon of Skinners, 114
Printing and publishing, 117–18

Privy Council meets in Haddington, 41; consulted as to town's finance, 45; at Lethington, 47
Provostship, antiquity of office, 94; not always coveted, duties of, 94–95; deacons of crafts and, 107
Public Library, 54, 141 n.
Punishments, barbarous, 102
Punton, Thos., bailie, 139

QUARRYING stone, 6
Quoits, 124

RAILWAY, coming of, 92; ill effects of, 93
"Ralph Eglyn's Acres," 27, 42, 85
Ramsay, Lord (Marquess of Dalhousie), his political contest, 69, 70
Ramsay, Allan, his Gentle Shepherd, acted by Haddington scholars, 131–32
Ramsay, Walter, preceptor, St Laurence hospital, 26
Reader of Scriptures in kirk appointed, also acts as schoolmaster, 32, 128
Redpath, Marion, teaches reading and sewing, 131
Reform, Parliamentary, agitation for, 68
Reformation, slow growth in Haddington, 31
Reid, John, town piper, 98
Reid, Robt., builds military stables, 62; contractor for town house, 140
Relief congregation in West Port, 36, 37
Richard II, invades town, 6, 7
Richard III, 8
Richardson, John, lawyer and antiquary, 143
Riding of the Marches, 86, 98, 123
Rifle Arms hostelry, 123
Robb, Jas., transcriptions of burgh records, 119
Robert the Bruce, King, 27; grants charter to town, 5
Robert II, 7; grants to burghers, 6; and Aberlady anchorage, 86; grants 250 merks from customs, 115; and grammar school, 128
Robert III, 7
Robertson, Joseph, nonjuring minister and Jacobite, 59
Robertson, Robt., merchant, 52 n.
Robswell, 86
Roger of Popil (Popple), gift to Abbey by his son, Patrick, 29
Roman Catholic disabilities, burgesses oppose repeal of, 64
Ronaldson, Dr J. R., 75
Ross, Thos., provost, 80
Ross, Rev. Wm., of Haddington, 77
Roughead, Provost, and raising of local volunteer corps, 75
Roundels, 143
Rudis of Friar Wall, 27
Rutland's army sets fire to town, 20

SABBATH Protection Bill, 70, 71
Saddler, —, Ferrygate, invents ploughing machine, 74
Saddlers, 110, 111, 112
St Andrews, bishop of, grant to Abbey, 29; prior of, his agreement with Haddington nuns, 29; convent of, and repair of St Mary's, 25
St Ann's Chapel, 26
St Ann's Place, 135
"St Clare's monastery at Haddington," 29
St Clement, altar of, Franciscan friary, 28

INDEX

St Crispin, altar of, St Mary's, 25
St Duthac, altar of, Franciscan friary, 28
St Eloi's altar, St Mary's, 25, 110
St John's altar, St Mary's, 25
St John's Chapel, 26
St John's Church, Newton Port, 36, 84, 85
St John's Fair, 91
St John's Free Church, 36 and note
St John's Kilwinning Lodge (No. 57), 126
St John's Port, 87
St John Street, 82
St Katherine's Chapel, 18, 26, 87
St Katherine of Sciennes, monastery of, 26
St Laurence, religious house of, incorporated with
   monastery of St Katherine of Sciennes, Edinburgh,
   26; suburb of, 65
St Laurence, village of, 126
St Martin's Chapel, 23, 135, 139; oldest edifice in
   town, 26; Jas. Carmichael, minister of, 33
St Mary's (Catholic) Chapel, 38
St Mary's Parish Church, 18, 22, 26, 27, 43, 101, 123,
   139, 145; David I and, 3; part played in siege,
   12, 24; French fire from tower of, 13; *not* "Lamp
   of Lothian," 23; history, architecture, structural
   alterations, 24–25; collegiate constitution, altars,
   town council and, 25; Wishart preaches in, Knox
   and, 25–26; chantry chapels, St Martin's Chapel
   and, 26; pavement of friary removed to, 29;
   Presbyterian worship, 32; seating insufficient, 36;
   burial-place of Rev. John Gray, 54; Defoe and, 55;
   Prince Charles Edward and, 59; regimental flags
   hung in, 80; trade incorporations and, 108, 110,
   113, 114, 120; grammar school and, 128; old road
   to, 129
St Michael's Fair, 42
St Ninian's Chapel, 26
St Peter's altar, St Mary's, 25
St Peter's Fair, 42, 91
Saltoun, 97, 124
Samuelston Loanhead, 86
Sands, The, 18, 83, 124, 134, 146; Little, 140
Sandybed House, Hardgate, erroneously known as
   Bothwell Castle, 39, 143
Savings Bank, 125
Sawers, —, clerk, Tarred Wool Co., 116
Sawers, Simon, pewterer, 112
Schetholme, Andrew, 31
Schillinghill, Court of, 101
School, Landward Public, 135
Schools, private, 137; modern subjects a speciality,
   134
Scots and French, disagree, 14, 15
Scott, Lieut.-Col., 75
Scott, Hew, compiler of *Fasti Ecclesiæ Scoticana*, 117;
   borrows from Gray Library, 138
Scougall, Richd., town piper, 121
Seal of burgh, 1, 2
Seals of Cause, 108
Searchers, fish and flesh, 99
Secession movement in Haddington, 34–35
Secondary education, 113
Seton, Sir Alex., gift to Franciscan friary, 28
Seton, Alex., schoolmaster, 130
Seton, Capt., his bequest, 126
Seton, Geo., of Barns, complaint against Provost
   Seton (1667), 96
Seton, Wm., first Lord, 28, 39

Seton, Sir Wm., of Kyllismore, provost, 95
Seton, Wm., provost, 130; confers with Monck, 95;
   tyrannical conduct, imprisoned, 96
Seton of Northrig, 96
Seven Years' War, town affected by, 60
Sharp, John, 102
Sheriff of Haddington, hereditary, 39
Sheriff Court, 121, 140; bailies' powers anent, 101
Shirreff, Patrick, pioneer of seed-breeding, 68
Shoemakers (Cordiners), 111, 114
Sidegate, 81, 85, 124, 126, 143, 144; inscribed panel
   marking height of Tyne flood (1775), 63
Siege (1548–49), 15, 55, 84, 95, 119
Simpson, Andrew, town drummer, 98
Simpson (Symson), Cuthbert, 120
Simpson, Geo., offers to sink mine at Gladsmuir, 86
Simpson (Sympsone), Isabel, wife of David Forrest
   of Gimmersmills, 41
Sinclair, Lord, of Herdmanston, 67
Sinclair, Sir Robt., 142
Sinclair, Wm., owner of *Advertiser*, 118
Sinclairs of Stevenson, and St Mary's, 25
Skene, Wm., schoolmaster, 136 *n.*
Skinners, 112; support Reform movement, 68;
   record of, 113–14; Pringles and Wilsons, crafts'
   ground on riverside, 114
Skinners' Knowe, 114
Slave trade, African, 67; town council petitions for
   abolition, 65
Sleich, John, provost, represents town at Convention
   of Parliament (1689), 50; municipal career, 96
Sleich, John, junior, provost, 96–97
Smail's Pond, 126
Smart, Alex., teacher of English, 133
Smart, John, blacksmith, 111
Smiles, Samuel, senior, 74, 117
Smiles, Samuel, author of *Self-Help*, 91, 135
Smith, Hay, and Tarred Wool Co., 116
Smith, Jas., Nungate, complained against for selling
   bread within burgh, 109
Smith, Rev. R. Nimmo, preaches sermon for Queen
   Victoria's jubilee, 77
Smiths, 111; United Society of, East Lothian, 125
Smuggling, 103–104
Social amenities, 119–20
Song School, 129
Souness, Wm., town crier, 91
South Port, 85
Spears, Geo., blacksmith, 113
Spence, Isabel, female teacher, 131
Spinning school, 116
Spittelrig at Haddington, 26
Sports and pastimes, 124
Spottiswood, Thos., 90
Spottiswoode, Jas., first dean of Guild Court, 101
Spring Gardens, 42
Sprott, Rev. Dr, of North Berwick, 75
Stagecoaches, 122
Stanfield, Sir Jas., New Mills Cloth Manufactory, 47;
   East Lothian representative in Scots Parliament,
   proposes to sell his interest in New Mills concern
   and start rival company, found drowned in Tyne,
   his son Philip involved in his death, 49
Stanfield, Philip, son of Sir Jas., convicted of murder
   and hanged at Cross of Edinburgh, 49
Star Inn, 123
Stead, Wm., card manufacturer, 116

INDEX

Steeple, town, 140
Steeplechase, East Lothian, 125
Steill, —, Provost Sleich's tenant, 97
Stevenson, A. C., town clerk, 97
Stevenson, David, provost, 97
Stevenson, Geo. H., town clerk, 97
Stevenson foot-bridge, 97
Stewart, Archd., Lord Provost of Edinburgh, his request to Haddington provost, 56
Stewart, Robt., of Alderston, M.P., 69
Stocks as mode of punishment, 120
Stoddart, Wm., swordslipper, 120
Streets, no armed person to walk, 120
Swinton, Wm., burgess, 96
Sydserff, Archd., merchant, 101
Sydserff family, and National Covenant, 34
Syme, Jas., friend of Knox, 32

TAILORS, 115
Tait, Geo., publisher and political reformer, 68, 118
Tantallon, James V and, 8
Tarred Wool Co., promoters, site of operations, chequered career, 116
Taverns, 120, 121
Tea-drinking discouraged, 104
"Telegraph" stagecoach, 122
Templedean, 66
Tenterfield, 85
Termes, Paul de, succeeds to French command at siege, 20
Terrot, Chas. H., Primus of Scottish Episcopal Church, incumbent of Haddington congregation, 37
Test Oath, refused by town councillors, 47
Teuchit Muir, 67, 85
Theatricals, 123–24; school, 129, 131–32
Thomson, Alex., baker, Nungate, 108
Thomson, Bernard, 32
Thomson, John, hanged at Nungate Bridge, 99
Thomson, Robt., provost, 62
Thomson, Robt., and bowling green, 124
Thomson, Wm., town clerk of Edinburgh, 101
Three Kings of Cologne, altar of, 25
Tinkers, Hammermen and, 112
Tinsmiths, 112
Tolbooth, 41, 89, 90, 92; injured during siege, 14; piping to prisoner, 121; history and description of, 142
Tolbooth Gait, 82
Tolbooth Wynd, 82
Toll-bars, opposition to additional, 65
Town Council, and St Mary's, 25; Haliburton charity, 28; James VII and, 49; military assistance, 50; petition regarding decay of trade, 51–52; and Queen Anne, 52; and George I, 53; address to George II, Jacobite army, 56; makes payment for damage done by rebels, 60; addresses to George III, 60, 62, 65; opposition to toll-bars, moves for abolition of slavery, and French Revolution, 65; and invasion, 66; navy recruiting, 68; and town wall, 84; self-elected, 94; early composition of, 95; poll election, 100; and smuggling, 104; burgh reform, 105; crafts and, 107; grants Seals of Cause, 108; and mill dues, 109; smiths and saddlers, 111; Fleshers and Seal of Cause, 114; patronises horse-racing, 125; and necessitous burgesses, 127; and school theatricals, 132; and Town House, 140; and Cross, 141; meets in Tolbooth, 142. See also Magistrates

Town crier, and "Coal and Candle" proclamation, 91
Town House, 142; earliest portion designed by Wm. Adam of Maryburgh, 140
Town lands, 85
Town officials, 98–99
Town Wall, course of, traced, 84–85
Trabroun village, 58
Trade, early, 5; incorporations and St Mary's, 25; town council's grievances enumerated, 51; injured by Jacobite rebels, 58; magistrates oppose proposed commercial treaty between Britain and Ireland, 65; improves, 92
Traill, Misses, Aberlady, gift of statue of Knox, 137
Tranent, 86
Transport, means of, 92
Traprain, 39
Treaty of Haddington (1548), 14
Tron weighing machine, 142
Tudor, Margt., queen of James IV, 8
"Tuesday's Chase," 16, 17
Turnbull, Rev. W. B., of Gladsmuir, 77
Tweeddale, Marquess of, 11 n., 71, 142; Sir John Cope and, 56; Geo., eighth Marquess, appointed Governor of Madras, 73
Tyne, inundations, 6, 20, 63, 64, 85; French forces posted at, 12
Tyneside Games, 78, 125
Tyneside Lodge of Oddfellows, 126
Tyninghame, 56, 97; John Wesley visits, 38

"UNION" stagecoach, 122

VAGRANCY, 88–89
Vallance, John, 120
Vass (Wauss), Thos., provost, 95
Veitch, Wm., clockmaker, 112
Vert, Geo., "meatseller," complies with Jacobite demand, 60
Vert Hospital, 79 n.
Vetch, Lieut.-Col., of Caponflat, raises local volunteer corps, 75
Vetch Park, 66
Victoria, Queen, addresses and celebrations, 72; Jubilee, 77–78
Victoria Bridge, 97, 146
Victoria Park, 78
Victoria Road, 85
Voluntaryism, 70, 71
Volunteers, Haddington, 97, 123; embodied, 66, 67; rifle corps raised, uniform, attend reviews by Queen Victoria, 75; entertained, 76

WALL, town, nature and purposes of, 83–84
Wallace, Hew, schoolmaster, 136 n.
Wallace, Wm., patriot, 5
Wallace-James, Dr, quoted, 85, 139; and antiquity of Nungate Bridge, 145
Wapinschaws, 124–25; tax on, 30
War of 1914–18, local efforts, 78–79; memorial to fallen, 80
Warbeck, Perkin, 8
Warrender, Sir Geo., Bt., 69; presents town's address to George III, 67; and Wellington monument, 73
Water supply, 91
Waterloo Bridge, 146
Waterston (Walterson), Wm., notary public, 30
Watson, Jas., rector of grammar school, 133

Watt, Thos., schoolmaster, author of Latin grammar, 131

Weavers, 115; divided into three classes, owns property in Poldrate, power-loom causes collapse of, 113; Constitutional Society of, East Lothian, 125

Wedderburn, Sir David, 77

Weights and measures, 102

Wellington, political opposition to, 70; town and county subscribes for monument to, 73

Wells, public, 91

Welsh, Dr John, 135

Wemyss, Earl of, signs National Covenant, 34

Wemyss, Francis, ninth Earl of, and Rifle Volunteer movement, 75; and recruiting, 79; purchases Aberlady anchorage, 87

Wemyss Place, 85; bowling at, 124

Wesley, John, visits Haddington, 37

West Barns Links, Dunbar, 67

West Church, 84

West End Park, 78

West Haugh, 97

West Hopes, reservoir at, 91

West Mill Haugh, 83

West Port, 36 n., 37, 42, 58, 84, 85, 124, 125, 126; New Lichts in, 36

West United Free Church, 36

West United Presbyterian Church, 36

White Hart, original name of Blue Bell Inn, 122

White Swan Inn, 123

Whittingehame, 77, 78

Whyt, Robt., tenant in Laverocklaw, 89

Whyte, Rev. Wm., rectorship of grammar school, 136

Widows' Society, 125

Wilford, Sir Jas., commander of English garrison in Haddington, 11, 16; retires before French, 12; appeals for fresh army, 17; reports pitiable state of garrison, 19; taken prisoner, 19; his portrait in Scot. Nat. Port. Gallery, 11 n.

Wilkie, Jas., of Gilkerston, complaint against Bakers 109

Wilkie, John, warded for abusing magistrates, 121

Wilkie, Wm., and Tarred Wool Co., 116

Wilkie, Capt. Wm., 66

William the Lyon, resides in burgh, 3, 139

William III, celebrations on accession, 50

Williams (Guylliame), Thos., influences Knox, 32

Wilson, Wm., bakes for plague victims, 88

Wilton, Lord Grey de. See Grey

Winton, 125

Winton, Earl of, 46

Wishart, George, 22, 31; condemns church festivals 22–23; preaches in St Mary's, 25; rebukes townsfolk, 32; guest at Gimmersmills, 32

Witchcraft, 97; punishments for, 102

Wood, John, his plan of Haddington, 82

Wood, Wm., his charity, 126

Wool, 106, 115; customs on, 6

Wright, John W., first minister of St John's, 36

Wrights and Masons, 107; their altar in St Mary's build convening room, trades included in, 113 property and funds, 115

YEAMAN, ISABEL, 52 n.

"Yellow and Blue Mail," 122

Yeomanry, East Lothian, 67, 68

Yester, Lord, a Covenanter, 42

York, Duke of. See James VII

Young, Geo., provost, 79

Young, Geo., blacksmith, 112, 113

Young, Patrick, clockmaker, 112